*Lacan Deleuze Bad

Lacan Deleuze Badiou

A. J. Bartlett, Justin Clemens and Jon Roffe

EDINBURGH
University Press

© A. J. Bartlett, Justin Clemens and Jon Roffe, 2014, 2015
This paperback edition 2015

Edinburgh University Press Ltd
The Tun – Holyrood Road
12 (2f) Jackson's Entry
Edinburgh EH8 8PJ
www.euppublishing.com

First published in hardback by Edinburgh University Press 2014

Typeset in 11/13pt Adobe Sabon by
Servis Filmsetting Ltd, Stockport, Cheshire,
and printed and bound in Great Britain by
CPI Group (UK) Ltd, Croydon CR0 4YY

A CIP record for this book is available from the British Library

ISBN 978 0 7486 8205 8 (hardback)
ISBN 978 1 4744 0145 6 (paperback)
ISBN 978 0 7486 8207 2 (epub)
ISBN 978 0 7486 8206 5 (webready PDF)

The right of A. J. Bartlett, Justin Clemens and Jon Roffe
to be identified as author of this work
has been asserted in accordance with
the Copyright, Designs and Patents Act 1988
and the Copyright and Related Rights Regulations 2003 (SI No. 2498).

Contents

Acknowledgements

A.J. Bartlett would like to thank Angela Cullip for her continuing support of these unsupportable endeavours. Justin Clemens would like to thank Michael Fee, Nicholas Heron, Helen Johnson and Ben Vaughan. The publication of this book was supported by the Faculty of Arts Publication Subsidy Scheme, and by the School of Culture and Communication at The University of Melbourne.

CHAPTER ONE

Introduction: Us Them

Neither people nor groups

We have written this book for four groups of people. The first are those new to the work of Alain Badiou, Gilles Deleuze and Jacques Lacan. These readers will find abstracts of selected concepts, directed exposition, and putatively helpful comparative discussion of these concepts as they range across the three authors. The second group includes specialised scholars of one or more of these figures. These will find ammunition here for their own preferences. For this book is not simply exegesis, but traces an ongoing philosophical war that the authors, attempting to follow the models of their masters, are continuing to fight against each other and themselves. The third group we address are those voyeurs who would like an aperture through which to enjoy the machinations of such theoretical confrontation. Whether tendentious, irritable, self-deceiving or aggressive, there may be choice selections of this text that will incite such readers to rage, terror or pity; or indeed to enthusiasm, complaisance and joy. The fourth group of addressees, finally, are we ourselves, the authors, who also simultaneously occupy the first three positions of amateur, professional and pervert. This book has been written to see if we could reconsider those thinkers and ways of thinking we find at once mystifying, titillating, precise, infuriating, disturbing – rendering them other to our own existing apprehensions and learned ignorance. Finally, and to put this another way, we hope that ultimately there are not really any groups of people – neither *people* nor *groups* – who have written this or for whom it has been written.

Justification by precedent

It is pertinent that such a composite authorship has its roots in the practices of the thinkers discussed here. For Lacan, following Freud, the problem of authorship that the unconscious opens up is so radical as to require a complete reinvention of a speaking-writing praxis, and not only that of speaking or listening alone. The unconscious is a writer, but also a non-writer in a strangely active sense, and also an unwriter, in that, in writing, it lays down lines that cannot be discerned, as it effaces its own invisibilities. The practice of impossible encounter that Freud enabled in his invention of free association, itself strictly impossible, entails a complete rethinking of the modes of possible presentation (speaking, writing, thinking, etc.): the speaker speaks, but without knowing what she is speaking; the listener listens, but without knowing what they're even listening to, let alone what they're supposedly listening for; what transpires is radical mis-recognition, mis-speaking, mis-hearing, etc. Even a glancing acquaintance with Lacan's work will strike the reader with a barrage of media (including speech, writing, radio, TV, and film), and a barrage of philosophical, philological and linguistic terminology (including signifier, signified, letter, language, discourse, etc.). For Deleuze, following among others Lacan himself, this engagement must be further radicalised, beyond the residual anthropology that sustains even Lacanian psychoanalysis, in theory as in practice. In practice, he and Guattari write a sequence of extraordinary non-books or post-books together, of a very odd character, and in those books the very order both of human language, and of supposed unity, are put into question. Rather than beginning with any putative unity, whether at the origin or end, as aim or fiction, they begin with multiplicities, a theory of substantive multiplicity, and work to sustain it through a syncopated movement of conceptual invention. With Badiou, on the other hand, we have a strange reversion to a classical model of a master: he is unquestionably the author and authoriser of the treatises that he signs. Yet, in his early Maoist work, Badiou had also proved to be an aficionado of the multi-authored, anonymous, pseudonymous or patchwork text, as one immediately sees from texts such as 'Thirty Ways of Easily Recognising an Old Marxist' or *The Rational Kernel of the Hegelian Dialectic*, among others.* So we cannot in turn take his reversion to be a simple act of regression to a prior image of philosophical authorship. On the contrary, it is linked with a particular authorial paradox of *identifiable public anonymity*, whose most recent analogue may be Foucault's well-known remarks about writing and authority.

---

* See Georges Peyrol (a pseudonym Badiou often used), 'Thirty Ways of Easily Recognising an Old-Marxist', trans. Nina Power and Alberto Toscano, *PRELOM: Journal for Images and Politics* (Fall 2006), pp. 177–9; Alain Badiou et al., *The Rational Kernel of the Hegelian Dialectic*, trans. Tzuchien Tho (Melbourne: re.press, 2011).

Not another effort! The question still remains: what sort of justifica-
tions can be found for writing a book that discusses
Lacan, Deleuze and Badiou in, as it were, a single breath (or a triple
breath, given the multiple authorship)? Surely there have already
been enough articles, books, special journal issues, blogs, radio docu-
mentaries, movies, podcasts, YouTube videos, and even television
shows dedicated to each of these difficult figures? Surely the extant
material already covers the entire gamut from anecdote and biogra-
phy all the way to specialised technical exegeses of fine-grained elements of their work? Surely it would be better to dedicate a study to
at best two of these thinkers, rather than all three, in which the
'compare and contrast' model so beloved of academese would be
more adequately served? Surely it would be even better to confine our
attentions to just one of these figures, or to a single central theme or
concept? Surely. At the same time, it only requires the opening of any
single text by these authors to be immediately confronted with something that remains yet to be thought.

The links are real Certainly, the empirical links between these figures
are very real. These links are not only national
('French'), culturo-institutional ('the metropolitan intelligentsia'),
disciplinary ('philosophical'), temporal ('mid- to late-twentieth
century'), personal (they all 'knew' or 'knew of' each other), and
vaguely part of a rather loosely delimited ethos ('continental philosophy'). Far more importantly, however, the links are immanent to the
work. These links, moreover, are fundamentally those of antagonism, and necessarily bear on a set of questions that Badiou himself
has posed very clearly. As he puts it: 'What is the new figure of the
master that results if one excludes all the validation of institutional
authority? Are there masters outside of the institution? Are there
masters at all?'* These questions are of the most extreme pertinence
in a contemporary philosophical context, one marked by an unprecedented intensification and commercialisation of 'critical' commen-
tary that simultaneously constitutes itself as a thoroughgoing rejection
of 'critique'. If we will speak at greater length of this situation in the
coming chapters, we can at once outline the stakes.

---

* Alain Badiou, 'Jacques Rancière's Lessons: Knowledge and Power After the Storm', in *The
  Adventure of French Philosophy*, trans. Bruno Bosteels (London: Verso, 2012), p. 105.

Rebroaching
transmission
First of all, Lacan is what Harold Bloom would call the 'prime precursor' of the conceptual divagations thereafter assayed by Deleuze and Badiou. Without Lacan's own radical praxis of psychoanalysis, the latter simply would not exist as such; moreover, and perhaps despite received opinions from and about Deleuze and Badiou themselves, Lacan provides a decisive impetus to their thought. Second, however, this is precisely *not* a question of 'influence' in the usual acceptations of this term. Rather, Lacan's radical retheorisation of precisely what constitutes the orders of the concept, of praxis, and the transmission of knowledge, issues a challenge to the discipline of philosophy which is taken up *in completely different – but strong and consistent – ways* by Deleuze and Badiou. Yet because the latter share the conviction that there is a necessity to rethink what such a 'taking-up' or transmission might mean, they themselves come to transform in their turn the very modes in which the thinking of such transmission proves essential to thinking itself. Third, this suggests the desirability of a re-intrication of the dispersion and divergences of all three thinkers' concepts vis-à-vis one another, in order to sketch not merely another genealogy of recent French philosophy, but to open such a genealogy to points of irresolvable undecidability that, when targeted in themselves, can suggest other ways forward from here in reconstructing the 'roads not taken'. To 'cut straight to the *sensitive point*',* as Badiou puts it, is to decide in such a way as to open up new means of thinking at the same time as one shuts down others which might appear from certain points of view to be 'equally viable'. To show how one must force oneself into restraint through philosophy – whether as an analyst, an ascetic, an aesthete, or something even less familiar – is an irreducible element of this project. As each of our thinkers might put it, if in their own vocabularies, one must affirm limits if one is to think the infinite.

Sophistry, anti-
philosophy, philosophy
So what we therefore attempt in this book has not, to our knowledge, been done (quite like this) before. We extract, from the problematic of the rethinking of the vicissitudes of transmission, a small set of key concepts in order to show how Lacan, Deleuze and Badiou themselves focus on particular resistances or inconsistencies within the crucial concepts, dredging

* Alain Badiou, *Deleuze: The Clamor of Being*, trans. Louise Burchill (Minneapolis: University of Minnesota Press, 1999), p. 5.

out of existing structures and operations even more intense or rigorous logics of thinking and praxis. In order to do so, we establish in each chapter a foundational problem, outlining its constitution, antecedents, elective affiliations and import – such as why we find it necessary to begin our thinking of the structuring of subjective time by means of an extra-psychoanalytic sophism – before showing how and why Lacan, Deleuze and Badiou take it up, what they do with it, and to what new ends. In doing so, we also sketch their background philosophical conditions as a force-field of limit-problems. What this means is very specific: when Lacan, Deleuze and Badiou respond to problems, these problems cannot simply be 'read off' their differing positions. A problem is not only not a 'thesis' affixed with a question mark; it is not always even formulable as a set of propositions. Rather, a problem is an 'un-place' or atopia of irreducibly multiple conceptual points that demand to be transformed, without necessarily having any possible representation or recognition as an index. As such, 'theses' emerge as the dissimulating, 'downstream' registrations of much more fundamental issues, ones which are 'unconscious' or 'imperceptible' or 'indiscernible'; for this reason, the 'problems' of which they are one partial outcome cannot always (or even often) be reconstructed by an analysis of the themes alone. This is one reason why it is misleading, perhaps even futile, to compare thinkers according to their differing positions regarding the alleged key traits of a thematic. Moreover, the seizure and extraction of 'key concepts' here does not tend to follow received opinions in the scholarship about their appearance and constitution; a different kind of modelling is required. Even the term 'problem' is a problem here, not least given the difficulties of establishing, formulating and separating questions and problems – and *question* from *problem* – that are at once shared and shattered by our three thinkers. This seizure-extraction will therefore often target marginal or under-remarked moments in the texts of Lacan, Deleuze and Badiou in the attempt to reconstruct a less-representational account of their problems than is usually offered.

Virtually real   One problem of the problem of influence is therefore precisely that it tends to efface problems as such. Instead, one is confronted by representations of problems as theses or other forms of positivity, and their inevitable articulation with a particular declension of the proper name. But proper names can take many declensions, and, if this declination-power is not

adequately investigated, those names can easily become territorial
facades. But a problem is, more profoundly, a no-man's-land in the
war over time, in all senses of that phrase. If there is a valuable point
made in the course of the contemporary 'critique of critique', it is
certainly due in part to the general conviction that critique as it stems
in its strong philosophical line from Kant has contributed to the
problem of the occlusion of problems, just as Heidegger famously
remarked at the inception of *Being and Time* that the forgetting of
the meaning of being had been forgotten so thoroughly that it had
been forgotten that it had been forgotten . . .* The present work is
therefore not a positive tracing of influence in the sense of source-
hunting, but a staging of the destinies of the objective virtuality of
problems and questions by attempting to take stock of their virtual
objectivity.

Shape-without-shape   Human beings are always confronted by problems
                           that they do not recognise and which are too diffi-
cult for them to solve. So-called 'solutions' or 'resolutions' are most
often low-grade and misleading responses to false problems – which
is why 'empiricism', if it is to be worthy of philosophy, must also be
'transcendental'; or 'Platonism', if it is to be worthy of the name,
must also be 'materialist'. But this is also why what goes under the
name of 'pragmatism' has a necessary but properly subordinate place
in philosophy: pragmatism is not so much an anti-philosophy as a
sub-philosophy; that is, a practice that inheres in philosophy itself as
its perennial idiot questioner, reminding it that there are indeed real
problems while itself so often mistaking not only these problems but
their real constitution as such. Being pragmatic is an unavoidable
demand, but deleterious if it is considered to dominate or exhaust the
field of philosophy. To deny the force of its operations is to abandon
philosophy for theology, but to affirm it without reservation is to
subordinate philosophy to stupidity. The pragmatist is, to invoke
Deleuze, a conceptual persona, a paradoxical one, one which denies
its own conceptual status in the name of humility, variability, relativ-
ity and effectivity, but there are also many others. Some of these are
entirely anonymous, 'shapes we would call them if shape they had
that had no shape', to parody John Milton's *Paradise Lost* on the

---

* Of course for Heidegger this was the question and not *per se* a problem, except insofar as the
  question itself produces as its effect the problem which is properly that to which the question
  is addressed.

non-figure of Death; others have proper names and well-defined outlines, names and outlines that call for their own undoing.

Proper names　　To put this differently, the status of the proper names 'Lacan', 'Deleuze' and 'Badiou' are at stake. A proper name for our thinkers is itself not, *pace* Saul Kripke, a 'rigid designator' assigned by a 'primal baptism', but something more remarkable. As Deleuze puts it in *Dialogues*, 'the proper name does not at all designate a person or a subject. It designates an effect, a zigzag, something that happens or that happens in-between as under a potential difference.'* So these names do not simply function as personages, conceptual or otherwise; they are not merely markers for important or interesting arguments; they are not only fodder for comparison and contrast; they are not just indices of trajectories of thought or of anxieties of influence; nor are they solely resources of conceptual power or potential. They are all these things, certainly, but they are more yet: they are misleading signposts to the real challenges of contemporary thought, challenges that they themselves designate, indeed have helped to identify and force, without for all that always being able to present those challenges so openly or clearly themselves. This is therefore fundamentally an attempt to outline some of their 'unthoughts'. This may be another way of stating that they are *our* masters – with the proviso, of course, and in accord with reason rather than presumptions to authenticity, that this 'mastery' too be rethought, as something other than a non-linear battery of order-words inflicting the stigmata of reactive obedience.

Incompletion, return, infinity　　It is our contention, finally, that no one is yet finished with these thinkers, has yet properly digested their work or rendered it purely operational. Rather than complete such a project, we wish to do what we can to make sure that such an eventuality will never take place. One separates 'knowledge' from 'power' by way of 'non-knowledge': the last-named of these is necessarily a new form of 'well-speaking', a 'line of flight', or 'praxis' that attempts to refound a position indifferent to a power that, from its beginning to its end, is essaying to insinuate itself everywhere. The same considerations have led us, little by little, to a peculiar methodological conclusion. Underlying this text is an attempt to elaborate

---

* Gilles Deleuze and Claire Parnet, *Dialogues II*, trans. Hugh Tomlinson and Barbara Habberjam (New York: Columbia University Press, 2002), p. 51.

a protocol of absolute disagreement. We travel to the end of the
dialogic program only in order to go beyond it, to the point where
the apparent parallels described as subjective and objective come into
contact, in thought. This means that the disagreement we seek no
longer invokes the affective, social, existential qualities of disagreement in the regular sense – Deleuze speaks of 'the fact that Foucault
existed',* the fact that he wrote what he did . . . Our disagreement is
predicated on a univocal agreement about the significance of the *fact*
of the thought of Badiou, Deleuze and Lacan, and nothing else. It is
our contention that the existing models by which thinkers are
brought together are one and all inadequate, have always been inadequate. This (hardly new) observation ought to lead to more significant consequences more often than it has. Correlatively, if we use the
image of parallels that meet at the horizon, it is not because we think
we have necessarily succeeded in our construction, but that we consider it a necessary effort nonetheless.

No name   What name or figure or form or concept is 'ade-
                   quate' to such a 'collective' enterprise? It is not a
Polis, a Republic, a Peripeteia, a Cosmos, a community or common-
wealth, an ideal speech community, an unavowable or coming
community, a community of those with nothing in common, a link or
a knot, a block of becoming, a rabble or swarm, or any other of the
gatherings that are today regularly invoked as types of (disavowed)
truth and grace. For the moment, let's just call this an *Us Them*, and
see where, if anywhere, it gets us . . .

---

* Gilles Deleuze, *Nietzsche and Philosophy*, trans. Hugh Tomlinson (New York: Columbia
University Press, 2006), p. 85.

CHAPTER TWO

Contemporary

This chapter locates our three thinkers at the heart of contemporary thought. More substantially though, it argues that it is the fact that the figure of the contemporary is also at once the milieu and a focus of their work that at least partially gives them their import. In a nutshell: for all three thinkers, to be contemporary is an injunction for contemporary thought.

Three ways of being contemporary with the contemporary   Lacan, Deleuze and Badiou take very different routes to this 'end'. For Lacan, in order to be contemporary, it is necessary to return to the origin. This 'return to' is different from the 'return of', and indeed the former must be effected in order that the second is not. For Lacan, as a psychoanalyst, one returns to Freud, albeit not so much to the latter's key propositions, but to the new fault-lines – 'problems'? 'questions'? – that those propositions at once open and occlude. A return to these problems is concomitantly thought of by Lacan as the conditions of the problems of the return, and the return of those problems in a contemporary way. For Deleuze, by contrast, to be contemporary is first of all to be untimely, which is to say, to not belong to the present. The present itself is what must be resisted in order to be contemporary. This is a difficult task because of the elasticity of our habitual mode of existence which yokes us to what already exists. As a consequence, to become is always to create (in life and in thought) in order to avoid being subsumed by the present: 'We lack creation. *We lack resistance to the present.*'* However, this creative relation to existence cannot be achieved once and for all, and must be constantly pursued, which is why, third, to be contemporary for Deleuze is to become. To become is to become-other, that is, to subtract oneself from every currently existing predicate through this act of creation. Thus

---

* Gilles Deleuze and Félix Guattari, *What is Philosophy?*, trans. Hugh Tomlinson and Graham Burchell (New York: Columbia University Press, 1994), p. 108.

Deleuze and Badiou are, at least *prima facie*, neighbours; for the latter, to be contemporary is to produce the *new*, the *truly* new. Yet to produce the new is also to be the contemporary of those that are not of our time but that, in the 'time of their own time', produced the new. To be contemporary is to partake of the trans-temporal, or really, trans-mundane, and not to be finally subject to time but to inscribe eternity in one's own time/world under the general name of Idea. Philosophy, for Badiou, is contemporary to the material and materialist conditions that in their own time produce the new discourses of time, and also to the Idea itself as the composition of this contemporaneity. As such, Plato, Descartes and Hegel are our contemporaries, just as are Euclid, Galileo, the Horses of Chauvet, Eloise and Abelard, the Paris Commune and Category Theory.

Afterlife of Meno's paradox   Whoever asks 'what is contemporary?' is already behind the times. If you are contemporary, then there's clearly no need to pose such a question; if you're truly posing the question, then it's because you don't know what the contemporary is. And not-knowing is already a kind of negative proof that you aren't it. Instead, you find yourself chasing the contemporary. But to chase the contemporary is also to be behind the contemporary, in its past or wake. Given, moreover, that you don't know what it is, then you may not have a clue what it is when you see it. Is that it, peeping out from behind the shadows at the edge of the forest? Or flickering dimly from the artificial light of an iPad? How can you chase something which you cannot recognise? Even posing the question, as Meno found out, can then be a sign that you're *never* going to be contemporary. Perhaps such a question can even be posed to simulate a quest for the very contemporary that you really don't want to seize at any cost. You might look like you're looking for it, while all the time having an impeccable alibi for your evasion of it. You pose the question so as not to ask. But the opposite might also then be true. Could the becoming-obscure of the contemporary, or the sense of the urgency of the question of the obscurity of the contemporary then be the contemporary itself? Time and non-knowledge thereby come to be linked, in this time of the end of times. 'We are the contemporary to the extent that we lack it' might be one attempt at a resolution. This answer does not get anyone very far; to pose the question in this way is simply to mark an epistemological limit (you can know that you can only not know).

❖

As sophistical as this flight of the contemporary into the zones of non-knowledge may appear, it doesn't for all that mean that you're entirely relegated to the past, since it can also mean that the organisation of time itself has become obscure or disordered – and to recognize this is to move beyond epistemology. 'The time is out of joint', as Hamlet laments – an extraordinary phrase that has had, unsurprisingly, an extraordinary fate in recent European philosophy. It might then be tempting to elevate this sentiment to a diagnosis of time's own self-wrenching (the untimely enigma of time itself to the times themselves, the problem of the contemporary as the problem of time itself, etc.), but one which has only emerged 'now', in a time that is no longer simply a time insofar as the question of time 'itself' has obtruded in a way that it hadn't or couldn't in previous times.

In sum, it can't not be significant that the 'contemporary' has become a necessary topic for thought today. Why? Because the problem of the contemporary is clearly a problem of the problem of time today. Time today is a problem for philosophy that has an essential link to the rubric of the contemporary, precisely because the received notions that have regulated the thought of time – past, present, future, of course, but also potential (or virtual) and actual, not to mention the distribution of other, more classical modal categories – have themselves been placed in question by the time or times in which we live. We say, then, 'time today', uncertain even whether there was time yesterday or whether there will be time tomorrow, somewhat worse off than at the Mad Hatter's Tea Party, where we could at least be assured of jam yesterday and jam tomorrow, if never jam today. Rather than entering into the problem of the contemporary through the problem of time, which would suggest that the medium of the contemporary is the present (contemporary as a name for the presence of the present), the problem of the contemporary presents something quite different. To begin with 'the contemporary' is already to suggest that the possibility of a complete temporal synthesis and of an adequate conception of this synthesis has become obscure. In fact, it implies that if there is or was or will be time, that such time is dependent on others, on other times and other non-times and on other places and placements, without that dependence being able to be thought as progression, sublation, supplantation, succession, protention, retention, status or even as différance.

Postulation and resolution of a Wittgensteinian problematic Characterising the situation in this way may itself be read as a symptom of a deleterious philosophical failure. As Boris Groys reminds us, writing of one of the last great (self-styled) critics of modern philosophy:

> Wittgenstein was highly ironical about his philosophical colleagues who from time to time suddenly turned to contemplation of the present, instead of simply minding their own business and going about their everyday lives. For Wittgenstein, the passive contemplation of the present, of the immediately given, is an unnatural occupation dictated by the metaphysical tradition, which ignores the flow of everyday life – the flow that always overflows the present without privileging it in any way. According to Wittgenstein, the interest in the present is simply a philosophical – and maybe also artistic – *déformation professionnelle*, a metaphysical sickness that should be cured by philosophical critique.*

Of course, Wittgenstein's mode of philosophical critique is itself the call for a more primordial passivity, 'thoughts that are at peace', a kind of morbid inactivity in place of the torment of thinking.† In this, Wittgenstein is at once the double, accomplice and antithesis of Heidegger, who also sought to characterise – if with a very different motivation and by very different means – recent philosophy as that of *Augensblickphilosophie*, philosophy of the moment and of the ground-abyss (*Abgrund*). Nonetheless, we might ask, *pace* Wittgenstein, whether the philosophical interest in the contemporary is just an unknowing reflex of a metaphysical inheritance, rather than a real project or programme for thought. Although we shall speak further of this difficulty shortly, and, indeed, will return to the problem of time in a later chapter, it is immediately worth emphasizing the paradox of this temporal closure of a certain sequence of the thinking of *temporality* qua *opening*.

This can also be put another way: time is of the essence *insofar as it is fundamentally no longer of the essence*. This becoming-inessential of time can therefore itself become the entrance to the present. One thinks here of the paradoxes of Kafka's little fable, 'Before the Law', much commented upon by contemporary philosophers, including Derrida and Giorgio Agamben, not to mention Deleuze himself. The

---

* Boris Groys, 'Comrades of Time', *e-flux journal*, No. 12 (2009), n.p.
† Ludwig Wittgenstein, *Culture and Value*, trans. G. H. Von Wright (London: Wiley-Blackwell, 1998), p. 50e.

paradox here is something like: we are *before* time. The entrance to the present as a synthesis of time is through the contemporary, and not through the present itself. Or, to put this another way, a contemporary way of thinking the present will have to be found if we are to be contemporaries of our present. In this sense, we are already outside of the Wittgensteinian determination: not a perverse metaphysical turn to the present in the present, but a post-metaphysical interrogation of the paradoxes of the syntheses of time by means of the a-temporal or pre-temporal category that is the 'contemporary'.

The contemporary as topological category Insofar as this is the case, the contemporary must become in some way a topological category. Why? To return momentarily to the Kafka fable, it is because the entrance to time, or at least the problematic of time, must be a *place* of some kind. We see in almost all recent European philosophy a shift from the conceptual routines that accord a primacy to time-as-sequence to a disposition of the organisation of space, spaces, spatiality, or as (deformed) form or (ungrounding) ground. Let us adduce here two critical remarks by Foucault as a kind of exemplum of this attitude:*

> 1) In the nineteenth century, philosophy was to reside in the gap between history and History, between events and the Origin, between evolution and the first rending open of the source, between oblivion and the Return. It will be Metaphysics, therefore, only in so far as it is Memory, and it will necessarily lead thought back to the question of knowing what it means for thought to have a history ... It is enough to recognize here a philosophy deprived of a certain metaphysics because it has been separated off from the space of order, yet doomed to Time, to its flux and its returns, because it is trapped in the mode of being of History.†

> 2) At the moment when a considered politics of spaces was starting to develop, at the end of the eighteenth century, the new achievements in theoretical and experimental physics dislodged philosophy from its ancient right to speak of the world, the cosmos, finite or infinite space. This double investment of space by political technology and scientific practice reduced philosophy to the field of a problematic of time. Since Kant, what is to be thought by the philosopher is time. Hegel, Bergson, Heidegger. Along with this goes a correlative devaluation of space, which stands on the side of

---

* It is worth noting too that for the Foucault of the archaeological works, the determination of an adequate historical method is always presented in spatial terms.
† Michel Foucault, *The Order of Things*, trans. Alan Sheridan (New York: Pantheon Books, 1970), pp. 219–20.

understanding, the analytical, the conceptual, the dead, the fixed, the inert.*

Although examples could so easily be multiplied – Lacan's topologies, Deleuze and Guattari's body-without-organs, Derrida's *spacing*, Kristeva's *chora*, Badiou's *splace* and *outplace* – for the moment we will only mark the necessity and ubiquity of this troping and transumption of time by space. The reader will therefore also note that this preamble has already implicitly sketched a *situation*, rather than a *period* of thought, and has done so by allusion to one of the strong lines of immediately available philosophy: the phenomenological tradition that stems, above all, from G. W. F. Hegel, and runs through Edward Husserl, Martin Heidegger, Maurice Merleau-Ponty and Jacques Derrida. For this tradition, at least in one of its dominant lines, the problem of time is paramount: sometimes time as history, sometimes time as process or development of the elusive tracks of interiorisation, sometimes time as the traces of the event of the withdrawal of being, sometimes time as self-absenting undoing, sometimes time as nothingness. It is the exhaustion of this tradition and its thought of time that gives rise to a contemporary situation in which thinking the contemporary appears as an urgent task.

A contemporary proliferation of categories of the contemporary   Something similar goes for those current descriptive attempts in a number of different zones to make distinctions intended at once to clarify and complicate the problem of the contemporary. There are, notably, a number of interesting attempts, many stemming primarily from the domain of contemporary art. This is not and should not be a surprise: as everybody dutifully repeats, modern art was characterised by its unique dialectical relation with avant-gardism, that is, the necessity to 'make it new' as an integral condition for art. The paradoxes of the avant-garde – that one must make it new, but without any clear directives available for doing so; that one must make it new, but not every novelty is significant; that one must declare something to be the case that does not and cannot exist in the supplementary form of the manifesto; that the identity of indiscernibles may no longer hold (e.g., the perceptually indiscernible may be conceptually antithetical); that the tradition of art becomes a tradition of ruptures with tradition,

---

* Michel Foucault, *Power/Knowledge: Selected Interviews 1972–1977*, ed. Colin Gordon (New York: Pantheon Books, 1980), pp. 149–50.

etc.* – have forced scholars of art towards quasi-philosophical interrogations of time and philosophers towards quasi-artistic theories of time, to the point at which art and philosophy have themselves occasionally become inextricably co-implicated. (We will return to this issue in subsequent chapters, because it bears crucially upon the differing yet essential roles played by art for Lacan, Deleuze and Badiou).

To give a specific example here: Terry Smith speaks of the 'immediate', the 'contemporaneous' and the 'cotemporal' in the zone of contemporary art. To the extent that these can be understood as concepts at all (and not as simply typological or descriptive rubrics): the *immediate* is what can be grasped as happening now, that which presents itself; the *contemporaneous* hinges upon what is happening or has happened at the same time, whereby at least two different presentations can be assigned to the same time; finally, the *cotemporal* is a recognition of at least two different processes of presentation that *happen together in time without being linked by or in (a) time*. Lacan himself once made a distinction between synchrony and simultaneity: that which happens *at* the same time is not the same as that which happens *in* the same time.† Clearly, it is something like this latter which we would characterize as the problematic of the contemporary. Hence Smith will remark that:

> the concept of the 'contemporary', far from being singular or simple – a neutral substitute for 'modern' – signifies multiple ways of being with, in, and out of time, separately and at once, with others and without them. These modes, of course, have always been there. The difference nowadays is that the multiplicities of contemporary being predominate over the kinds of generative and destructive powers named by any other comparable terms.‡

Yet such distinctions, valuable as they are, immediately start to proliferate to the point of derangement. Take some of the other crucial conceptual distinctions the avant-garde philosophical movements of the nineteenth and twentieth centuries gradually unearthed as they dug their own graves; for example, the further gaps between 'innovation', 'novelty', 'the up-to-date', and 'the untimely' that one could

---

* For a helpful general overview of some of the historical issues, see Thierry de Duve, *Kant After Duchamp* (Cambridge MA and London: MIT, 1998), esp. Chapter 1.
† Jacques Lacan, *Seminar IX*.
‡ Terry Smith, *What is Contemporary Art?* (Chicago: University of Chicago Press, 2009), p. 6.

easily add to Smith's list. 'Innovation' itself has today been exposed
as having become a pure question of *technique*. One *innovates* by
creating a new drug, by eminently reproducible technical means
(think of the work of Bernard Steigler on such topics here). 'Novelty',
on the other hand, is what *appears* now-as-new, presents itself as
newly appearing *now*: it need not be new, even happening now, just
until now unknown by its audience. But novelty is certainly not necessarily up-to-date; these days, whatever's up-to-date won't be new
for twenty years. As Lord Mountbatten once remarked of modern
technology: if it works, it's obsolete. The up-to-date differs from the
innovative insofar as it doesn't have to take a new step in the realm
of technique: it just has to be there at the right time. But to do so it
must be acceleratory in principle: it keeps up. As such, the up-to-date
must be counterposed to the 'untimely': that which is contemporary
insofar as it appears as wrong-in-time, the contemporary as the
disruption of the contemporary. Against the untimely, moreover, we
could invoke the theses on the messianism of time (Walter Benjamin,
Giorgio Agamben), time as the time-that-remains between the
arrival of the messiah and his return as final total obliteration. So we
quickly have eight quite different internal, relational figures which
complicate the very 'contemporary' that conditions the necessity of
their introduction: innovation, novelty, up-to-dateness, immediacy,
contemporaneousness, cotemporality, untimeliness and messianism;
or, to put these another way, technicity, apparition, acceleration,
spectrality, simultaneity, disjunction, irruption and messianism.
Such intra-temporal relations could easily be further diversified and
nuanced.

Kant Kant Kant Kant
Kant   Should our proliferation and connection of these
              categories seem excessive and beside the point, we
would simply insist that this complexity is precisely part of the
problem. To enter into a thought of time via the contemporary is
already to enter into a labyrinth of complications that threaten to
dissolve the investigation from the start. The moment we take the
various attempts in contemporary thought to think the contemporary seriously, we find ourselves within this categorical labyrinth.

Nonetheless, we can avoid remaining lost in it by following the
thread back to a common precursor, the first thinker (as Foucault
so clearly demonstrates) to raise the question of the contemporary
in philosophy, Immanuel Kant. There are two critical elements to

mention in this context. The first is that philosophy for Kant is a thought of time insofar as it thinks time at the level of conditions. As Deleuze says in his little book on Kant: 'Time is no longer related to the movement which it measures, but movement is related to the time which conditions it: this is the first great Kantian reversal.'* Deleuze quickly adds that for Kant there is a 'giddiness that constitutes time'. The environment of time which subjectifies a subject is that very subject's secretion; a subject is a subject to the extent *that it secretes and excretes itself in time*. This leads Deleuze himself to insist that time not only conditions experience but literally corrupts the subject, constituting subjective experience in relation to the objects of experience only in the form of an irremediably split subject.

This corruption of the subject, second, has an irreducible if obscure political valency. And if modern philosophy has often been convinced that this valency must somehow be articulated with and by means of Kant's own transcendental categories, the attempt to do so proves difficult, even aporetic. As Foucault argued in a sequence of famous presentations, Kant thereby renders the problem of truth coterminous with the problem of 'minority', or what a subsequent tradition of philosophical thought will denominate 'infancy'. In a Collège de France seminar of 5 January 1983, Foucault comments on the concepts of *Aufklärung*, *Ausgang*, and *Unmündigkeit* (the latter translated variously as immaturity, minority, or tutelage) as they are presented in Kant's famous essay of 1784, *Was ist Auflklärung?*† For Foucault, *Ausgang* means, first of all, an exit without established aim or end. Second, it is an exit *from*, an exit from immaturity. Third, it is an exit from *self-imposed immaturity*. One can see at once that Foucault is emphasizing the resolutely *negative* dimensions of Kant's claims, in order to underline that the latter's negations bear upon a radical utopianism that does not for all that provide false images of what is to be done. The key for Foucault is the introduction of the problematic of the production of the present itself – the contemporary political context – into the heart of philosophical conceptuality. As such, it is a form of resistance to governmentality that is at stake here, a governmentality whose logic is equivalent to that of the educating of infants.

❖

* Gilles Deleuze, *Kant's Critical Philosophy*, trans. Hugh Tomlinson and Barbara Habberjam (Minneapolis: University of Minnesota Press, 1984), p. vii.
† Michel Foucault, *The Government of Self and Others: Lectures at the Collège de France, 1982–1983*, trans. and ed. A. Davison and G. Burchell (London: Picador, 2011).

What is this immaturity? The word itself is of crucial importance in the context. As Jörg Volbers explains:

> *Unmündigkeit*, signifies the absence of *Mündigkeit*. But what is *Mündigkeit*? It can be translated as 'maturity,' 'accountability,' 'responsibility,' 'self-ownership' or, what seems to be the best fit for Kant's specific use, 'autonomy.' ... A certain behaviour is *unmündig* if it resembles the doings of a child, if it does not display the signs of mature, rational self-control. But you could also call a person *unmündig* in the second, formal sense. In this use, the *Unmündigkeit* describes a legal state, an exclusion due purely to formal criteria.*

In Foucault's reading, however, *Unmündigkeit* cannot simply be natural powerlessness nor the deprivation of a right; on the contrary, it is a peculiar, paradoxical state of self-abnegation. Humans, who have already the power *to not be* immature, have nevertheless, immaturely, chosen to abrogate their autonomy. For Kant, this abrogation is due, as Foucault underlines, to a certain moral failure, of laziness and cowardice (*Faultheit, Freigheit*). Courage – Kant famously asserts that *sapere aude*! is the very maxim (*Wahlspruch*) of Enlightenment – is required. An aporia immediately arises: this courage cannot be simply given by the subject to itself, but it can only be given by the subject to itself. This aporia is essentially political. Autonomy must pass through heteronomy to become itself. The subject requires external guidance to achieve the freedom it always already enjoys, but the necessity of a recourse to external guidance is precisely the index of immaturity. One immaturely refuses to exit from immaturity insofar as one abrogates one's own autonomy to others, but the only remedy for such abrogation involves a recourse to the very others who are agents of that abrogation. In the background of Kant's strictures, one can certainly discern a struggle with Rousseau, and with the generalised eighteenth-century problematics of a 'sentimental education'. For our philosopher, however, humanity is not a sensible vegetable.

The process of enlightenment is therefore at once temporal and non-temporal. One *becomes* free insofar as one becomes what one already is, insofar as this becoming is an exit from infancy without a determined goal. The goal cannot be determined, because it at once

---

* Jörg Volbers, 'Natural Conditions of (Kantian) Majority', in V. Brito and E. Battista (eds), *Becoming Major/Becoming Minor* (Maastricht: Jan van Eyck Academie, 2011), pp. 26, 28.

demands knowledge and self-knowledge, and to acquire either is to go forward in both. To go forward, one finds novelty: what is new to oneself, naturally, but also, in doing so, making oneself anew, and, finally, the world anew too. This is clearly a question of the time of the subject, if one that is un-determining itself in its universalising exit from its own particularity. Time itself here, moreover, receives a third characteristic, that of the essential openness of the future. Its unimaginable, its literally un-imagable, quality is the index of the adulthood-to-come-already-here, that is, the place of freedom. Time is at once a condition of experience conditioned by the subject of experience, yet unconditioned insofar as its 'to-come' is a non-place of potential development.

Beyond Kant   Any post-Kantian consideration of time and the transcendental therefore directs us towards the aftermath of this subject and its becomings, that is, to the phenomenological subject, the subject that must also be embodied, whose act is at once passion and process, reflection and non-reflection, thrown and projected, a subject whose own unity is a problem for it – and for its philosophers. These are therefore the most important aspects of the situation of the contemporary as post-phenomenological. To mention certain prevalent traits found in contemporary thought: the exhaustion of time (the non-presence of the present), the exigency of its double nature as both universal medium of experience and derived category of being (the quasi-transcendental), and the underdetermination of the subject by time (the aporia of ontogenesis). Furthermore: this situation raises the problem of politics and ethics again, in a way that implicates the problem of the insistence of the 'past' in the 'present' on the basis of the 'future' (minority and majority, infancy and adulthood, etc.), as it scrambles the commonsensical acceptations of these terms. To think in a truly post-Kantian way, then, is to rebroach the problem of time and the transcendental from the point of the actual – that is, the current, the contingent, the contemporary – even if this ultimately means adverting to the virtual. Foucault's own notorious programme for 'an ontology of the present' remains a limit-Kantianism in this regard.

The contemporary as polemical *topos*   Yet these cannot be the contemporary as such, but the proliferation of possible temporal relations that emerge. To adapt a syntagm of Lacan's: *the contemporary is what has not yet failed not to insist.* In this sense, though Plato is certainly not new, nor up-to-date, nor innovative, etc., he is still a *contemporary* – with and against whom we cannot not think. So we will return to the problem of the contemporary by displacing its terms: what Lacan broaches, and Deleuze and Badiou take up, is *an an-ontology of the con-temporary*. Each of our authors – Lacan, Deleuze, Badiou – reflects upon these issues in their own way, which, being 'dialectical' in its primary sense of establishing and affirming a polemical space, constantly reuptakes its enemies' propositions and powers into its own elaboration. As we will argue throughout this book, all three agree that the limits of the situation to be rethought must be those of the subject, time and transformation, but this is to be done by proceeding from immanence rather than transcendence – however virulently they differ on the sense of this immanence, on the means of treating it, and the consequences they draw from it.

Psychoanalysis will be contemporary, or it will not be   This is self-evident in the case of Lacan, whose career was marked by institutional wars over innovations in clinical praxis, and whose concomitant elaboration of the theory of psychoanalysis provides one key to the seminars and writings. Notably, 'contemporaneity' is itself a crucial term and task for Lacan in his redevelopment of the Freudian subject. As we can immediately see from the essays collected as the *Ecrits*, Lacan insists that: 1) psychoanalysis will be contemporary or it will not be; 2) to be contemporary is to be attentive to the situation in which one finds oneself; 3) this situation is a media situation, that is, one must be attentive to all its communicative modalities, including those that are given in their absence; 4) through such attentiveness, it is necessary to find a contemporary formalism of the contemporary in order to treat of the times, and time itself. In this programme, it is just as necessary to attend to the 'psychopathologies of everyday life', that is, to the language of the everyday, as it is to attend to the new technologies of communication and the current developments in science, mathematics and logic. As we shall later see, this programme finds its *ratio ultima* in a minimalist, materialist theory of the 'letter'.

Notably, this programme begins very early, even before Lacan has become Lacan. In the essay 'Beyond the "Reality Principle"', first presented in 1936, Lacan adverts to the transformed context of psychoanalysis insofar as it has itself transformed the context into which it intervened. The specific signposts he gives are of crucial importance, given that, 'for the psychiatrist or psychologist of the

1930s, initiation into psychoanalytic method no longer involves a conversion that constitutes a break in one's intellectual development, a conversion that thus attests less to a carefully thought out choice of an avenue of research than to the outburst of secret affective strife'.*
For the young Lacan, then, what matters for the second generation of psychoanalysts must be of a different order: rather than pursue intellectual rupture, it must invoke and intricate certain key problems in order to establish an intellectual continuity. Note that these are eminently psychoanalytic questions: of indebtedness, education and inheritance. Note, too, that these questions essentially involve delay, deferral and divagation. If the Freudian revolution was indeed a revolution in psychological thought and practice, this can finally be gauged by how it illuminates the very context it overturned: that of the 'scientific psychology' of the nineteenth century, whose hallmark was its (idealist) *associationism*. It is here that the problem of the contemporary is explicitly linked by Lacan to the problem of the *inheritors* (the aforementioned 'second generation'). Lacan asserts: 'In order to oppose it simply to a conception that is more or less judiciously defined in the theoretical foundations of various contemporary schools by the term "function of reality," let us say that associationist theory is dominated by the "function of truth."'†
So the problem of the contemporary is here linked by Lacan to, first, the problem of schools (in this case, psychoanalytic ones) – therefore, to the motif of transmission, exemplified of course in early psychoanalysis by the relation between an infant and its parents – and, second, to a shift in the relation of the foundations of these schools from 'truth' to 'function', a shift which at once raises the question of the *principles* of transmissibility-as-transformation.

Free association, not associationism   It is this set-up that enables Lacan to broach an archaeology of the foundations of associationism. Associationism, despite its claims to objectivity and materialism, failed to be either. Rather, in placing the emphasis on the problem of perception (hence its putative 'materialism') and on linkages through similarity (hence its putative 'objectivity'), it thereby covertly presupposed within the phenomena it studied the idealist signature of what Taine called 'veridical truth'. As Lacan points out, this means that the image in associationism is reduced to *a reflection of an illusion*.

---

* Jacques Lacan, *Ecrits*, trans. Bruce Fink (New York: Norton, 2006), p. 73.
† Lacan, *Ecrits*, p. 60.

Worse still, science itself need have nothing to do with truth in order to be a science, and it is a confusion to think otherwise. Why? Because 'scientists', at least as Lacan considers them at this early moment in his career, 'do not realize how much their truth is relative to the walls of their tower'.* Not only that, but the psychologists thereby missed the essential: it is not the installation of knowledge in the place of truth that should orient practice, but precisely the opposite, the concern for treatment as the control for theory. Truth as praxis should determine the function of knowledge-beyond-its-institution.

Here, Lacan calls this attitude of Freud's one of 'submission to reality', a submission which directly induces Freud to attend to a subject's own account of what his or her 'reality' is. Lacan proposes:

> If we wish to recognise a reality that is proper to psychical reactions, we must not begin by choosing among them; we must begin by no longer choosing. In order to gauge their efficacy, we must respect their succession ... This is the way in which what we may call 'analytic experience' is constituted: its first condition is formulated in a *law of non-omission*, which promotes everything that 'is self-explanatory', the everyday and the ordinary, to the status of interesting that is usually reserved for the remarkable; but it is incomplete without the second condition, the *law of non-systematization*, which, positing incoherence as a condition of analytic experience, presumes significant all the dross of mental life.†

In the present context – which is precisely to do with the status of the present! – we should underline the following pertinent aspects of Lacan's discourse. Above all, it concerns the specificity of the Freudian post-phenomenology: rather than a transcendental *epoche* à la Husserl, Freud introduces an immanent suspension, viz., *nothing* is bracketed. Second, this immanent suspension is primarily in the service not of knowledge but of *action*. Third, the radical operator of this double action is the fundamental Freudian principle or law of 'free association'. One can immediately see how, from Lacan's point of view, the Freudian revolution introduces a real cut into the history and practice of the sciences, from the allegedly medical on the one hand, to the allegedly purely philosophical on the other. As

---

* Lacan, *Ecrits*, p. 64.
† Lacan, *Ecrits*, p. 65.

Lacan elsewhere puts it, psychoanalysis is something that takes place *between* the scientific regime and the traditional regime of care-for-the-self as philosophical therapy.

However, we also need to add a fourth point to this departure, which is this: Lacan is still explicitly placing psychoanalysis in a *phenomenological* frame. The subheading immediately following the above quotations in fact reads: '*A Phenomenological Description of Psychoanalytic Experience*'.* This would already have been evident from Lacan's vocabulary ('phenomenon', 'experience', etc.), as well as from the ways in which he characterises the fundamental psychoanalytic principles. That Lacan is fully aware of the consequences of this affiliation is evident from his later references to the contemporary. In the famous essay 'Kant avec Sade' (1963), Lacan notes: 'we now know that humour betrays the very function of the "superego" in comedy. A fact that – to bring this psychoanalytic agency to life by instantiating it and to wrest it from the renewed obscurantism of our contemporaries' use of it – can also spice up the Kantian test of the universal rule with the grain of salt it is missing.'† This is part of the problem, then, for Lacan: to give Kant a place in a psycho-topology that does not succumb to the problem of the contemporary as 'renewed obscurantism'. Although Lacan is famous for his declaration of a 'return to Freud!' (doubled, as it happens, by a peculiar shadowy 'return to Descartes' as well) as well as his recurrent bickering with Hegel, it is worth noting that Kant is also another consistent interlocutor (perhaps above all in *Seminar VII*), and precisely regarding the psychopathology of the metaphysics of morals and its integral links to a problematic of time.

We have already seen that this obscurantism is irreducible; we can add that this is also the case on Lacan's account, for essential psychoanalytic reasons. 'Indeed', as he says in 'On a Question Prior to Any Possible Treatment of Psychosis' (drawing on material from 1955–56), 'this play of signifiers is not inert, since it is animated in each particular case by the whole ancestral history of real others that the denomination of signifying Others involves in the Subject's contemporaneity'.‡ The contemporary is a place of obscurantism,

---

* Lacan, *Ecrits*, p. 66.
† Lacan, *Ecrits*, p. 648.
‡ Lacan, *Ecrits*, p. 461.

divided according to orientations which literally cannot *speak* the principle of their division, though the division is real – and is *bespoke*, if you'll pardon the pun.* This is a comedy that analysis precisely sets out to *ana-lyse*, by showing how the inexistent but fundamental operations of language itself necessitate such an un-knowing split. The upshot of the Freudian intervention for Lacan is thus further clarified. First and foremost, the contemporaneity of the subject is formalised as a split between others and the Other, the imaginary and the symbolic. The imaginary – which itself is inter-nally split in a particular way, between narcissism and aggression, between the fantasy of totality and its tearing to scraps, between one and another – is subtended by the symbolic, as an extrinsic place which is itself lacking its key element, and it is this immemorial constitutional lack that is transmitted through its inexistence. Yet it does so only in its trafficking with the materials provided 'by the whole ancestral history' of the subject. The key to unlocking these routines of the subject's contemporaneity is through psychoanalysis's praxis of free association, with its peculiar characteristics already noted above. So we already have an approach from Lacan which rebroaches the problem of time from that of contemporaneity, and enters contemporaneity by means of a radicalisation of the thought of structure and an incitation to free association as revelatory of the anachrony of the subject. That this project immediately encounters the moral thought of Kant and the language of phenomenology as an intimate (or, perhaps, to use Lacan's own hilarious pun, *extimate*) enemy is no accident.

Two senses of the contemporary in Deleuze   Now Deleuze, though he rarely uses the term, is a thinker of the contemporary in two senses. The first is critical, and relies upon the theme that runs from the begin-ning of his work to the end, according to which the advent of novelty is perennially resisted by existing structures (from individual habits to the functioning of States as apparatuses of capture). In this regard, the contemporary, as a name for what obscures the new and the important, is the object of a critique: 'philosophy has an essential relationship to time: it is always against its time, critique of the present world'.[†] This critical strand of Deleuze's argument is, as it is

---

* See Samuel Beckett's joke about the tailor, the world, and the pair of trousers.
† Gilles Deleuze, *Nietzsche and Philosophy*, trans. Hugh Tomlinson (London: Continuum, 2006), p. 100.

here, often marked by the disjuct deployment of the terms 'contemporary' and 'present'.

In the second sense, the contemporary is thought as the disjunction between becoming and history, and which arises on the side of becoming. The contemporary is thus the object of an affirmation in Deleuze, and speaks to the capacity for novelty to arise in the first place. If these two points are reorganised according to the order of reasons, we see we are dealing with a serial position that passes from the conditions of novelty to the advent of novelty, and from the advent of novelty to its subsumption in (and by) the present. This means, correlatively, that the opposition between becoming and history is not an exclusive one, and that the two processes are intertwined – or better, *intercalated* – where untimely becoming interrupts and asserts itself within the movement of history (the becoming-untimely of history itself?).* The contemporary is thus the name for the structural dehiscence that gives rise to history and the present from within history and the present. Deleuze's account of the contemporary has, furthermore, three sites of expression: ontology, a critical conception of thought, and a theory of time; or again, what the thought of the contemporary reveals about being, what the thought of the contemporary reveals about the creative act, and what it reveals about the structure of temporality (since it is time itself that grounds this non-coincidence of the present with itself that is the contemporary; it is also this dehiscence within the present that is the form of time as such).

The untimely
In any event, the first heading under which Deleuze will treat the contemporary is that of the *untimely*, what stands between the present and itself. Or, as Deleuze will write with Guattari in *What is Philosophy?*, the untimely is what resists the present: 'books of philosophy and works of art . . . have resistance in common – their resistance to death, to servitude, to the intolerable, to shame, and to the present'.† Deleuze's use of Nietzsche's untimely always draws attention to a *substantive non-coincidence* of the

---

* One development of this kind of theme can be found in the work of Craig Lundy. See in particular his *History and Becoming: Deleuze's Philosophy of Creativity* (Edinburgh: Edinburgh University Press, 2012) and 'Deleuze and Guattari's Historiophilosophy: Philosophical Thought and its Historical Milieu', *Critical Horizons*, Vol. 12, No. 2 (2011), pp. 115–35.

† Deleuze and Guattari, *What is Philosophy?*, p. 110.

present with itself. It is only because this non-coincidence exists – or, better, subsists or insists – that history becomes possible, qua the sequentially ordered passage of past presents. More importantly, it is only by attending to this untimely facet of the present, what is contemporary *in* the present, that the problematic of the event appears in all of its importance for philosophy.

This point about the Nietzschean untimely is intertwined in Deleuze's work with the claim that to be contemporary is an essential requirement of philosophy. This is due to the philosophy's primary enemy, stupidity. Unlike the figured foes in Badiou's pantheon of villainy (the sophist and the anti-philosopher), it is the fog of stupidity, the only true global community – one that links together the high and the low alike in the purveyance of blank looks and common sense – with which philosophy struggles. Moreover, stupidity has a crucial relationship, on Deleuze's account, with the present. It is on the basis of the habitual mooring of the present that, despite the incalculable shocks that impact us on all sides (due the ubiquity of the event in Deleuze), we are able to maintain our semi-stupefied state, and to which is attached the primary affect of fear, the fear of what there is here and now losing shape, becoming unrecognisable. It follows, then, that the worst capitulations to the present are symptomatically marked in philosophy itself – we have made some brief indications to this point above.

Philosophy and communication   *What is Philosophy?* details three interrelated ways in which the failure of philosophy manifests itself. The first is the extent to which philosophy has been subordinated to the ideal of universal communication and the harmonious and frictionless society of friends. By grounding philosophy in the facility and right of communication, philosophy entirely abdicates to the present. Famous passages in this book address the absolute inadequacy of the communicative conception of philosophy that constitutes one of the points at which our three authors are undoubtedly in consonance:

> Philosophy has a horror of discussions. It always has something else to do. Debate is unbearable to it, but not because it is too sure of itself. On the contrary, it is its uncertainties that take it down other, more solitary paths. But in Socrates was philosophy not a free discussion among friends? Is it not, as the conversation of free men, the summit of Greek sociability? In fact, Socrates

constantly made all discussion impossible, both in the short form of the contest of questions and answers and in the long form of a rivalry between discourses. He turned the friend into the friend of the single concept, and the concept into the pitiless monologue that eliminates the rivals one by one.[*]

As we shall see in the coming chapters, the situational and conceptual necessity of rendering discussion impossible even becomes one of the central aims of our three authors, which has consequences for their styles, their concepts and their derangement of existing forms of address. It is, however, crucial to underline that such positions are not anti-argumentative: on the contrary, the refoundation of the grounds of reason, logic and presentation are at stake, in the name of (why not say it directly?) *truth*. Even Deleuze, who is so often held to elaborate a position that valorises the interesting over the true, only does so – to the extent that he does – as an attempt to evade the Scylla and Charybdis of 'discussion' on the one hand, and unthought pseudo-demonstrative piety on the other.

Philosophy and marketing

This leads to the second manifestation. Since philosophy is happy to render itself, its creative capacity and its resistance to stupidity, equal only to the ideal of dinner table opinionating, it finds itself unable to resist being made subordinate to the creative communication of ideas as it is practised at its most frenetic and enthusiastic: marketing. 'The most shameful moment came when computer science, marketing, design and advertising, all the disciplines of communication, seized hold of the word *concept* itself and said "This is our concern, we are the creative ones, we are the *ideas men*!"'[†] Only philosophy could have resisted this subordination, and, *precisely*, it did not ('What is most distressing is not this shameless appropriation but the conception of philosophy that made it possible in the first place'[‡]). And on the side of philosophy, shameful compromises continue to be made – as though philosophers are so little philosophical, so little resistant to the present, that they could easily find themselves at home in a marketing department or a private business school, itself attached like a leech to the side of a university.

---

[*] Deleuze and Guattari, *What is Philosophy?*, p. 29.
[†] Deleuze and Guattari, *What is Philosophy?*, p. 11.
[‡] Deleuze and Guattari, *What is Philosophy?*, p. 99.

Philosophy and capitalism

Third, capitalism, as the social organisation of the present, is in no manner troubled by this conception of philosophy, which does nothing to resist it. Since the opinions that circulate at the table of discussion have an *a priori* and *de jure* equality, the communicative model of philosophy does nothing to trouble the immediate equation of opinion and commodity. In sum, this ideal of communication, this ideal communicability, cannot be the *métier* of a contemporary philosophy, which must instead necessarily *break* with this theoretico-capitalist orthodoxy: 'We do not lack communication. On the contrary, we have too much of it. We lack creation. *We lack resistance to the present.*'* It is at this point that Deleuze and Guattari invoke – though not without noting its unfortunate tonality – the term *utopia*. Rather than indicating an idealisation (rapturous or cynical), it makes for them '*that conjunction of philosophy, or of the concept, with the present milieu*'.† This takes us back, once more, to the Nietzschean *untimely*: 'true philosophy is no more historical than eternal: it must be untimely, always untimely'.‡

Creation in thought

What we lack, they say, is *creation* in thought. Deleuze and Guattari's definition of philosophy as the creation of concepts is well-known, but the point is a more general one, namely that critique cannot be a merely (or purely) negative category, the posing of an oppositional stance, since this too is a way of being present in the present (in a landmark late essay, Deleuze will oppose the negativity of war with a positivity of combat). Creation and not opposition is the locus of resistance because the present is a perennial problematic, and to merely oppose it is to be entirely a part of it. Deleuze's many remarks on the facile nature of the negative have this as their ethical correlate – as he says of Hegel's labour of the negative, 'if the truth be told, none of this would amount to much if it was not for the moral presuppositions and practical implications of such a distortion'.§ Deleuze and Guattari are thus closer (at least to the letter) of Trotsky than Marx in these terms, in the sense that they too insist on the need for a

* Deleuze and Guattari, *What is Philosophy?*, p. 108.
† Deleuze and Guattari, *What is Philosophy?*, p. 100.
‡ Gilles Deleuze, *Pure Immanence: Essays on a Life*, trans. Anne Boyman (New York: Zone Books, 2001), p. 72.
§ Gilles Deleuze, *Difference and Repetition*, trans. Paul Patton (New York: Columbia University Press, 1994), p. 268.

permanent – which would have to be heard as untimely – revolution.

Becoming The same point is made repeatedly by Deleuze and Guattari in *A Thousand Plateaus* in particular, under the rubric of becoming. Despite the voluminous and occasionally arcane terminology they deploy there, the concept is a straightforward one. Since the untimely contemporary does not allow what exists in the present (existing structures of thought, organisation of bodies, matter, etc.), by holding it open to what might otherwise be the case, there are always a range of trajectories available to become otherwise. These trajectories are not subjective enterprises in the banal sense, but involve genuine transformations for whatever engages in them, and in whatever they engage – this is the famous double articulation involved in becoming: the wasp eats from the orchid, while the orchid uses the wasp to disseminate its pollen. Crucially, becomings are trajectories of transformation illegal from the point of view of the present situation. In sum, processes of becoming are the contemporary, insofar as they render the present incommensurate with itself. Thus the following reference to Nietzsche in the plateau devoted to the theme of becoming:

> There is no act of creation that is not transhistorical and does not come up from behind or proceed by way of a liberated line. Nietzsche opposes history not to the eternal but to the subhistorical or superhistorical: the Untimely, which is another name for haecceity, becoming, the innocence of becoming.[*]

In a series of remarkable passages, which bring together these points, Deleuze will characterise the untimely contemporary as a form of absolute, violent engagement with the present. At the risk of raising the ire of the gods of copyright:

> The image of the philosopher is obscured by all his necessary disguises, but also by all the betrayals that turn him into the philosopher of religion, the philosopher of the State, the collector of current values and the functionary of history. The authentic image of the philosopher does not survive the one who can embody it for a time, for his epoch. It must be taken up again, reanimated, it must find a new field of activity in the following epoch. If philosophy's critical task is not actively taken up in every epoch philosophy dies

---

[*] Gilles Deleuze and Félix Guattari, *A Thousand Plateaus*, trans. Brian Massumi (Minneapolis: University of Minnesota Press, 1987), p. 295.

and with it die the images of the philosopher and the free man.
Stupidity and baseness are always those of our own time, of our
contemporaries, our stupidity and baseness. Unlike the atemporal
concept of error, baseness is inseparable from time, that is from
this rapture of the present condition in which it is incarnated and
in which it moves. This is why philosophy has an essential relationship with time: it is always against its time, critique of the present
world. The philosopher creates concepts that are neither eternal nor
historical but untimely and not of the present world . . . There is no
eternal or historical philosophy. Eternity, like the historicity of philosophy amounts to this: philosophy is always untimely, untimely
in every epoch.*

What is centrally at stake in the Deleuzian philosophical programme
is the necessity of becoming-imperceptible as the untimeliness of
the contemporary, entirely in and out of its time at once. Peculiarly
enough, this simultaneous necessity for self-situation inseparable
from time and situational-derangement qua uncanny untimeliness
is also an aspect of Badiou's philosophical project. Yet Badiou also
explicitly opposes himself to the Deleuzian programme at a certain
key point.

The contemporary   For Badiou the question of the contemporary, of
renders the old new   what it is to be contemporary, is bound up with the
question of innovation, of the new, of the production of the new and
so of the 'present'. The contemporary as a category of stasis, as a
nomination for what exists *here* and *now* in time, is problematic. For
if, as Badiou contends, his key effort is to think the new in situations,
then this would suggest that what concerns his philosophy most is to
have done not with what is, but with what it is that determines that
existence or the possibility of existing is a matter of its being 'contemporary' to what the 'temper of the times' recognises to be (known to
be) here and now. So the question arises: what is it that is here under
the logic of the 'here and now'? Alternately, what, for Badiou, does
the contemporary name, if not the *here and now*?

The primacy of self-   Badiou always opens his works with an essay in
situation   self-situation: *Theory of the Subject* begins with a
short polemic addressed to the political failures of contemporaneous
France; *Being and Event* with a triple localisation vis-à-vis Heidegger

---

* Deleuze, *Nietzsche and Philosophy*, p. 100, translation modified.

as 'the last universally recognizable philosopher', analytic philosophy as keeping alive the scientific thread of philosophy, and anti-philosophical practices as opening up unprecedented modes that challenge philosophy; *Logics of Worlds* opens with a barrage against 'democratic materialism'. But even the shorter essays or polemics invariably begin with exercises of self-localisation too. In other words, each work of Badiou's begins self-reflexively with a mapping of the contemporary situation with which he will attempt to break.

In doing so, however, Badiou necessarily also recognises and affirms the difficulties: the very phrase 'attempt to break' is itself a cover (an *asylum ignorantiae?*) for a multitude of possible specifications. As he so carefully and powerfully phrases the difficulties in the opening paragraphs of *Being and Event*, 'there is disagreement over knowing whether this opening [of the contemporary] ... manifests itself as a *revolution*, a *return* or a *critique*'.* How can one not see in this brilliantly compressed résumé a designation of the strongest active philosophical elements of the situation, respectively Marxist, psycho-analytic and Kantian? As Badiou responds: to be contemporary is to 'draw a diagonal', to move transversally, point by point, against the topological prescriptions of the contemporary. His own programme will therefore be neither revolutionary, returnist, nor critical, but it will not therefore simply repudiate these options in their entirety. The point is to move point by point. In doing so, however, the goal is the inscription of an eternity in and through this point-by-point production of the present itself.

From here to eternity   Let's now approach this regulated movement from the other side, from the side of 'eternity', specifically the eternity of the Idea. For Badiou, the new in situations, which is to say, the step-by-step production of the truth of situations, is also simultaneously the realisation of Truth as Idea. The Idea is not specific to the time of the situated production of truths (lower case), nor is it a substance, fullness, purity or perfection from which all else issues or to which all is subordinated; it is that which is thinkable as thought of each process of innovation and invention, of event and consequence, in whatever field of thought it takes place – political, artistic, scientific or amorous. The step-by-step subjective production of truths, truths particular to specific situations (in the sense that this

---

* Alain Badiou, *Being and Event*, trans. Oliver Feltham (London: Continuum, 2005), p. 2.

situation is configured and counted as secure by a knowledge that circulates as its very guarantee of stability, order and regularity *here and now*), in other words, the traceable bodies incorporated and manifest for discrete worlds, is at the same time the participation of these bodies and subjects (as subjectivisable bodies!) in the manifestation of the Idea of Truth manifest in each and every such production, in each and every epoch, situation, world and condition. That truths are made manifest, or are 'not impossible', in disparate worlds and regardless of time – that they are in fact exceptions to the time of their time* – is what is named by the Idea. Idea is 'the name given to what is thought insofar as it is thought', the 'mediating instance between the act of thought and the act of being'[†]: and this applies not only to mathematics but to all *forms of thought*. Every disparate procedure of truth, from, for example, the slave revolt of Spartacus to that of Toussaint L'Ouverture in Haiti, to the Spartacists in Berlin to the unnamed (im)possibility yet to come, as Badiou contends, participates in and manifests at once this Idea of Truth as the truths of their time.

To put this another way, and in relation to the art of theatre, the Idea as 'an eternal and incomplete idea caught in the instantaneousness ordeal of its own completion' presents a choice: between the 'chance-laden scenic configurations that complete the (eternal) idea by means of the instant that it lacks, and . . . the often very seductive configurations that nevertheless remain external to and aggravate the incompleteness of the idea'. 'Truth', Badiou concludes, 'must be granted to the following axiom: A theatrical representation will never abolish chance.'[‡] The contemporary straddles eternity and the present without being reducible to either – neither to transcendence nor to that vague relativism which underpins both subservience and reaction in our (capital) times. 'What interests me', Badiou avers in the *Second Manifesto*,

> is that a truth is produced with particular materials in a specific world, yet, at the same time, since it is understood and usable in an entirely different world and across potentially vast spans of time –

* 'Pour aujourd'hui: Platon!', Séminaire d'Alain Badiou, 2007–8, available at http://www.entretemps.asso.fr/Badiou/07-08.htm (accessed 6 May 2013).
† Alain Badiou, *Theoretical Writings*, ed. and trans. Ray Brassier and Alberto Toscano (London: Continuum, 2004), p. 167.
‡ Alain Badiou, *Handbook of Inaesthetics*, trans. Alberto Toscano (Stanford: Stanford University Press, 2004), p. 74.

we understand the artistic power of cave paintings executed 40,000 years ago – it has, well and truly, to be trans-temporal.*

In other words, truths are both conditional and absolute but never one or the other – hence the capital T (as for Truth as Idea) marks, as he says in the *Manifesto for Philosophy*, only the 'empty' or 'void' place of truths, a void that pertains to every situation as per the formal elaboration of situation as such and which insists as the situated site for an event – precisely that which marks the impossibility of the abolition of chance.†

Point of a recommencement

The Platonic referent is plain to see – to the Idea as that which marks the aporetic point of a recommencement 'rendering immanence and transcendence indiscernible'.‡ Yet its formalisation today is also *extra-* or perhaps *citra-*Platonic,§ given that for Badiou the ontological condition is itself 'contemporary' (set and category theory), the conditional arrangement includes art, the art of that which inexists 'rendered visible',¶ love as scientifically articulated in psychoanalysis (Lacanian), revolutionary and thus non-state and non-party politics and, as such, commends a resolutely contemporary and post- but not anti-Cartesian theory of the subject.** While Plato shares this set of philosophical conditions, the

---

* Alain Badiou, *Second Manifesto for Philosophy*, trans. Louise Burchill (London: Polity, 2011), p. 129. Parallel in a lecture given by Deleuze to cinema students: 'Malraux developed an admirable philosophical concept. He said something very simple about art. He said it was the only thing that resists death . . . Think about it . . . what resists death? You only have to look at a statuette from three thousand years before the common era to see that Malraux's response is a pretty good one . . . even if it is not the only thing that resists.' Gilles Deleuze, 'What is the Creative Act?', in *Two Regimes of Madness*, trans. Ames Hodges and Mike Taormina (New York: Semiotext(e), 2007), p. 23.

† See Alain Badiou, *Conditions*, trans. Steven Corcoran (London: Continuum, 2008), p. 11. And see also: 'Today, in the extremely obscure situation that is the general system of contemporary politics, philosophy can attempt to clarify the situation without having any pretense to creating it. Philosophy has as its condition and horizon the concrete situation of different political practices, and it will try, within these conditions, to find instruments of clarification, legitimation, and so on. This current takes seriously the idea that politics is itself an autonomy of thought, that it is a collective practice with an intelligence all its own.' Alain Badiou, 'We Need a Popular Discipline', *Critical Inquiry*, No. 34, Summer (2008), pp. 645–59. This same relation articulated here as between philosophy and politics is that of philosophy to all its conditions – any thinking of the contemporary has to be thought in its immanent division as Two. Note that chance is correlated to a public in *Handbook of Inaesthetics* and thus theatre is the possible site of the crossing of art and politics qua truth.

‡ Badiou, *Theoretical Writings*, p. 50.

§ Badiou, *Theoretical Writings*, p. 168.

¶ Alain Badiou, *Polemics*, ed. and trans. Steve Corcoran (London: Verso, 2006), p. 148.

** Unlike in Deleuze's reading in *Difference and Repetition* (p. 50), Badiou, following Lacan some way, already sees in Descartes' 'I think' a split constitutive of the subject. Deleuze contends that Descartes runs 'together the ontological, the formal and the numerical' in

various inventions, interventions and novelties that those conditions produce realise themselves in the epoch that is our own, distinct from those of Plato or Descartes or Kant or Hegel. In other words, while it is true to say, as Badiou points out, that Plato concerns himself with mathematics, art, love and politics, and that these animate and condition the dialogues in their search for the form proper to philosophy, these conditions have their own discursive history. Hence the conditions today are different from those in the days of Plato, Descartes, etc. Not only is the existence of such discursive truth procedures at stake, however, but it is also the case for Badiou that they continue to operate in a similar fashion. The realisation of the conditions in their disparate 'times' still links them to certain ideal operations, which simultaneously manifest a distinct and 'compossible' trajectory. The conditions always produce the truths of *their* times, which philosophy makes contemporary for all time under the empty nomination 'Truth', 'a category which operates but presents nothing'— here and now.*

Matheme versus poem   There is one further thing at stake here that is key to Badiou's paradoxical nomination of Plato (among others) as 'our contemporary'. This concerns the immanent rivalry between the poem and the matheme. In terms of philosophy at least this rivalry is key to understanding how being contemporary has nothing to do with time or proximity per se and everything to do with the Idea.

For Plato the poem itself – the pre-eminent tool of sophistic teaching, as Protagoras announces, and, as such, its pre-eminent condition – presented philosophy with its greatest rival in terms of what it is to know. By recourse to mathematics, Plato was able to interrupt the transmissible dominion of the poem. The reconfiguration of philosophy qua 'dialectic' has as its effect the demonstration that sophistry, the poem's political 'representative', did not, ultimately, know what it supposed and claimed to know. The deployment of the mathematical operation against the *knowledge* of the poem conditions the philosophical assignation of sophistry 'to its place'. That is to say, as Badiou recounts, mathematics for Plato constitutes a discourse

his distinctions and thus is guilty of 'analogising' thought and self, as it were. But not every crossing of mathematical thought and philosophical composition is Pythagorean!
* Badiou, *Conditions*, p. 11.

that could not be reduced to the vagaries of experience, the contentions of language, or the force of opinions and majorities. If such a discourse existed, one for which the real was at stake – 'things, not words' as the famous philosophical declaration has it – then it had to *be thought*. Mathematics is intelligible beyond opinion, and thus conditions a possible *and* actual exception to the rule of 'bodies and languages'.*

This is not to say that mathematics is the last word on being or truth, just that its sheer existence as the discourse it is – incomplete *as such* and consistent in terms of its deductive capacities and articulated effects – means that poetry, with its characteristic analogic, metaphoric, metonymic and oratic operations, cannot maintain its monopoly over the *forms* of thought, nor sophistry over the means of its transmission. Mathematics effects this at the point of the paradoxes that the discursive adaptation of the knowledge of the poets themselves logically generates. In his essay 'What is a Poem?' (and elsewhere) Badiou nuances this 'old quarrel' between poetry and philosophy, situating it as between poetry and mathematics, not poetry and philosophy per se, thus making possible a recalibration of poetry as a thought in itself, as is, he argues, mathematics.[†] For Badiou, it is the turn to language in its various guises, the pre-dominance of an 'aestheticised' logic, phenomenology, language games, etc., rather than poetry as such, which for Badiou turns ultimately, ontologically, on or towards (*pros en*) some conception of the One.[‡] For Badiou, it is to this linguistic complex that today the name sophistry refers – later we will note the ways in which 'great modern sophistry' remains contemporary to 'great ancient sophistry'. The point remains that the thinking of being qua being is always that of mathematics, demonstrable now vis-à-vis set theory's handling of infinite infinities; while language, logic, etc., avers in one way or another the sets of relations, rules of appearance, forms of representation, discernments of objects, of what mathematics presents as the real of being qua being. To be contemporary is to be contemporary with whomsoever, in whatever way, participates in or decides for (it's the same thing) this Idea – which this very participation makes manifest.

---

* Alain Badiou, *Logics of Worlds*, trans. Alberto Toscano (London: Continuum, 2009), p. 1.
† See *Handbook of Inaesthetics* and *Theoretical Writings*. The latter has to be argued for, against mathematical Platonists as against Heidegger, Hegel and ultimately Plato himself.
‡ Badiou, *Theoretical Writings*, p. 166.

This means, then as now, now as then, that what is known as thought, what counts existences, has to be thought again, at least *for philosophy* – time and again subject to what conditions it – ontologically and, in terms of what it is for being to appear, logically as well (although the latter, for Badiou, is an *onto*-logic, a mathematised and so de-aestheticised logic). Certainly, Plato would agree with Lacan that 'the human animal is such that it can get by very well without truth' (and as Plato pointed out, without philosophy too) – at least up to the point of questioning what this 'well' might be. As Giorgio Agamben puts it in his own essay 'What is the Contemporary?', 'success' here is 'evaluated . . . by our capacity to measure up to this exigency'.*

If Plato is 'our contemporary', then what it means to be contemporary is to think in such a way that one is not subject to what Badiou calls the authoritarian regime of the true or its relativist counterpart:

> An authoritarian regime exists when the truth of a statement depends, not on the argument that supports it, but on the position of the one who pronounces it, whether God, king, priest, professor, or prophet. A relativist or sceptical frivolity reigns when the critique of the authoritarian regime of the true leads to the suppression of the absoluteness and universality of truths.[†]

As he puts it in *Theory of the Subject*, 'when one abdicates universality, one obtains universal horror'.[‡] As ever with Badiou's conception of philosophy we shouldn't overlook the *polemos* involved in this motif of making Plato our contemporary. Indeed, it's as much in what this Platonic framework makes impossible as possible for philosophy today, which as conditioned is always 'contemporary' or not at all, that Badiou is interested. Thus 'Plato's problem – which is still ours – is how our experience of a particular world (that which we are given to know, the "knowable") can open up access to eternal, universal and, in this sense, *trans-worldly* truths.'[§]

---

* G. Agamben, 'What is the Contemporary?', in *What is an Apparatus?*, trans. David Kishik and Stefan Pedatella (Stanford: Stanford University Press, 2009), p. 39. In speaking of success here Agamben is referring to his seminar, but the context is the texts and authors 'many centuries removed from us' as well as those more approximate.

† Alain Badiou, 'Plato, Our Dear Plato!', trans. Alberto Toscano, *Angelaki*, Vol. 2, No. 3 (2006), pp. 39–41; p. 40.

‡ Alain Badiou, *Theory of the Subject*, trans. with intro. Bruno Bosteels (London and New York: Continuum, 2009), p. 197.

§ Badiou, *Second Manifesto for Philosophy*, p. 106, translation modified.

Not only is Badiou repeating the alignment he makes between his philosophy and that of Plato as the founder of philosophy (most prominently in *Manifesto for Philosophy*), he is also marking out in the contemporary situation that discursive configuration and those philosophical positions that reject this Platonic identification and, paradoxically, are therefore not 'our contemporaries' despite having the closest temporal, situational and even spatial proximity. These latter temporal and spatial categories are not critical to what Badiou means by contemporary – if Plato is and the anti-Platonists of the twentieth century are not. The latter, spread across the discursive fields of hermeneutics, Anglo-American analytic philosophy, and post-modernism,* are in one way or another in thrall to the authority of language or the scepticism its inherent excess permits sanctuary: 'after all, "Platonist" is in general not a flattering epithet – not for Heidegger, Popper, Sartre, or Deleuze, nor even for the hard Marxists of the golden age, or for the logicians, whether Viennese or Yankee. "Platonist" is almost an insult, as it was for Nietzsche, who argued that the mission of our age was to "be cured of the Plato sickness"'.† Nor – we can add – for Lacan. Thus time, language and spatial proximity are not the conditions of possibility for what is 'contemporary'.

Anti-Platonism regnant It is not true, however, that amongst this timely anti-Platonism there is no nuance. On the contrary, we could invoke: Deleuze's overturning of Plato's difference on the basis of Plato's own internal division; Lacan's subversion of Plato vis-à-vis his 'avatar' Socrates; the generalised reduction of Plato to Aristotelianism, the better to 'include' the division and so reduce it to 'nothing', and so on. Indeed, these differences are enough (or part thereof) to set them against each other, but one should not mistake diversity of opinion for difference as such. The former, as our democratic age attests, is merely cover for a shared manifest antipathy to the mathematical *condition* and therefore to the conception of 'truths' it makes 'not impossible'. This conditioning is for Badiou that which

---

* Alain Badiou, *Infinite Thought: Truth and the Return to Philosophy*, ed. and trans. Justin Clemens and Oliver Feltham (London: Continuum, 2003), p. 46, and *Deleuze: The Clamor of Being*, trans. Louise Burchill (Minneapolis: University of Minnesota Press, 2000), pp. 101–2. 'Let us say in passing that since (philosophical) remedies are often worse than the malady, our age, in order to be cured of the Plato sickness, has swallowed such doses of a relativist, vaguely sceptical, lightly spiritualist and insipidly moralist medicine, that it is in the process of gently dying, in the small bed of its supposed democratic comfort.' Badiou, 'Plato, our Dear Plato!' p. 40.
† Badiou, 'Plato, our Dear Plato!', p. 39.

displaces language as the medium of the expression of being, of what is sayable of being qua being (or 'difference' or 'rules' or 'norms' or 'selves' or 'consciousness' or whatever the term for 'what is' might be), and so as the sole recourse of any articulation or manifestation of the true or truths, whether thought, as sophisticated as it may be, as unconscious or as sense. It is this rejection, this negationism, no matter how rigorously worked through – Deleuze's spatial geometry and Lacan's knots— which unites this disparity. It's the point of their indiscernibility, we might say, which is not the same as their similarity.

To be the contemporary of Plato, with the Idea of Truth, then, is to be resolutely non-contemporary to what Badiou nominates with generality, the linguistic turn, to great post-modern sophistry at its worst, to philosophies or anti-philosophies of the One at its best. To the former Badiou remains un-contemporary, just as was Socrates to his sophistic interlocutors – present to, but divided from, demonstrably, eternally. With the current non-philosophies Badiou establishes protocols of non-relation, of minimal difference; with contemporary philosophies insofar as they take up the question or problem of philosophy itself: those of being, truth and subject, under condition of their elaboration and in a way that is itself a manifestation of what it is to think through the *discipline* of philosophy.

Obviously, other concepts and categories than those of language, experience, authority and opinion, or in fact those of time, nature and history, give us the constitution of 'contemporary' in Badiou's telling. The key question, as he remarks in *Second Manifesto for Philosophy* is: 'What is thinking in our times?' Still, we need to note that when it comes to thinking about some of the figures of what Badiou designates as *contemporary* anti-Platonism – such as, say, Wittgenstein, Lacan, or Nietzsche – it is precisely their status as contemporary anti-philosophers (thus anti-Platonists) that becomes important for Badiou's conception of philosophy itself. Moreover, it is in rivalry with two twentieth-century (nominally) anti-Platonist philosophers, Heidegger and Deleuze, that Badiou also sets out his two great works of philosophy, *Being and Event* and *Logics of Worlds*. But even here we need to realise that both these works are constructed with regard to the discoveries of contemporary mathematics as well as contemporary politics, art and love, in conformity to the Platonic conditions.

❖

Even as the contemporary anti-philosophers are, well, contemporary, in the sense that they inhabit and draw from (but also ignore, falsify and foreclose) the temper of the times, they still do so in a way which accords with the approach, emphasis and commitments of those pre-Socratic 'anti-Platonists' such as Heraclitus or Democritus; or of Plato's sophistic contemporaries Protagoras and Gorgias; or of the post-Platonists – if not Aristotle directly, then, in no particular order and making no particular reference, the Stoic, Cynic or Epicurean types, to say nothing of the neo-Platonist anti-Platonists. For Badiou, anti-philosophy is a category immanent to that of philosophy. As such, contemporary anti-philosophy has ancient anti-philosophy as its contemporary, just as does 'sophistry'. What this means, though, is that despite anti-philosophy's position on the question of truths and of Truth as such, its relation to the Idea – and despite the fact that anti-philosophy prides itself on being untimely at all times – something Ideal insists between the two, something that makes 'Heraclitus the contemporary of Nietzsche or Wittgenstein that of Arcesilaus'.*

So, again, contemporary in the sense of (temporal) proximity and contemporary in the sense of (the eternity of) the Idea (in this case of philosophy itself) and contemporary in the sense that what is near is far away and what is far away is most near. In other words the contemporary is subjective *and* formal, conditional *and* philosophi-cal, proximate *and* eternal – philosophical or anti-philosophical. The difference is that the former will conceptualise this, while the latter disavows any such division; the former will affirm this, while the latter, in one way or another, like Nietzsche, will consider such a formalisation exemplary of the illness of the times, and not at all 'untimely'.

Still, the notion of the contemporary insofar as it can be thought only gets us so far. We have a sort of an impasse in that it is possible that two forms of the contemporary exist side by side: the contemporar-ies of the poem and those of Plato, of language against mathematics. The 'old quarrel' which marks our contemporaneity is re-enacted, if

---

* Arcesilaus was head of the Academy for a time and it seems he developed his notion of suspending judgement from a selective reading of what Plato understood by aporia. Thus it is not so much the starting point but the consequences of thought that reveal the anti-philosophy of philosophy.

subtly reconfigured,* under the conditions of a contemporary mathematical invention whose consequences, ontological and logical,
must not go un-thought, thus affirming again the non- or not-just-
temporal dimension of the contemporary, such that it is simultaneously a participation in the eternity of the Idea (of what it is to live)
and the place of its evental and subjective renovation.

A new present   As we have remarked, what this contemporary
                       impasse calls forward, as the same contemporary
impasse called forward for Plato 'our contemporary', is the formation of what Badiou calls 'a new present'. We must pass from the
contemporary, as the name for what subtracts itself immanently
from the time of this time, to the present as that which must be made
manifest, affirmed *here and now*. To forge a new present – which
'neither perfectly coincides' with its time nor 'adjusts itself to it'† – is
what it is to be Plato's contemporary (or Saint Paul's or Marx's or
Freud's) and simultaneously to not be contemporary, insofar as philosophy, which thinks the thoughts of its time after all, is concerned
with those contemporaries of the 'suture of language to being'. The
present, then, which exists and must *be thought*, depends on the
enacting of a procedure which, in its act but not in its principle, is a
de-suturing of what can be thought from the dominance of a single
condition, the repetition of a definitive (conception of) logic, or the
'exorbitant excesses of the state'.‡

Philosophy circulates, Badiou argues, between its conditions, which,
insofar as they accomplish what is true of the situations in which they
are manifest, affirmatively subtract themselves from the norm, rule
or states of these specific situations. This movement, which Badiou
names compossibility (after Leibniz) is key, for it links philosophy
qua discourse to the thought (or forms of thought) of its time and
at the same time provides for its irreducibility to this time alone.
Philosophy in-exists when this circulation, this capacity for compossibility, is given up in favour of one or other of the conditions, as
if that condition could itself be the sole and single condition for all
thought.§ This is what Plato's Socrates was up against in fifth-century
Athens: the sophistic shackling of the poetic as condition or currency

---

* Badiou, 'What is a Poem?', in *Handbook of Inaesthetics*, pp. 16–27.
† Agamben, 'What is the Contemporary?', p. 40.
‡ Badiou, *Being and Event*, p. 282.
§ Alain Badiou, *Manifeste pour la philosophie* (Paris: Seuil, 1989), p. 41.

of all possible knowledge, whether political, amorous, scientific, etc.* The domination by one condition of the general capacity for knowledge means, despite the multiple disavowals of the contemporary sceptics (including relativists, constructivists and hermeneuts), that this condition sets itself up as the place of truth. From its occupation of this place it comes to dominate all the other generic conditions for thought such that, for example, under the positivist suture that locates all truth within science, the thought of the poem is relegated to the function of supplement in the sphere of culture or a matter of linguistic analysis; that the amorous condition is ignored altogether or at best relegated to the inconsistent complex of 'sex and sentimentality'; that the political condition is conceived as a technical problem of administration and management.†

Some consequences of philosophy's default What we can say, then, is that when philosophy ceases to circulate and to compose, and instead delegates its function of thinking the thought of its time qua generic procedures, then there is, as such, no present or at least no Idea of the present. In other words, what is thought in this time, cannot be *thought* precisely because what it is to be contemporary lacks any access to an Idea beyond the immediacy determined by the suture of which philosophy has become the support and, in some archaic sense, the guarantee. Philosophy fails to think the thought of its time, which is to say, be conditioned by and circulate as the discourse of the four generic procedures and, as such, it subordinates the thought of the present to the determinations of the most recent, most up to date, most 'current'. Knowledge turns to *oikonomia*.‡ We have said enough on this to forestall any supposition of nostalgia or 'idealism' in the sentimental sense: Badiou certainly offers no comfort to the Restoration tendencies that periodically do the rounds. We need to note that today this progressive reductionism goes even further and that the generic conditions for thought – as discourses in themselves

* A. J. Bartlett, *Badiou and Plato: An Education by Truths* (Edinburgh: Edinburgh University Press, 2011).
† Badiou, *Manifeste pour la philosophie*, p. 42. Cf.: 'and, finally, on the level of knowledge ... the strange concoction we're supposed to swallow of a technologized scientism, the crowning glory of which is the visualisation of stereoscopic brains in colour, combined with a bureaucratic legalism whose supreme manifestation is the "evaluation" of all things by experts hailing from nowhere who invariably conclude that thinking serves no purpose and even proves harmful'. Badiou, *Second Manifesto for Philosophy*, p. 5.
‡ For the genealogy of this notion or, really, the reverse genealogy, see Giorgio Agamben, *The Kingdom and the Glory: For a Theological Genealogy of Economy and Government*, trans. Lorenzo Chiesa and Matteo Mandarini (Stanford: Stanford University Press, 2011).

capable of conditioning a contemporary philosophy – have been reduced in the contemporary world, the pedagogic world of 'democratic materialism' as Badiou calls it, to mere techniques of the market.* In his *Saint Paul and the Foundation of Universalism*, in the chapter entitled 'Paul: Our Contemporary', Badiou declares:

> The contemporary world is thus doubly hostile to truth procedures. This hostility betrays itself though nominal occlusions: where the name of a truth procedure should obtain, another, which represses it, holds sway. The name 'culture' comes to obliterate that of 'art.' The word 'technology' obliterates the word 'science.' The word 'management' obliterates the word 'politics.' The word 'sexuality' obliterates love. The 'culture-technology-management-sexuality' system, which has the immense merit of being homogeneous to the market, and all of whose terms designate a category of commercial presentation, constitutes the modern nominal occlusion of the 'art-science-politics-love' system, which identifies truth procedures typologically.[†]

Like Plato, Paul is 'our contemporary' because, as this repressive litany shows, the contemporary world lacks precisely the *courage* to be present. This same lack of the present confronted Plato and Paul (and Marx and Freud, etc.). But this shared lack, really, and somewhat paradoxically, can only be retroactively asserted, on the basis precisely of the courage of Plato, Paul, etc., to act and so to think despite the time of their time, despite the knowledge and the law current to their world, and to make such a thought intelligible and transmissable. This is to say, to subject themselves to what, for that world, *inexists* within in it, and to be seized by what signifies this *inexistence*: an inexistence that must mark itself as such.

Courage as act not virtue   However, it's not as if the knowledge which circulates of this world, which is itself 'contemporary' and which works to make itself known as *the* knowledge (or *encyclopaedia*) of the world per se, experiences itself as lacking. On the contrary, it is full: excessively so and indeed the encyclopaedia by definition not only disavows lack but controls excess. What this means, moreover, is that to be the contemporaries of Plato and Paul, Spartacus or Luxemburg, Rousseau or Alexander, to use Badiou's examples from *Logics of Worlds*, is to 'take courage'. Courage, like

* Badiou, *Logics of Worlds*, p. 1.
† Badiou, *Second Manifesto for Philosophy*, p. 12.

fidelity (its alter ego, so to speak), is not a virtue of the present (in fact, it's not a virtue at all), but its *act*. The present, which *inexists*, is the effect of the courage to decide against what represents itself as 'contemporary'. Such representations in the guise of knowledge must be contested *for* the truth of the present whose construction is the traceable effect of this courage. This courage is therefore the courage to 'keep going', 'to continue to be this someone' as Badiou says in *Ethics*, 'striving to hold fast to some true thought, whatever it be', that is, to some single 'point'.[*]

Thus we return to the Idea of the eternity of the true and, as such, to what is *contemporary* in the present, which is to say, we reverse the appearance of the present in the contemporary world. In the terms of *Logics of Worlds*, as we have already noted, this present inexists for the contemporary world. We must activate the Idea, which remains the same Idea as Plato, as Paul, as Marx, as Freud, 'our contemporaries'. To inexist is not not-to-be. As in *Being and Event*, in *Logics of Worlds* the key is to demonstrate as rigorously as possible and by the involvement of the four key philosophical conditions that what belongs to a world can come to appear there and so disrupt, reverse and reconfigure that world in such a way that *the truth of that world be present* and coterminous with its very presentation as such. Put another way, to ensure that this new world not be simply another instance of the state.

The subject manifests   It is the same to think as to be, insofar as the subject is the finite trace or instance of an infinite process of making manifest what an event opens up to the possibility of being true, for that situation for which the event is an event is thought in its being by mathematics and in its appearing to a world by a mathematised logic: two contemporary onto-logical conditions for any contemporary Idea of truth. As Badiou's series of examples in *Logics of Worlds* illustrates, this subjective work is the actuality of courage, of the affirmation of what is as opposed to what counts, or the praxical fidelity to that which is demonstrably other than, exceptional to, the timely, coincident, discursive form described by Badiou as that of 'bodies and languages'. This world, timely and 'atonal' as he says in *Logics of Worlds*, and thus 'pointless', in which opinion is

---

[*] Alain Badiou, *Ethics: An Essay on the Understanding of Evil*, trans. Peter Hallward (London: Verso, 2001), p. 90.

raised to the level of the constitution of the subject, its authentic virtue in fact, retains, he says in *The Century*, the signature of an earlier romanticism.[*] It's less a world without qualities than one saturated with them, to that 'atonal' point where life and its representations are thought inseparable, uninterruptible, and so where the 'times' overwhelm the present and, not-coincidently, repetition overwhelms interruption and interpretation formalisation.[†]

It is at this point of indiscernibility – between presentation and representation or, in another register, void and excess – that the contemporary becomes present as consequence. Yet this is not to say that everything is given over to the act or to action. For Badiou, this double articulation of act and totality, which he presents as the twentieth-century dialectic between nihilism and romanticism (both of which make declarations as to their contemporaneity under the synthesis of what Badiou nominates as 'the passion for the Real'), are both limited, insofar as their engagement with this Real is concerned, and excessive, insofar as this effort to so engage with it yields destruction as its only terminus, either of self or all.[‡] This is the result, Badiou says, using the condition of art as illustration, of the general failure of the century's dominant tendencies to 'discover another articulation of the finite to the infinite' (or of their compulsion to repeat).[§] For Badiou, this 'new articulation', itself the effect of a *new* orientation to this same world, is what 'formalisation' names and effects, such that form is not opposed to matter or content but is instead coupled to the real of the act. Thus

> every creation of thought is in reality the creation of a new formalisation and at the same time this new formalization establishes a relation or takes part in an interaction with the particularity of what we are trying to express. In this case, we determine the formalisation as a universality, but it is ultimately a particularity that carries universality in the model. Because, at base, we can say that, even if we take, for example, a painting by Picasso, that is, if we are taking a cubist painting by Picasso or by Braque in 1913, we find the creation of a possibility of a new type of pictorial formalization. That is to say, it renders possible a way to formalise in the space of

---

[*] Alain Badiou, *The Century*, trans. Alberto Toscano (London: Polity, 2007), p. 153.
[†] Badiou, *The Century*, p. 164.
[‡] This coincides with Plato's designation of the dual nature of tyranny as either individual or mass. In the first, the individual is all '*l'état c'est moi*'; in the second, the mass is itself One.
[§] Badiou, *The Century*, p. 155.

painting something that was previously unacceptable. On the other hand, it realises itself in a particular context, with respect to the materials used or in the sorts of cultural references that render the painting a particular painting. It is a model.*

Art, mathematics, politics and love cross, then, or are compossible as a matter of form, each in its own right being a form of thought, proposing to the present, as the present, its own formalisation. The essence of this new formalisation of which every creation is an act, every singularity 'the possibility of a new universality', is of being devoid of pathos, of finitude – sublime or transcendent, consecrated or sublimated – and at the same time a matter of the exception, thus of truths and so of the subject, and as such 'far removed from the business of humans',[†] and so far removed from organics and representation too.[‡]

On their terms   In the context of Badiou's formalisation of the twentieth century, however, three things come into play concerning formalisation and its contemporaneity. First, given that to think the new – which is already to decide against 'obscurantism'[§] and 'disorientation'[¶] and so for a single impossible point, an existence without measure – is to think a new formalisation, whether in art, mathematics, love or politics, then whoever thinks the *truly* new (or the new as truth perhaps) is 'our contemporary'. Second, this highlights the 'links' between proposition, hypothesis, projection and actualisation or manifestation.[**] Here, for Badiou, the nineteenth century is primarily obsessed with the former, the twentieth with the latter. It is, in his reading, that minimal difference between *declaration* and act *that* divides one century from another, on the basis of the perspective of their passion or their subjective capacity. Third, it prompts consideration of the success or failure of these manifestations, comprising the question of the place of this qualitative assessment; whether we take a position immanent to their projects and

* Alain Badiou, *The Concept of Model: An Introduction to the Materialist Epistemology of Mathematics*, ed. and trans. Zachary Luke Frazer and Tzuchien Tho (Melbourne: re.press, 2007), pp. 90–1.
† Badiou, *The Century*, p. 160.
‡ As in the supposed anti-Aristotelianism of Chapter 1 of *Difference and Repetition* where Deleuze defines form as an 'organic representation' (p. 37).
§ Alain Badiou, 'On Contemporary Obscurantism', available at http://www.lacan.com/symptom11/?p=163 (accessed 17 July 2013)
¶ Alain Badiou, 'The Courage of the Present', available at http://www.lacan.com/symptom11/?p=163 (accessed 17 July 2013).
** See Deleuze, *Difference and Repetition*, p. 44.

their manifestation *or* subject to judgement, external criteria, the logics of determination, existence, knowledge itself.

Submission to the trace The basis of any 'present' is a formalisation of what there is, subtracted on the basis of one 'impossible point', *eventally* 'shown', declared and subjectively seized, from all determinations of time, logical instruments, and the various pathologies or rights, norms and bodies that subtend the atonicity of worlds. In Quentin Meillassoux's summary, and starting out from the 'impossible point' of a new orientation to the situation opened by an event: 'The form of the faithful subject consists thus in the subordination of the split body to the trace of the event by which it constitutes, point by point, a new present.'* Meillassoux is referring to the example of the Spartacus slave revolt given by Badiou in *Logics of Worlds*. Badiou remarks the same thing in *The Century*, regarding the 'great failure of Bourbaki', which is nevertheless a requirement of all thought: 'what matters is that the formal presentation of mathematics [or art, love, politics] envelops a founding radicality which characterises the nature of its act'.† To hold fast to such a point, to construct in a world the body of the truth this founding radicality marks to be there, is to mark what is decisively present and, as such, to mark the eternity of this present insofar as it becomes the contemporary or marks what is the contemporary of every present – just as the declaration of the vast body of slaves, 'I am Spartacus', renders that name *generically* present in every world in which slavery is in 'logical' revolt: Haiti, Germany . . . Hence, to categorise such revolts as failures, just as to categorise Bourbaki as a failure, requires a logic of dis-orientation and obscurantism, in short a pedagogy of the construction of un-readability, by which a time renders itself without contemporary or, really, as contemporary only with that which is always already counted to exist, for which there is no exception. In other words, the invention, practice, fidelity and subjective attention and incorporation required of any such project is pathologised, rendered 'opaque', which is not to say forgotten but, worse, memorialised as what it was not; or at least *was* in the least of its aspects, or attested at the worst of its effects (like ego psychology is to the truth of Freud). Pedagogy is always obscure, always partial,

---

* Quentin Meillassoux, 'History and Event in Alain Badiou', trans. Thomas Nail, *Parrhesia*, No. 12 (2011) 1–11; p. 5.
† Badiou, *The Century*, p. 163.

and eminently productive of incapacity. On the contrary, for Badiou, marking the ignorance that accompanies any 'lesson in infinity':

> to partake in a truth is also to measure that other truths exist, truths we do not yet partake in. This is indeed what separates formalisation, as both thought and project, from a merely pragmatic employment of forms. Without ever being discouraged, one must invent other axioms, other logics, other ways of formalising. The essence of thinking always resides in the power of forms.[*]

In lieu of a summary   Against the Kantian heritage for which the atemporal temporalising of the immaturity-maturity dialectic is primary, our three thinkers are united in their hostility to this heritage and its implications: no to discussion, no to representation, yes to the untimely. Yet such a 'uniting' comes with new forms of strenuous dissension: Lacan insists on the psychoanalytic problematic of the contemporary as a question of inheritance itself, of the vicissitudes of transmission and the constitutive anachrony of the subject; Deleuze ups the ante on untimeliness in order to affirm an atemporal becoming; for Badiou's part, he attempts to extract and formalize the traces of the eternal from a conditioning by the worldly praxes that actively create a present. This unity and dissension are only further intensified when we return from our thinkers' rethinkings of the contemporary to their new thoughts on time.

[*] Badiou, *The Century*, pp. 163–4.

CHAPTER THREE

Time

The contemporary problem regarding the problem of time has a post-Kantian (or pre-Aristotelian) character. In the previous chapter, we showed how Lacan, Deleuze and Badiou all attempt to reconstruct a praxis of the contemporary as the gateway to a thought of time – and not the other way around. As such, time can no longer be thought of in a still-Kantian frame, and therefore the temporal syntheses of past, present and future must be complicated and revised, while the subject itself can no longer be considered a constitutive, ideological or active agency. This will lead us in coming chapters to a reconstruction of the problem of the event – as something that happens at once in time, to time, out of time and despite time – as an attempt to consider what an immanent genetic concept of what happens might look like shorn of transcendental unifying presuppositions. At this point, the problems of the contemporary and the event start to expose the problem of time in its relation to varieties of *timelessness*: eternity, pure form, perpetuity, endlessness, of course, but also their apparent others, such as the instant, the moment and the *kairos*.

Peregrinations   While Badiou, Deleuze and Lacan all develop decisive engagements with the category of temporality, they do so by simultaneously deepening and rupturing the main traditions of European philosophy, which is to say the various heritages of Kant, post-Kantian philosophy and phenomenology. Here, a major interlocutor proves to be G. W. F. Hegel, and his binding of time, the concept and negativity by means of totality, a.k.a. 'the circle'. At issue in this chapter will be the attempt to situate our three figures in relation to the new problematics of temporality they introduce and develop, with particular attention to the consequences of their various doctrines of the event, discussed in the next chapter. This chapter focuses especially on the problem of the figure of the 'return' as key to the redevelopment of the relationship between negativity, change and time. In sum, for Lacan time moves from being thought as the imaginary registration of the event of retroaction as structural repetition to the singular enigma of the presentation of matter. For Deleuze time 'is the most radical form of change, but the form of change does not change'*; time is the name in Deleuze for the necessity of contingency. Finally, for Badiou, time is derivative: a time is always and only the time of a situation or world; a truth is always novel, trans-mundane and therefore 'eternal'; yet a truth always refounds the time or times of a situation or world. Time comes in second place to truth, a self-doping silver medallist in the Olympics of Being.

The spectre circus of Rome | From the first, Lacan recognised that Freudian psychoanalysis had done something irreparable to the thought of time and the event. Freud himself constantly emphasised that one of the sources of the scandal of the unconscious was not just its sexual nature, but its *an-archaic* constitution. Even the psychoanalytic schools and institutes that Lacan spent much of his life arguing against recognised: 1) that infantile fantasies condition adult behaviours; 2) that these fantasies are integrally fantasies *in time* and *about time*; 3) that there is, concomitantly, a certain 'timelessness' in the continuing effectivity of these fantasies. Take the most famous Freudian image of psychoanalytic archaeology, the city of Rome. Freud writes:

> Now let us, by a flight of imagination, suppose that Rome is not a human habitation but a psychical entity with a similarly long and copious past – an entity, that is to say, in which nothing that has once come into existence will have passed away and all the earlier phases of development continue to exist alongside the latest one. This would mean that in Rome the palaces of the Caesars and the Septizonium of Septimius Severus would still be rising to their old height on the Palatine and that the castle of S. Angelo would still be carrying on its battlements the beautiful statues which graced it until the siege by the Goths, and so on. But more than this. In the place occupied by the Palazzo Caffarelli would once more stand – without the Palazzo having to be removed – the Temple of Jupiter Capitolinus; and this not only in its latest shape, as the Romans of the Empire saw it, but also in its earliest one, when it still showed Etruscan forms and was ornamented with terracotta antefixes. Where the Coliseum now stands we could at the same time admire

---

* Gilles Deleuze, *Difference and Repetition*, trans. Paul Patton (New York: Columbia University Press, 1994), p. 89.

Nero's vanished Golden House. On the Piazza of the Pantheon we should find not only the Pantheon of to-day, as it was bequeathed to us by Hadrian, but, on the same site, the original edifice erected by Agrippa; indeed, the same piece of ground would be supporting the church of Santa Maria sopra Minerva and the ancient temple over which it was built. And the observer would perhaps only have to change the direction of his glance or his position in order to call up the one view or the other.*

This late anti-image of psychic life as an impossible, spectral archaeology, in which nothing is destroyed but rather haunts, impossibly, the same topography as that which still incontrovertibly exists, had, however, been with Freud from the start. The unconscious is 'timeless' in the sense that it is a junkyard of non-experienced, unrecallable experiences, and these 'experiences' re-emerge or return constantly in everyday life *as* everyday life, unrecognised and unrecognisable. The present is constituted by what preceded it, by its past that insists in it, and which it sustains, unsustainably, in a mode of affective antithesis. The structural diagnoses of psychoanalysis – hysteria, obsession, melancholia, schizophrenia, and so on – are themselves names for some of the generic ways in which each psyche incarnates itself as *a singular relation to time.* For psychoanalysis, ontogenesis is always also nomochronic: its own constitution repeats a phylogenetic inheritance in the form of dictatorial singularity. 'Hysterics', as Freud and Breuer stated, 'suffer mainly from reminiscences'[†]: obsessionality, as exemplified by the Rat Man, is a supplementary labyrinth of mirrors erected on top of an originary hysterical reaction to the trauma of sexuality; melancholia is the active refusal to mourn the loss of an incorporated object (i.e., not just a lost object, but the possibility of loss itself); and so on. As such, the 'regression' that Freud so often invokes cannot simply be thought of in the form of a linear return to an earlier state of things.

1, 2, or 3 Things I Know About Death

What makes the later Freud even more unacceptable for classical philosophical theories of time and the subject is that, in his post-First World War supplementation of sexual aetiology with the speculative hypothesis of the death drive,

---

* Sigmund Freud, *Civilization and its Discontents,* in *The Standard Edition of the Complete Psychological Works of Sigmund Freud,* Volume XXI (1927–1931), ed. J. Strachey et al. (London: The Hogarth Press and the Institute of Psycho-analysis, 1961), p. 69.

† Sigmund Freud and Josef Breuer, *Studies on Hysteria,* in *The Standard Edition of the Complete Psychological Works of Sigmund Freud,* Volume II (1893–1895), ed. J. Strachey et al. (London: The Hogarth Press and the Institute of Psycho-Analysis, 1955), p. 220.

three further themes are introduced; or, rather, three existing themes are disturbingly modified. The first of these themes is that the organism – constituted by the pleasure principle – is also traversed by another, countervailing drive that is the representative of the most primordial, minimal existence: inorganic matter. As Ray Brassier puts it:

> The death-drive understood as repetition of the inorganic is the repetition of the death which gave birth to the organism – a death that cannot be satisfactorily repeated, not only because the organism which bears its trace did not yet exist to experience it, but also because that trace is the marker of an exorbitant death, one that even in dying, the organism cannot successfully repeat. Thus, the trace of aboriginal death harbours an impossible demand for organic life: it is the trace of a trauma that demands to be integrated into the psychic economy of the organism, but which cannot because it expresses the originary traumatic scission between organic and inorganic.*

The organism is driven to end as it began-before-it-began, as disorganised, disseminated primal matter. Second, the representative of this drive is the latter's expression as 'pointless', 'destructive' repetitions inassimilable by the psychic organisation; the rhythms of this repetition have no discernible schedule or possible reintegration by the organism; they have no *binding* function, unlike the repetitions of the symptom. Third, the time of the drive is the time of the end of time, the inscription of final universal dispersion as immanent to all life. Time is the drive to return to a time before time. If drives for Freud always invoke their pressure, aim, object and source, the paradox of the death drive is that it can only find satisfaction in its own obliteration. This triple intrusion of inassimilable inorganicity, disjunctive repetition and cosmic dissemination is all the more distressing – intellectually speaking – because, as Freud is forced to admit under the heading of a 'speculative hypothesis', the death drive must do its work 'in silence'. On the one hand, the death drive may not exist at all, and its features may simply be better understood as unprecedented ruses of symptom-formation – meaning they may still ultimately be dictated by the creative vicissitudes of *eros*. No *positive* evidence can possibly be provided of its operations. On the other hand, even if its workings are silent, indiscernible, the hypothesis of such a drive explains certain gaps in the evidence: for example,

---

* Ray Brassier, *Nihil Unbound* (Houndmills: Palgrave Macmillan, 2007), p. 238.

how shell-shocked soldiers can suffer repetitions without relief that contravene the staple Freudian theses regarding the motivating factor of desire that have held since the *Interpretation of Dreams*, and, in doing so, expose disturbing continuities between the extra-volitional actions of the traumatised mind and the gestural activities of pre-volitional infants. Not only do we have, with Freud, a moment in his temporal revisionism which is that of deferred action, of the present acting upon the past in such a way that elements of the past intrude into the future as differentially repetitive, self-dissimulating interruptions of action beyond both volition and cognition, but this moment is also doubled by another. This other moment involves the 'return' of cosmic time within the first series of returns.

Becoming your own result Freud himself acknowledged that by such theses he had 'steered his ship into the harbour of Schopenhauer's philosophy', and there is of course also an implicit tacking vis-à-vis Friedrich Nietzsche's late 'revelation' of the eternal return. Leaving aside the putative 'nihilism' of Freud's propositions – which, despite Freud's own sense of the matter, are not really pessimistic in the sense of Schopenhauer's blind will endlessly pulsing beneath all representations without possible fulfilment – the real consideration hinges on the interpretation of the metaphysics of time projected by the image of eternal return. In all of these cases, the metaphysical enemy is, whether intentionally or not, the circle of Hegelian absolute spirit becoming its own result at the end of its dialectical historical becomings. In Hegel, this 'circle' (Hegel's own word) is and must be unique. At the end of the cycle there can no longer be any possible repetitions within or of the cycle itself, precisely because the entire *piste* of spirit is to proceed throughout the travails of every possible expression of negativity, until, exhausting the most radical powers of its own relentless differential negations, it absorbs and absolves negativity in the ultimate closure of totality.* To do so, it must concretely become its own projections, and it must do so temporally: as Hegel himself objects to Kant, for instance, in the Preface to the *Phenomenology of Spirit*, the concept is not a fixed form but the turbulence of a temporal becoming.† What is crucial to understand here is that Hegel has – or rather takes himself to have –

---

* For example, see G. W. F. Hegel, *Science of Logic*, trans. A. V. Miller (Atlantic Highlands: Humanities Press International, 1989), pp. 71–2.
† G. W. F. Hegel, *The Phenomenology of Spirit*, trans. A. V. Miller, foreword. J. N. Findlay (Oxford: Oxford University Press, 1977).

generated the becoming of world and thought out of the most minimal presuppositions possible,* from the pure and void point of being itself. In the *Science of Logic*, this programme engages not only the possibility of formal logic, but another 'logic', that of the logic of the necessity of the latter's emergence, not to mention how this in turn conditioned the emergence and elaboration of Kantian 'transcendental logic', as well as Kant's own necessary limitations in regards to thinking the relationship between subject and substance.† The contingent will be retrospectively transformed into necessity by a thought that marks the necessary contingency of prior thoughts, and it can only do this by inscribing temporal vicissitude as determinate negation within the becoming-concept of the concept itself.

Negativity beyond negation   Although we shall return to this issue below in more detail – Lacan, Deleuze and Badiou all taking very strong and different positions in their evaluations of Hegel, Nietzsche and Freud – we need to mark here, in a preliminary fashion, that Hegel, in re-establishing essential links between the circle, negativity and temporality in the wake of Kant, himself thereby becomes the target of the Schopenhauerean, Nietzschean and Freudian critiques precisely regarding the status of these links. What all three especially target in the Hegelian armature is the necessity for thinking precisely what Hegel's system was fundamentally calibrated to exclude (or rather *include*, given its genius for including-the-unincludable): *that there is a negativity that escapes the concept.* Indeed, there may be multiple forms of negativity that cannot be captured conceptually – and, moreover, the name 'negativity' itself, the primary name for such an excess in the Hegelian schema, might itself mislead. Nonetheless, logically speaking, it would only be necessary to show that *one* such irrecuperable power (or operation or non-being) exists in order to falsify or derail the Hegelian theatre. If there is not such a negativity, then Hegel cannot be contravened. At least, such a belief implicitly persists through two centuries in 'continental philosophy' up to Bataille, Foucault and Derrida, in whom one continues to find very nuanced declarations regarding the difficulties of eluding the world-historical cunning of the Hegelian dialectic.‡ To announce the

---

* Not, we would insist, none.
† Hence Hegel explicitly declares the contemporaneous necessity for philosophy to 'begin again', but 'gratefully acknowledge' the 'meagre shred' and 'disordered heap of dead bones' of the logics that preceded it. *Science of Logic*, p. 31.
‡ In this context, one should refer to the excellent study by Ben Noys, *The Persistence of*

problem in the most basic terms: if there is indeed such a negativity, then how can it be discerned, conceived or represented, precisely because any such re-presentation is always already able to be recuperated by the dialectic, by definition and by demonstration?

Logical time   It is on the basis of these difficulties and in line with his call for a 'return to Freud', that Lacan found himself forced to engage in a radical rethinking of time. This rethinking, however, proceeded by a series of unexpected steps, each of which, in supplementing the Freudian legacy, also introduced new difficulties which then inspired further (ultimately dissatisfactory) innovations.* Notably in this context, one of Lacan's first published articles is entitled 'Logical Time and the Assertion of Anticipated Certainty', commissioned for the March 1945 recommencement of the journal *Les Cahiers d'Art*. Let us note, in passing, the essay's ironic subtitle 'A New Sophism', which may well put readers in mind of J. L. Borges's equally stunning 'A New Refutation of Time': in both cases, we are confronted from the first by the paradox of time, which means that, following the famous Augustinian meditation regarding its eluding cognitive capture, in reflecting upon it, one can only lose that for which one grasps. For such a tradition, time vanishes Eurydice-like in the very act that might constitute its capture – and that is part of its essence, not simply our incapacity.

❖

Negativity: A Critique of Contemporary Continental Theory (Edinburgh: Edinburgh University Press, 2010).

* One of the best recent books on precisely this topic is Adrian Johnston, *Time Driven: Metapsychology and the Splitting of the Drive* (Evanston: Northwestern University Press, 2005), which proposes an ingenious reinterpretation of the psychoanalytic theory of the drive as essentially split, and that this constitutive split within drive is essentially *temporal*. Taking up and explicating this position in great detail – which, moreover, intersects with many of the same references invoked here (especially in regards to Kant) – Johnston provocatively yet persuasively concludes that: 'The pain of a malfunctioning, internally conflicted libidinal economy is a discomfort signaling a capacity to be an autonomous subject. This is a pain even more essential to human autonomy than what Kant identifies as the guilt-inducing burden of duty and its corresponding pangs of anxious, awe-inspiring respect' (p. 341). However, his formulations remain compromised precisely because, much like Slavoj Žižek (who provides the book's Foreword), he continues to run psychoanalysis together with philosophy, e.g., Johnston's first 'Central Thesis' reads: 'Psychoanalysis is, fundamentally, a *philosophical* insight into the subject's relationships with temporality' (p. xxix; our emphasis). But it precisely isn't, as we show here, and elsewhere: psychoanalysis should rather be considered an 'anti-philosophy', because its relation to its own *means* are antithetical to those of philosophy insofar as it injects literary elements into scientific ones. See Justin Clemens, *Psychoanalysis is an Antiphilosophy* (Edinburgh: Edinburgh University Press, 2013). Johnston argues for his own continuist position most directly in his Chapter 3: 'Psychoanalysis and Modern Rationalism'.

Lacan's essay notoriously begins by establishing a 'prison scenario', in which three prisoners are informed by their warden that, if they solve a puzzle and are able to provide an adequate explanation of their solution, they will be freed. The warden has a choice of three white and two black discs; he fastens one of these to the back of each of the prisoners, and the winning prisoner must inform him which colour he has if he is to be released; the warden then fastens a white disc to each. Hence the 'sophism': how to work out from the reactions of the others alone what colour one is? One can see immediately the post-war 'literary' elements of the sophism: human life is carceral, and one can only exit the prison by means of a self-knowledge that is delivered by meditating rationally upon the behaviour of others meditating rationally upon oneself, whereupon it turns out that one cannot exit without the others, nor exit with them. Thus Lacan adds, explaining the 'classical sense' of the word 'sophism':

> a significant example for the resolution of the forms of a logical function at the historical moment at which the problem these forms raise presents itself to philosophical examination. The story's sinister images will certainly prove to be contingent. But to whatever degree my sophism may seem not irrelevant to our times, its bearing their sign in such images is in no way superfluous.[*]

One might think that to 'solve' the sophism requires putting oneself in the position of each prisoner. Lacan thus offers 'the perfect solution': 'I' must be white, given the two others have white discs, and, if I had been black, then each of the others would have been able to infer that, if one of them had been a black, then the third would have immediately left, and, since that has not happened, neither of them can be black, and, if that is the case, then neither am I. We are all whites!

Note that the problem of *hesitation* in the logic is crucial. Lacan underlines that this solution could be given only after '*a certain time*', given that it requires each prisoner to think the others' thinkings-through as evidenced by their persistence in non-movement. Yet this solution is inadequate, as Lacan hastens to demonstrate. Not only does the logic of the sophism hinge on the double presumption, first, *that the others think* (at least, that 'we' all think in an eminently logical way), and, second, that the non-movement of the others is

---

[*] Jacques Lacan, *Ecrits*, trans. Bruce Fink (New York: Norton, 2006), p. 163.

tied directly to their thinking. It also thereby exposes something very odd about the logic of the situation. For given that each prisoner can only take into account the 'outward' *behaviour* of the others, even if he 'can correctly impute to the others a thought process', as soon all the prisoners move, having proceeded alone together through the same ratiocinations – then they are all forced to stop again. Why? Because, given they are all in exactly the same situation, then the very movement of the others induces them to think again: maybe I am in fact black? Another suspended moment. Then, realising that, if 'I' was indeed black then the others would have just kept going, each prisoner can start off again, all now absolutely convinced of their own whiteness. As Lacan says, 'the sophism thus maintains all the constraining rigor of a logical process, on condition that one integrates therein the value of the two *suspensive scansions*'.* It is critical for Lacan that the *suspensions are immanent to the logical process* itself; this very fact points to the 'infirmity' of classical logic, which has always resorted to localisations (Lacan's term here is 'spatialization') that 'never give us anything which cannot already *be seen all at once*'.† Classical logic, in its 'view from nowhere' of the totality of situations, is a pure panopticism; in being so, it is blind to time, much like certain orthodox versions of the Christian God Himself.

Lacan proceeds to extract three key elements from the 'modulation of time in the sophism's movement: the instant of the glance, the time for comprehending, and the moment of concluding'.‡ These evidentiary moments have the following character. The first moment is the immediate apprehension of the situation: if I could see two blacks, then I would be white; I see no such thing, rather only two whites. The next step, the time for comprehending, thus follows. If I were a black, then the whites would leave as soon as they saw me. The third step requires haste or what Lacan carefully denominates 'precipitation': for, if I am beaten to this recognition by the others, then I will no longer be able to ascertain what I am. This is the moment at which 'I' must subjectively seize myself as 'I', as Lacan points out. Whereas the two preceding moments, which Lacan respectively calls 'apodosis' and 'hypothesis', require a kind of 'third-person-ratiocination' in that 'one' literally thinks about what 'one' (i.e., the 'other' or

* Lacan, *Ecrits*, p. 165.
† Lacan, *Ecrits*, p. 166.
‡ Lacan, *Ecrits*, p. 167.

'others') must be thinking in the situation, this third moment is a moment which requires a logical subjectification: *I* must move now! Moreover, 'the assertive judgement finally manifests itself here in an *act*'; although the 'verification' of the reasoning behind this act can indeed be validly put in the form 'One must know that one is a white when the others have hesitated twice in leaving.'* For Lacan, an act is therefore the rational consequence of apprising the others' failure to act . . . *twice.* Something has (to be seen) to be unaccomplished twice for something to be accomplished once, and what is accomplished is failure. Lacan thereby presents an exemplarily logical process as a combination of propositions and acts (which are paradigmatically inactions), braided together in a disjunctive sequence of inevitable loss.

From logical time to the logic of the signifier

The brilliance and difficulty of this early essay project a number of possible forms of continuation: time as a logical *combinatoire*; time as intersubjective logical conundrum; time as irregular action constituted by the partiality of position; a lack (in this case, of vision) coupled with a failure (of an act) as the *arche* of the action itself. Lacan, however, did not take these propositions up in a fully analytic mode, but began to reconsider the problem of logical time on the basis of the Saussurean science of the signifier, coupled with a rethinking of the legacy of Hegel. Under the pressure of the work of Claude Lévi-Strauss and Roman Jakobson, but also retaining elements from his longer-standing interest in phenomenological existentialism, especially in the neo-Hegelian form given it by Alexandre Kojève, Lacan started to reimagine the Freudian intervention as a kind of media pragmatism: if human beings are defined by language-use, then it is a science of language that will give us the directions for understanding the consequences for an animal body that is subjected to language. The articulation runs something like this: psychoanalysis's specificity is geared to the specificity of the experience of language; this experience is determined by the structure of language itself; the structure of language is given by the science of linguistics as delivered by Saussure; this science confirms the necessity of 'repression' qua material-literal barrier between signifier and signified; psychoanalysis is the treatment of the consequences of this repression in individual suffering subjects.

---

* Lacan, *Ecrits*, p. 173.

As such, Lacan develops – with an extraordinary inventiveness, subtlety and range of reference – a position regarding the articulations of the symptom, language and negativity ('death') that can be formalised as follows. For our purposes here, there are four issues that Lacan introduces, on the basis of his own idiosyncratic encounters with post-Saussurean linguistics, and which he remorselessly re-interrogates:

1) the signifier as constitutively lacking;
2) the inconsistency of any thought of the whole;
3) the subject as empty, split, unreflective support for a signifying chain;
4) the rift between statement and utterance.

If Lacan relies heavily on post-Saussurean linguistic science – and let's not dismiss the claims of 'science' here too rapidly – he immediately remarks something about structural linguistics that is at once very simple, yet has extraordinary consequences. For Lacan, the Saussurean conception of the sign has a peculiarity that Saussure himself falsifies with his little diagrams. It is this: one never encounters a signified anywhere. Ever. One only ever encounters signifiers. A simple, stupid point. If each language, as an ensemble of diacritically defined signs, must cut up the sound- and thought-planes differently (to use Saussure's own terms), then one cannot think of the signifieds of any particular language as having any direct or privileged lock onto the real. On the contrary, human language is distinguished from other sign-systems by precisely being, in Hegel's terms, 'the murder of the thing'. Not only is there no possible grounding referent outside of language, nor any transcendental signified, but language itself creates the things of the world for a language-user. Yet no signified can ever be met with directly, anywhere; one has to go through signifiers. Yet there is no such thing as a pure signifier 'in itself' without at least the presumption of a signified (for a signifier by definition must at least 'signify'!). That 'signified' can only be encountered as lacking from the signifier that nominally conveys it; moreover, every signifier materially leads only and always to others. At one stage, Lacan will even translate this structural double-differentiation in terms drawn from classical rhetoric: metaphor (the signified does not exist except as troping) and metonymy (the signifier does not exist except by referring to others). Language is constituted by inflections, deflections, defections, misdirections and reflections.

❖

Language can therefore only function as language because it is internally 'barred', lacking from itself, yet always and everywhere presuming what it misses. The sense of a signified *insists*. This bar – to which we will give another sense in a moment – is a cut *within* the word. For Lacan, this gives a precise sense to the 'castration complex' of Freud: any language user is literally castrated by words that are themselves *cut cuts*. What, for psychoanalysis, can be the signifier of this irreparable lack? Nothing other than the 'phallus'. The phallus is the signifier of the constitutive lack that founds signifying, significa-tion. The phallus is the signifier of lack that is itself lacking from its place – i.e., there is no sign in language that exemplifies it, although it is presupposed in and by every sign. It is thus a simulacrum in the strict sense, undoing any relation between original and copy. It is also always only 'veiled', because no signifier in language can *be* that phallus, and so the phallus can only 'function', to use Lacan's term, as veiled. The fantasy of un-veiling, however, therefore becomes one fundamental fantasy of the neurotic language-user.

This is a crucial point made by Nathan Widder in his *Reflections on Time and Politics*: 'Deleuzean repetition here converges with Lacanian repetition.'* He proceeds:

> The Oedipal story . . . refers not to a trauma occurring in time but to the traumatic organization of time itself. In this revised story, the Oedipal trauma may or may not be established by a real childhood event. Its effect, in defining sexual difference in heterosexual and genital terms and introducing the castration threat, is at once to separate and join together two orders, one infantile and pregenital and the other adult and genital, each having divergent body images and both real and imaginary objects of desire, memories of the past, and expectations of the future. The expression of this event is the phallus, the signifier of the mysterious paternal Law, which seems to give sense and cohesion to the psyche but is never entirely incomprehensible. Because it constitutes the separate series through a radical break, it cannot be localized within either series, appear-ing at the margins at each. But the phallus does not establish an identity between the series, because it has no identity itself.†

There are some further issues to underline. What Lacan manages to do with this revision of Freud in accordance with Saussure is to find

* Nathan Widder, *Reflections on Time and Politics* (University Park: Pennsylvania State University Press, 2008), p. 87.
† Widder, *Reflections*, p. 94.

a way of 'saving' the Oedipus complex from its immediate intra-psychoanalytic critiques. In doing so, however, he also accomplishes a reconciliation of the problem of the symptom with the problem of the death drive: the 'phallus', qua missing element, *insists* as what is not, that is, as 'death'. Human beings are therefore creatures whose paradigm is to be caught 'between the two deaths', as Lacan points out in *Seminar VII* regarding the status of *Antigone:** between the animal death and the death given by signification or, if you prefer, between biological dissolution and linguistic negation. This, as we shall see in the next chapter, has an integrally ethical consequence.

One can also see immediately how Lacan uses this strikingly simple algorithm of the barred sign to rewrite an entire sequence of classical psychoanalytic themes. Where Freud would speak of *Nachträglichkeit* as double-causality, the traumas of infancy being triggered later by the adolescent hormonal rush, Lacan will speak of the structure of the signifier; whereas for Freud 'anatomy was destiny', for Lacan 'desire is destiny'. To summarise Lacan's position as clearly as possible, then, we will resort to the following dot-points (which, by the way, will enable the reader to see immediately how close Lacan is with several of these theses to Wittgenstein, confirming Badiou's diagnosis of the pair as 'anti-philosophers'):

- Human beings are animals 'tormented by the signifier' (language is always spoken by *some-body*).
- Human beings are born into language (it necessarily pre-exists you . . . just like your parents).
- There is no private language (it is necessarily 'shared' with others).
- No individual can control language (to speak it you have to conform to its rules).
- The learning of language is a *problem*, not a given or an inevitability (there is no 'language instinct' as such).
- No particular division of language can be considered 'foundational' or 'original' (even the 'simplest' human language is already defined by complex bundles of differential traits).
- The key to language is what it 'lacks', or rather what *enables it to lack* (the bar or cut between signifier and signified).

---

* See Jacques Lacan, *The Ethics of Psychoanalysis 1959–1960*, trans. D. Porter (New York: Norton, 1992).

- No person knows 'all' of 'language' (therefore each person neces- sarily has his or her own 'idiom').
- Language does not exist: instead, 'language' is a *fantasy* that we have to have in order to speak at all (there is no all of language, or, as J.-F. Lyotard will say, language is an Idea in the Kantian sense).

We will call the upshot of the above account Lacan's 'second solu- tion' to the problem of time as repetition. If the theses of logical time couldn't ultimately stand for Lacan, it is because the sophism on which they are founded fails to capture the problems of encounter and novelty that are at the heart of the psychoanalytic experience; to capture them requires turning to the sciences of language; these sciences enable a formalisation of the repetition compulsion as the insistence of the cut within all and any signs as an ineradicable, constantly mutating symptom. The primacy of topology over dynam- ics is therefore key in Lacan's innovation: a hostility to privileging forces, energies and powers is sustained throughout his oeuvre, as subordinate to a theorisation of the subject through the topological distribution of places.

Again, it is explicitly Hegel who proves to be a key interlocutor for Lacan from first to last, from the quasi-psychoanalytic writings of the 1930s through to the seminars of the 1970s. Certainly, Kojève is initially the key teacher for Lacan in regards to Hegel, as has been well documented, but it is also the case that other major French com- mentators on Hegel, such as Jean Hyppolite (who contributed per- sonally to several of Lacan's seminars on precisely this topic), proved important interlocutors. But it should now be clear why Lacan is not a Hegelian: Hegel, on the contrary, is crucially the strongest philo- sophical enemy with which psychoanalysis must struggle, and there- fore the form of thought whose propositions must be confronted at every point through unrelenting hostilities. In Lacan's words, what his own project 'hones in on' 'is certainly not absolute knowledge but rather the position from which knowledge can reverse truth effects'.*
Moreover, as Lacan is keen to emphasise, in a highly significant passage for the aetiology and import of concept-formation:

> Without criticizing the Hegelian dialectic for what it leaves out –
> the lack of a bond that would keep the society of masters together
> was pointed out long ago – I simply wish to stress what, on the

* Lacan, *Ecrits*, pp. 306–7.

basis of my own experience, strikes me as blatantly symptomatic in it, that is, as indicative of repression. This is clearly the theme of the cunning of reason, whose seductiveness is in no wise lessened by the error I pointed out above. The work, Hegel tells us, to which the slave submits in giving up jouissance out of fear of death, is precisely the path by which he achieves freedom. There can be no more obvious lure than this, politically or psychologically. Jouissance comes easily to the slave, and it leaves work in serfdom.[*]

This is why it was important to flag up above not only the results of Freud's constant self-critique with regards to the problem of the symptom, death and the return. Lacan was urgent in his call for a 'return to Freud', which already evidently places the thematic of the return 'front and centre', as it were, as providing the necessary orientation towards a set of essential problems, rather than a simple reclamation of a truth that had been unfortunately covered over by contingencies such as misunderstanding, stupidity or malice. As Lacan reiterates, this return 'has nothing to do with a return to the sources that could, here as elsewhere, signify no more than a regression';[†] rather, it is the exigency to read Freud's texts in their literality, and, therefore, their materiality. In doing so, one must base the return 'on the subject's *topology*'.[‡] The real problem involves how to *repeat differently differently*: how to 'experience', in one's own differential repetitions, a repetition that shows itself as repetition and, in such self-showing, transforms the status of such repetition by way of an eminently paradoxical 'act'?

This is, at least for much of Lacan's life, the challenge of psychoanalytic *treatment*, as well as its *ethics*, for both analysand and analyst.

---

[*] Lacan, *Ecrits*, p. 686. Note here, then, the quite outrageous assertions by such critics as Slavoj Žižek and his epigones, who consistently attempt to reduce the gap between Lacanian psychoanalysis and the propositions of German idealism (above all, Kant and Hegel), e.g., in every text from *The Sublime Object of Ideology* (London: Verso, 1989), through *For They Know Not What They Do* (London: Verso, 1991), *Tarrying with the Negative* (Durham, NC: Duke University Press, 1993), *The Metastases of Enjoyment* (London: Verso, 1994), *The Plague of Fantasies* (London: Verso, 1997), *Did Somebody Say Totalitarianism?* (London: Verso, 2001), to *In Defence of Lost Causes* (London: Verso, 2007) and *Living in the End Times* (London: Verso, 2010). What is symptomatic in Žižek's work is his procedure which runs precisely counter to the gap Lacan consistently seeks to open up between psychoanalysis and philosophy, as if they were continuous with one another, as if the propositions each offered were translatable, and, worst of all, as if the details of their *Auseinandersetzung* were essentially irrelevant. On the other hand, Žižek has effected a quite brilliant montage of Lacan and Hegel, which has revivified certain aspects of their work for our contemporary era.

[†] Lacan, *Ecrits*, p. 306.

[‡] Lacan, *Ecrits*, p. 306; our emphasis.

In a nutshell, the former ought to act in such a way as to not give way on his or her desire; whereas the latter must incarnate a 'positive non-acting', that is, act in such a way that the analysand is interrupted in the milieu of a symptomatic repetition. What is very odd about this account is how it manages to separate novelty from the 'act' (or what Deleuze or Badiou might call the 'event'). The symptom is, for Lacan, always new, as it produces new sets of signifiers in leaping the bar. As differential repetition, it dissimulates itself by its ever-shifting metastatic presentations. Yet this is precisely not a transformation in structure, but its very expression and exemplification. We will encounter some further complexities of this doubled, asymmetrical phenomenon in the next chapter, in regards to the event; here, it is necessary to note that the rethinking of time as differential repetition is explicitly conceived and denominated as an *ethical* problem. Time *is* ethics, which subtends being; it is thought topologically, which subverts dynamics.

But this is also why Nietzsche needed to be invoked – not as another authoritative reference for Lacan, whose paucity of allusions to the former is striking in the context – but as the index of a different orientation to the same problem. Indeed, Lacan, occasionally acknowledging the apparent proximity, will declare: 'It is repetition itself whose face [Freud], as much as Kierkegaard, renews for us in the division of the subject, the fate of scientific man. Let another confusion be dispelled: it bears no relation to Nietzsche's "eternal return."'* In an intellectual context that was later marked by a thoroughgoing enthusiasm for Nietzsche – and whose notable adherents include Derrida, Deleuze and Foucault – Lacan only rarely invokes the former, and, when he does, it is in terms that are often quite derisory. Hence we can read of 'Nietzsche's inflatable super-man'† or of his links to a chain of humanistic moralists.‡ There are two further points to be broached here. First, despite the possible attraction of doing so, one can't really consider Lacan's hostility to Nietzsche the emblem of a kind of 'anxiety of influence': Lacan is too cool, too clear and too indifferent in this regard for such a possibility to be plausible. Second, however, given that Deleuze and the other neo-Nietzscheans are simultaneously anti-Hegelian and, to

* Lacan, *Ecrits*, p. 307.
† Lacan, *Ecrits*, p. 106.
‡ Lacan, *Ecrits*, p. 407.

a noteworthy extent, stringent critics of Freudianism (or at least of a certain Freudianism, a certain strand of Freud, and in ways that differ dramatically depending on the context in question), one should read this as a sign of their own implication in the same post-Hegelian problematic, and their own recognition that there is in some way a fundamental decision to be made designated by these proper names: Nietzsche *or* Freud? The fundamental problem that forces such a distinction takes the name of 'Hegel' in the form we briefly outlined above. 'How to think the power of time as differential return beyond any possible experience?' is its basic question, and a reconceptualisation of ethics is its consequence.

The third way   Towards the end of the 1960s a long-standing motif in Lacan's work awakens in a new and stronger incarnation. This involves an upping of his attentiveness towards the mathematisation and formalisation of results. It also means a new assault on Hegelianism. A third account of time as repetition is in the offing. This 'third way' is of a far less settled nature than the second, and Lacan – from about the late 1960s, and certainly from *Seminar XVII* on – is constantly reformulating it, often unclearly and with inapparent success. It is marked by a proliferation of formalisation, a relentless self-critique, new concepts or the savage revision of older ones, and a mode that is manifestly even more hermetic than Lacan's already-notorious linguistic tactics. Perhaps unexpectedly, we are going to finger Deleuze as an important influence in this development.

Lacan's revised account – or, probably more accurately, his presentation of the necessity for developing a new account – derives from a number of intra- and extra-psychoanalytic developments of the 1960s. These include not only the vast social upheavals of that decade, and emblematically May '68, but, ironically enough, the post-Lacanian critiques of Lacan issuing primarily from the young philosophical bandits of the ENS, Derrida and Deleuze perhaps above all. We know that Lacan even tried to court them both, with a notable rapture of unsuccess.* These matters are of more than merely

---

* For Lacan's encounter with Derrida, see Elisabeth Roudinesco, *Jacques Lacan*, trans. B. Bray (New York: Columbia, 1999); also, Derrida's own accounts in *Resistances of Psychoanalysis* (Stanford: Stanford University Press, 1998); for Deleuze (and Guattari, who, of course, had cheerfully spent a good deal of his early working life as a card-carrying Lacanian), see François Dosse, *Deleuze and Guattari: Intersecting Lives* (New York: Columbia, 2010).

circumstantial or anecdotal interest to the extent that they have left their traces in the subsequent conceptual derangements of Lacan's work. In fact, there is an absolutely critical remark to be made at this point regarding Lacan's second, classical account of the phallic signifier, because it is in response to it that Deleuze and Badiou find themselves both forced to make a decision regarding the priority of thought or life and, in doing so, take different routes to the construction of a philosophical system that evades the psychoanalytic critique. Indeed, it can be argued that it is in large part Deleuze who forces Lacan to shift his position, above all, regarding the status of psychosis.

The issue is this: Lacan rigorously applies his adapted theory of the phallus-as-lack to formalise psychopathological structures. As can easily be seen, there are three and only three relations that can be taken vis-à-vis the bar: neurosis, psychosis and perversion. As an analyst who gives an absolute priority to language, Lacan clearly treats neurosis as primary: the neurotic, whether hysterical or obsessional, must at some stage have said 'yes!' to the barrier within signification. What makes hysteria determining in particular here is that it is the hysterical protest – the 'No!' – that enables the relation of language to its living support to be staged most starkly and intensely, to show itself as dissimulation, and simultaneously show this dissimulation as essentially of a sexual nature. It is therefore in terms of this operation that Lacan reconceives *repression*. No longer simply a psychological defence, repression is necessitated by the structure of language itself. The hysteric's No exposes the Yes with which it is always necessarily implicated. Lacan's famous reinterpretation of Roman Jakobson's essay on the metaphorical and metonymic poles of language in fact takes off by considering these poles as integrally tied to the neurotic structure: given the acceptance of the bar, then desire slips from signifier to signifier along the top of the bar ('metonymy'); the phallic insistence literally 'leaps' the bar as difference ('metaphor'). The psychotic, by contrast, *forecloses* the bar from signification, with the consequence that the difference between words and things necessarily collapses: words become things, such that when one says the word 'chariot', a chariot runs through one's mouth. Under such conditions, metaphor and metonymy do not serve a central place for the psychotic, but are rather local operations in a more general field. The psychotic cannot say No because he or she has already said No to saying itself. Perversion, however, works by *disavowal*: it simultaneously accepts the bar, but acts 'as if' it didn't; it says 'yes' and 'no' simultaneously.*

Beyond all the fulminating critiques and erudite explications of Lacan's alleged 'difficulty', note how simple Lacan's theory actually is. It begins with the very basic – if stunningly profound – recognition that the bar in signification must be considered primary, and then identifies three logical positions that can be taken in regards to the bar as providing the matrix of the three fundamental psychopathological structures . . . and that's it! Yes to the bar (neurosis); No to the bar (psychosis); Yes and No, or neither Yes nor No (perversion). This is also, by the way, why psychoanalysis is anti-Aristotelian, not only in its subversion of the principle of non-contradiction and its denial of substance, but in its rejection of all taxonomy according to predicates. If, as psychoanalysts of all orientations maintain, subjectivity appears only by dissimulating itself, then philosophical or psychiatric classifications of this kind, supposedly based on this or that distinguishing feature, can only be based on a fundamentally stupid-yet-motivated misrecognition. Any alleged 'empiricism' which believes non-appearance = absence or non-existence is not only counter-indicated in the regime of the subject, but tyrannical in its essence. The 'content' of the statements of anybody can indeed be 'identical' to the statements of anybody else, without that bizarre identity compromising the singularities, the radical non-homology, of psychic life.

Lacan turns into Deleuze, Deleuze to Lacan   To our mind, one of the most distressing consequences of the (no-doubt unavoidable) polemics against each other's masters that have characterised at least the last forty years of Lacanian and Deleuzian scholarship is that the crucial – and reciprocal – points of influence have been almost totally ignored. In going unrecognised, however, not only is the complexity of influence completely misrepresented, but the partisans also miss some of the key philosophical problems, points, decisions and operations at stake. What Deleuze, in his work from the late 1960s onwards, did is quite brilliant: he takes up the Lacanian *description* of psychosis, but perverts Lacan's account of its genesis by *taking*

---

* Hence the well-known formula of Octave Mannoni's which runs: 'I know very well that X isn't the case, but all the same . . .' On the basis of a quite strict rendition of this Lacanian account, Deleuze will analyse the fiction of Leopold von Sacher Masoch.

the psychotic operations as primary – and not as the *consequences* of a foreclosure of the phallic signifier. Having effected this reversal of priority, Deleuze then rigorously follows through on the implications, by proliferating the forces and blocs with which a psychotic works, and for which 'language' is only one among very many possible lines. We want to underline this point, as we believe it shows something absolutely essential about Deleuze's method: he often accepts the *analyses* of those who force him to think, but then literally inverts their accounts of *genesis*, in order to trace out something new by following through the consequences of this inversion. It is on this basis, and on the basis of his work with Bergson, Nietzsche and Spinoza too, that Deleuze and Guattari can come to assert:

> If desire produces, its product is real. If desire is productive, it can be productive only in the real world and can produce only reality. Desire is the set of *passive syntheses* that engineer partial objects, flows, and bodies, and that function as units of production. The real is the end product, the result of the passive syntheses of desire as autoproduction of the unconscious. Desire does not lack anything; it does not lack its object. It is, rather, the *subject* that is missing in desire, or desire that lacks a fixed subject; there is no fixed subject unless there is repression. Desire and its object are one and the same thing: the machine, as a machine of a machine. Desire is a machine, and the object of desire is another machine connected to it.[*]

This is also to say that Deleuze can thereafter only consider formalisation as secondary, as a royal or arborescent science, and the subsequent development of Deleuze's work bears this logical consequence out. Deleuze (like Derrida), with utter consistency, seeks out what he considers the illegitimate points of fixity – or, to use a Lacanian term, *fixion* – in any form of formalisation. Perhaps the epitome of this is evinced by his and Guattari's remarks in *A Thousand Plateaus*, where they praise the diagrammatic as disarraying all or any semiotic systems.

This consistency, this willingness to pursue the consequences of one's thought all the way along the line, is, as Badiou will later admiringly recognise, a genuine assumption on Deleuze's part of

---

[*] Gilles Deleuze and Félix Guattari, *Anti-Oedipus: Capitalism and Schizophrenia*, trans. R. Hurley. M. Seem and H. R. Lane (London and New York: Continuum, 2000), p. 26.

the philosophical consequences of his decision to render language derivative in such a way; it also enables us to see how Badiou must have learned from Deleuze's decision here about the only real *ways* to circumvent the Lacanian critique of anti-philosophy. Rather than attacking the formalisations of Lacan, then, à la Deleuze, Badiou takes the other route out as it were, by going further in his formalisations than Lacan himself, and more rigorously too, to the point of formalising inconsistency itself. Perhaps more surprisingly, however, we can also suggest that Lacan himself recognised – having been confronted with the Deleuzo-Guattarian critique – that he needed to go further with his own formalisations in order to answer the anti-Oedipal charges against the primacy of the signifier, even in the radical form that he, Lacan, had given it.*

The force of psychosis   To return to the pressing issue of structure in this context: if psychoanalysis for all sorts of reasons has often privileged neurosis as its central category, it has also dedicated a great deal of attention to the problems posed by psychosis. One of the great case-studies of Freud examines the absolutely extraordinary work by Judge Schreber, *Memoirs of my Nervous Illness*, which has thus become a central document in the subsequent dossier – and certainly for both Lacan and Deleuze. Lacan himself literally began his career by investigating psychosis, notably with the notorious case of Aimée, a young woman who had attempted to murder a well-known actress, and that of the Papin Sisters, servants who dismembered their mistress and her daughter, an event later to be immortalised by a number of writers, including Jean Genet. But it is in his *Seminar III* that Lacan gives his most extended account of the constitution of psychosis, above all regarding the doctrine of foreclosure elaborated above.†

Although Deleuze's assaults clearly made a big impression on Lacan, the latter's shift is surely not due to Deleuze alone. With the

---

* Notably, though, Deleuze and Guattari's remarks on this point always insist on the fact that Lacan himself was not trapped in the retrograde formulations of these concepts: 'Lacan himself says "I'm not getting much help." We thought we'd give him some schizophrenic help. And there's no question that we're more indebted to Lacan, once we've dropped notions like structure, the symbolic, or the signifier, which are thoroughly misguided, and which Lacan himself has always managed to turn on their head to bring out their limitations.' Gilles Deleuze, *Negotiations*, trans. Martin Joughin (New York: Columbia University Press, 1995), p. 14.

† Jacques Lacan, *The Psychoses: The Seminar of Jacques Lacan Book III 1955–1956*, trans. with notes R. Grigg (London: Routledge, 1993).

diminution of the pertinence and powers of high structuralism in the Lévi-Straussian and Jakobsonian modes, as well as with the sense that 'language' itself was no longer the single most important causal agent in the creation of subjectivity, Lacan had already begun to turn away from a structural analysis of the signifier, or, more precisely, had already begun to *supplement* it with his notorious 'rings of string' of the early 1970s. *Seminar XXIII*, of 1975–76, dedicated primarily to the study of the case of James Joyce, is exemplary in this regard.*
One of the striking things about this seminar – and all the more strikingly, since, as we have just shown, it is in some way a response to *Anti-Oedipus* – is that Lacan returns here to what turns out to be a paradoxical case of psychosis, the 'untriggered psychosis' of the great Irish writer – an ingenious move, in a number of ways. First, it constitutes a radical auto-critique of what we have been calling Lacan's own 'second classicism', and it does it through an analysis of one of the greatest re-creators in and of signifiers themselves. Second, it does this by 'fractalising' the Deleuzo-Guattarian critique by pinpointing the peculiarities of a central figure who simultaneously escapes any structural diagnosis (whether psychoanalytic, psychiatric or philosophical), and, in doing so, presents something that cannot be satisfactorily explained by their accounts. Third, as already intimated, it does this by exacerbating Lacan's own enthusiasm for formalisation, here using developments in mathematical topology.

Yet the seminar still relies on Lacan's fundamental orientation towards signification: it will be the consequences for interpreting psychosis on the basis of a foreclosure of the paternal signifier which alerts Lacan later to the *disconjunctive* operations (or what Deleuze would call 'inclusive disjunction') which Joyce exacerbates and extends beyond all prior attempts without ever being able to be diagnosed as such. Speaking of the production of neologisms in the context of Judge Schreber's *Memoirs*, Lacan asserts that:

> This is the language ... of the delusional. It's a language in which certain words take on a special emphasis, a density that sometimes manifests itself in the very form of the signifier, giving it this frankly neologistic character that is so striking in the creation of paranoia ... At the level of the signifier, in its material aspect, the delusion is characterised by that special form of discordance with common language known as neologism. At the level of meaning,

---

* Jacques Lacan, *Seminar XXIII: Le sinthome* (Paris: Seuil, 2005).

it's characterised by the following, which will appear to you only
if you set out with the idea that a meaning always refers to another
meaning, that is, precisely, that the meaning of these words can't be
exhausted by reference to another meaning.[*]

An attention to materialism and meaning transformed through
neologising qua designed discordance and signifying inexhaustibility
by the delusional operations of paranoia is therefore in the background of Lacan's orientation towards *Ulysses* and *Finnegans Wake*.
Yet these features are, as we have already declared, not quite enough
to locate what's singular about Joyce. Hence *Seminar XXIII* opens
with an announcement that lists three key recent developments of
Lacan's. The first of these concerns 'the figures on the blackboard',
reproduced at the top of the edited text in greyscale: the 'Borromean
knots' of which Lacan had already been speaking for several years,
including in *Seminar XIX* and *Seminar XX* (1972–73).[†] The second
is introduced in the first line: '*Sinthome* is an old way of writing
what had previously been written *symptom*.'[‡] The first canonical
mention of the new term had come in the previous year's seminar
R.S.I. (the letters standing for 'Real Symbolic Imaginary', but which
must suggest to an English-speaker, albeit anachronistically, and, if
you'll pardon the neologism, *analingually*, the acronym for 'repetitive strain injury'). The third key innovation immediately follows
the first two: *lalangue*. This para-concept, introduced by Lacan as
a kind of bridge between the pre-linguistic and the linguistic proper
– and hence integrally as the mark of an a-temporal interval and
para-practice that expresses itself anasemically – designates an infant
babbling that is not-yet-signifying-yet-not-not-signifying either. This
articulability-as-variation can no longer be thought diacritically, but
only 'experimentally': it is constitutively an *enigma*, for everybody,
and will remain so. Finally, and to pick up on our prior remarks on
the event *chez* Lacan, the material enigma of *lalangue* designates
the necessary possibility of irretrievable disconnection without any
reference to its prior state.

Taken together, what these three developments also amount to,
placed at the entrance to the seminar, is yet another retake on time.
Even if Lacan throughout adverts to his formalisation of the S1 and

---

[*] Lacan, *The Psychoses*, pp. 32–3.
[†] See Jacques Lacan, *Seminar XIX*, ed. J.-A. Miller (Paris: Seuil, 2011), p. 91, where he intro-
    duces the figures for the first time.
[‡] Lacan, *Seminar XXIII: Le sinthome*, p. 11.

S2, the master signifier and knowledge, fulsomely introduced in *Seminar XVII*, and which he extends here, notably through the 'tetradic schemas' of the master's discourse (e.g., p. 23), this particular triplet moves away from the preceding accounts of the 1950s and 1960s in a number of ways. Above all, the Borromean knots place the emphasis on the *knotting* itself, on the interlinking of 'rings of string' that are all necessarily singular and do not necessarily have a standard form of articulation. As Lacan further underlines, citing Philippe Sollers, Joyce 'wrote in English in such a way that the English language no longer exists'.*

Back to time   Crucially, the sessions make direct allusion to the themes of 'Logical Time': 'Function of haste. It's necessary that I haste myself [*Il faut que je me hâte*].' The self-speeding-subject goes a little fast through the imprudent buckling of itself, through its linkages, and this turns out to be a way of isolating and proposing an enigma. Lacan continues: 'an enigma, as the name indicates, is an enunciation such that one cannot find a statement'.†
The enigma proves to be a crucial theme throughout this seminar, and Lacan regularly adverts to an algebra:

> I write this E*e*, E index *e*. It is a question of the enunciation and the statement. The enigma consists in the relation of the big E to the little e. It is a question of why the hell such a statement has been pronounced. This is a matter of enunciation. And enunciation, it's the enigma borne to the power [*puissance*] of writing.‡

This writing, moreover, must partake simultaneously of the formula and the heresy (as *hairesis*, decision, choice, etc.). On the one hand, 'the writing of little mathematical letters is what supports the real'; on the other, 'when one writes, one can even touch on the real, but not on the true', even if 'the real is found in the tangles of the true'. This real 'has no sense' and, moreover, Lacan *believes* (he emphasises himself that this belief is his symptom) that it is 'without law'. The consequences? Speaking of what there is in philosophy of *philia*, Lacan asserts: '*Philia* is time, insofar as thought. Time-thought is *philia*.'§ The subject is a friend or lover of time – not a friend of truth or wisdom, mind you, not being a philosopher nor philosophical

---

* Lacan, *Seminar XXIII: Le sinthome*, p. 11.
† Lacan, *Seminar XXIII: Le sinthome*, p. 67.
‡ Lacan, *Seminar XXIII: Le sinthome*, p. 153.
§ Lacan, *Seminar XXIII: Le sinthome*, pp. 68, 80, 85, 134, 137, 145, respectively.

– and such 'friendship' must be taken in the fullest sense of the word, as bound with the other-in-death.

Moreover, 'the Other of the real Other, that is to say impossible, is the idea that we have of artifice, insofar as it is a making [*faire*] that escapes us, that is to say which greatly overflows the *jouissance* that we can have of it'.* Joyce as artificer is the artificer of impossibles, that is, of enigmas: not nonsense nor paradox nor even simple babble, but what is a-decipherable. Why, then, name or rename Joyce as *Joyce the Sinthome*? Because 'the sinthome is very precisely the sex to which I do not belong, that is to say, a woman'.† Joyce the Other Sex, without the supplement of copula: Joyce's writing his own sexual an-equivalence to self requires this ever-escalating inventiveness on 'his' part, which proliferates enigmas as a form of absolutely singular self-binding. For late Lacan, then, what becomes of time in this process is *literally enigmatic*: time is an enigma; and the enigma is the inscription of technical lawlessness as captivating invention. This invention is, in turn, given as singularity, without any possible generality. We see a proliferation not simply of circles, but of rings and links (these not being the same thing) formalised by way of endless play-demonstrations with Borromean knots. Unsurprisingly perhaps, Lacan's very last seminars forlornly essay to evade the aphasiac implications for conceptuality of such presentations: not being and time (too philosophical!), but 'topology and time', the endless binding and unbinding of little rings of string, the endless scratching and rubbing of chalk on boards. This is Lacan's late problematic of the borromeanising of the poem-event with regard to the letter-event of *lalangue*: the work of creation (the poem) counterposed to the problematic of pure irruption (materiality) and that non-relationship formalised in the silence of the knots (ana-lysis): Lacan's final doctrine of Event-Work-Thought.

From anti-philosophy to Deleuze   Here perhaps we can note one of the things that so strongly characterises anti-philosophy in the Badiouian sense, namely, its resistance (rejection? foreclosure?) to the link between topology – or, better, topologies – and being. While philosophy insists on the connection, anti-philosophy, if it ever gets that far, renounces it, declares it fantasmatic, delusory, ethically

---

* Lacan, *Seminar XXIII: Le sinthome*, p. 64.
† Lacan, *Seminar XXIII: Le sinthome*, p. 101.

problematic, intellectually corrupt. In Deleuzian terms, Lacan's analyses appear to remain at the level of the figure or even – a crueller accusation – the *icon*. If topology opens onto figures, it tends towards an artistic mode of thought; if onto icons, religious 'conceptuality'. Such general broadsides are warranted here not just to annoy our Lacanian brethren, but because they once more return us to the figure of the circle in its Hegelian provenance. This figure (let's insist on the word) is the object of Deleuze's most severe criticism of Hegel's philosophy, and no single moment of Hegelian thought is as often attacked by Deleuze as is his formal investment in the figure of the circle: 'Hegel's circle is not the eternal return, only the infinite circulation of the identical by means of negativity.'* The delirious, 'orgiastic' passage to the Absolute, the Absolute of repetition itself figured in the Hegelian circle, is for Deleuze nothing but smoke and mirrors, the most refined mirage that conceals only the infinite instantiation of the self-identical. This Circle is, for Deleuze, nothing but a grounding principle that assures 'the monocentring of circles', and 'while this foundation is not the identical itself, it is nevertheless a way of taking the principle of identity particularly seriously, giving it an infinite value and rendering it coextensive with the whole, and in this manner allowing it reign over existence itself'.†

On the terrain of time, this means that Hegel, the first thinker adequate to History, is nonetheless inadequate to time. He cannot think it, subordinates it to a non- or para-temporal concept of repetition which denatures temporality as such. For this reason, 'Hegel's innovation is the final and most powerful homage rendered to the old principle',‡ which is of course nothing but principle as such taken as what is 'oldest', archaic, archonic: the superiority of the Concept over temporality.

The entirety of the Deleuzian theory of time aims to broach this Hegelian figurine by showing how temporality is irreducible to but also productive of the apparition of identity enshrined in Hegel's account. The assaults are mounted from a variety of directions, and, as is always the case, Deleuze synthesises his position from the materials at hand. Certainly, however, the sources most frequented

---

* Deleuze, *Difference and Repetition*, p. 50.
† Deleuze, *Difference and Repetition*, p. 49.
‡ Deleuze, *Difference and Repetition*, p. 51.

when reflecting on the question of time are Freud (and, after him,
Lacan), Kant, Bergson, Proust and Nietzsche; this somewhat perverse
menagerie is foundational.

Proust and time   Proust is to Deleuze what Mallarmé is to Badiou: a
literary figure whose work makes decisive contri-
butions to philosophical thought from its margins. Deleuze's engagement with Proust takes place throughout his early work (the final
entry is made in 1972, the year of publication for *Anti-Oedipus*) – a
point notable because this is also the period during which he is
closest to Freud and Lacan. From Proust, Deleuze derives the notion
that time is multiple, and that it is necessary to engage with it in the
context of a generous nexus of concepts, primary among which are
those of signs and of truth. However, what makes this Proustian
position particularly striking is that it shows time as the ground of
subjectivity and what inexorably and repeatedly breaks the subject
open. As in Kant, time is not subordinate either to human consciousness or to the movement of bodies, but provides subjectivity and
objectivity with a necessary form – which is just to say that it is time
that is the most profound level of subjectivity, the chain that joins the
rest. However – and here Deleuze and Proust depart from Kant –
time is not interior to phenomenal reality but is what broaches the
division between the intrasubjective space of phenomenal experience
and the maelstrom of being.

Proust's signs   According to Deleuze, Proust's account unfolds
this view by considering four moments in the serial
arrangement of time, truth and signs: worldly signs, signs of love,
sensuous signs and the signs of art. In each case, Deleuze finds in
Proust a certain configuration of these three terms, and as the series
progresses, shows how the signs of the previous regime are provided
with a new significance by the new regime. Since the category of truth
is to be addressed in a later chapter, we will focus here on the time-
sign relation in particular.

It is important to insist at the outset that signs in this Proustian sense
are irreducible to a linguistic category for Deleuze. For this reason,
the positive account implies a set of strong criticisms of Saussure,
but also Chomsky and Benveniste, criticisms that hold *ipso facto*
for aspects of Lacan. Signs, on this account, are not the matter of
meaning but the vectors of a primarily – and primary – asubjective

affect. In the first instance, a sign does not *mean* but only *takes place at the level of sensation*. When its force is registered at this level, it engenders a thinking activity – interpretation, first of all, but ultimately thought as such will be produced in this fashion. Already in *Proust and Signs* Deleuze will insist – a central element of his 'transcendental empiricism' – that it is the encounter with signs that makes us think.

Now, each regime of signs is individuated on the basis of the temporal mode that it expresses. Thus, for example, the signs of love each express a past lost in advance, an inaccessible past (memorial mourning, or memory-melancholia) belonging to the beloved that the lover has no place in. This is why every gesture (sign) on the part of the beloved wounds, since all signs of love remind the lover that they are excluded in principle from the originary meaning of this gesture. However, the inverse is also true, since the time of the past is found both in love and in the phenomenon of involuntary memory (for example, in the memory of Combray that the sensation-sign of the tea-soaked madeleine engenders). What distinguishes the two, at least in part, is the fact that different signs are in play: the signs of love, on the one hand, and sensuous signs on the other.

The four registers of time in Proust Deleuze describes four temporal regimes at work in Proust: time wasted, time lost, time rediscovered and time regained. But what does the word time mean here? It is not – clearly, cannot be – a mere container, the time of physics, since this latter is a unified and neutral conception time that can bear no differences in kind. Time is the synthetic element in which subjective experience is organised. The various times (wasted, lost, rediscovered, regained) are modes of subjectivity.

It is not that there is a neutral passage of time that I am free to use or waste. Rather, time wasted is time necessarily wasted, time that cannot support the presence of love or art. Likewise, the lost time of love is not lost contingently, but as such and in general. The time of love, the time capable of gathering together the signs of the beloved, constitutes time as such as what is always already gone. It is that framework of subjective experience in which my acts and choices are always revealed to be too late – I only know what I ought to have been paying attention to after the decisive experience which would have revealed the truth of my lover's world to me. Time rediscovered is the time in which involuntary memory can constitute a mode of experience. Here, time is rediscovered *as* time, as the reality of time that insists beneath the previous times and which, unbeknownst to the subject who exists as a function of these times, makes them possible. The suffering that the lover experiences in the (fundamental) moment of jealousy, for example, involves the being of the past of the beloved as such. When I suffer from jealousy, though, I only have access to the always-already-lost feature of the past as such, as if to my beloved's body as she turns the corner, seen out of the corner of my eye. Finally, time regained is the subjective access to eternity, to time as absolute. Here, the synthesis involved is of the other times as such, since once I can adopt the position of time as such, wasted, lost and rediscovered time are equally affirmed *as* time, in their irreducible differences and as the ways in which certain signs can come to matter. It is from the point of view of time regained that the subject can affirm (in the manner presented by Nietzsche in his first elaboration of the idea of the eternal return) even the prosecutors of her worst experiences, of boredom, jealousy and anguish. In other words, time regained offers the point of view from which these differences can be affirmed in their difference.

Proust, then, is a kind of phenomenologist on Deleuze's account, but the subject in question is not a human subject, even that of the narrator, but time itself. Time is the Proustian subject.

Signs and time   In turn, signs play two different roles. On the one hand, they are what are synthetically organised by the time in question: time wasted, for example, as a mode of organisation of experience, gathers together the empty signs of the dinner party and the polite conversation, thereby constituting a subjective orientation undergone by the narrator at the Guermantes'. On the other, signs are what introduce a rupture into the synthetic rhythms of the time in question, forcing the subject into a serial investigation that may effect the passage to a new time. The encounter with Albertine, the signs that she emits, will give rise to the passage to the lost (in advance) time of love, just as the sensuous signs, those that are obscurely connected to involuntary memories, will make the demand on the subject to pass beyond the worlds of the amorous and the everyday.

Proust's split subject   From the subjective point of view, the taking-place of the sign as sensation marks precisely the point at which the world of Proust's narrator as it currently exists – and analogously, the phenomenal regime of Kant's empirical self – is ruptured. The reality of time from the subjective point of view is thus the cracking open of the subjective point of view through the agency of the sign. Proust's novel is in turn the account of the subjectivation/counter-subjectivation of the narrator by way of a serial encounter – an apprenticeship in Egyptology, Deleuze remarks, which is also a temporal apprenticeship – with the different regimes of signs. The narrator is not then one subject but rather a chain of different subject positions that arise on the basis of the encounter with these various signs, and with the temporal orders that they open the subject onto.

From Proust to Bergson   We will say more on Proust in a later chapter when truth is at issue (though, for Deleuze, that time is at issue is already to implicate truth, since nothing, not even truth, escapes the rule of time). Already, though, the essentials of Deleuze's entire early position are in place, at least *in nuce*: differential time, sign as sensible encounter, difference as foundational. It may seem odd to dwell on the Proustian moment in Deleuze at all when it is Bergson who is his 'true master'. But the Proustian lesson *is* the Bergsonian lesson. From Bergson we also learn that time is multiple, that it is the fundamental level of reality, the Subject from which particular subjects are produced, and that it is time that also cracks open existing subjects in order to give rise to new ways of thinking and being.

The Bergsonian account of time revolves around a dramatic ontologisation of the category of memory as the past as-such and in-itself. This is not to say that he has no interest in the present or future, but that these latter are, and must be according to the architecture of his argument, accounted for on the basis of this past. When Deleuze presents this famous position, he invariably does so – following Bergson himself – starting with the inadequacy of the present as a temporal modality to account for the nature of memory, and recollection in particular.

The temporality of memory   The capacity to recollect is not absolute. Aside from the hardly insignificant fact that it is troubled by forgetting, recollection seems to require a peculiar temporal torsion in order to take place at all. Bergson asks us to consider the following question: *when* are memories created? Of the three available options (before the experience, at the time of the experience, after the experience), Bergson argues (and Deleuze agrees) that only the second is viable. If memories are created before the experience, they are not really memories; if after, they must be somehow created *ex nihilo* by the subject in question.

However, another question now arises from a different point of view. When I recollect in the present a past present, there is a qualitative difference between the perception of the present and the memory of the past. The difference, as Deleuze notes, concerns the fact that 'reflection implies something more than reproduction: this something more is only this supplementary dimension in which every present reflects itself as present while at the same time representing the former'.* In other words, there is something supplementary in both the image of the present and the image of the past when they are subject to active consideration, namely the *having-been-past* of the past and the *being-present* of the present. Thus there must be a temporal register in which present and past are situated in order for them to be present and past at the level of conscious thought – or, as Deleuze puts it, *'there must be another time,'*† in which the present as passing is located or on which it is grounded. This is the case however radically the time of the present is conceived: the point holds equally for the simple stupidities of psychological accounts of the mind that privilege human agency, for the logico-physiological positions adumbrated by analytic philosophers, but also for the Humean account according to which the present is the result of a passive habitual synthesis (a view Deleuze also holds), not to mention any of the grand empty gestures towards the present qua moment of *kairos* that sometimes can be found in the discourse of sophisticated radicals.

Constitutive paradoxes
of the past   Bergson will go further again, in a direction that anticipates several of the central insights of psychoanalysis, and insist that this supplementary register is not just characteristic of representations that I actively consider (*she's changed her hair since yesterday*), but of experience as such. Over

---

* Deleuze, *Difference and Repetition*, pp. 80–1.
† Deleuze, *Difference and Repetition*, p. 79.

every present experience hovers a fog or haze of memories that are required in order to orient or make sense of it.

This second time is the past, as the ground of the present, and is the element in general in which present experience is possible. Now, Bergson goes on to show – and Deleuze each time follows in his characteristically metaphysical mode of reading the discussion in *Matter and Memory* when elaborating these points – that this situation has a number of surprising consequences which in turn provide us with the scaffolding for a theory of the past: four theses which Deleuze will call its 'constitutive paradoxes'.[*]

The first thesis we have already seen, and consists in the claim that the past is necessarily co-extensive with the present. For every current sensible encounter with the world, there is a corresponding memory of the present. This is what leads Bergson, in 'Memory of the Present and False Recognition',[†] to speak of time as a stream that splits into two jets in the present, one which constitutes the passing present, and the other the past as such (a claim which allows for a striking explanation of *déjà vu*). The second thesis follows from this. If the past co-exists with the present, it is not simply the present memory that does so, but the past as such. Deleuze writes: 'The past does not cause one present to pass without calling forth another, but itself neither passes nor comes forth [as such]. We cannot say that it was. It no longer exists, it does not exist, but it insists, it consists, it *is*. It insists with the former present, it consists with the new or present present. It is the in-itself of time as the final ground of the passage of time.'[‡] This leads again to the next, third, point, since if the whole of the past insists as such, alongside the present as it passes, the past as a temporal element must *pre-exist* the passing present. This is not to say that there already exist memories of all that will occur – at the level of content – but that – at the level of form – memory insists. Finally, the fourth thesis: the past as a whole co-exists with itself. The structure of this co-existence of the totality of the past (a totality, important to note, that is necessarily open, an open system-in-heterogenesis)

[*] Deleuze, *Difference and Repetition*, p. 81.
[†] Henri Bergson, 'Memory of the Present and False Recognition', in *Henri Bergson: Key Writings*, edited by Keith Ansell-Pearson and John Mullarkey (London: Continuum, 2002), pp. 141–56.
[‡] Deleuze, *Difference and Repetition*, p. 82.

is figured by Deleuze as a differential system of relations between memories as singular points in the co-existent matrix of the past.

The irreducibility of Deleuze to Bergson   Note that, in this account, Bergson goes no further than the associationist-Humean position does in treating the future on its own terms. In both cases, there is a pact between the present and the past (one grounded in the present for Hume, and at the point of intrication between present and past for Bergson), one that constitutes a practical orientation towards the future, which stands at a varying distance from what we expect it to be. In neither case is a positive account of the future provided, one which would not present it as an implication, a tracing from the present and the past. Note too that Deleuze will not hesitate to assert Proust's superiority over Bergson in an important respect. In *Difference and Repetition*, he says:

> The entire past is conserved in itself, but how can we save it for ourselves, how can we penetrate that in-itself without reducing it to the former present that it was, or to the present present in relation to which it is past? How can we save it *for ourselves*? It is more or less at this point that Proust intervenes, taking up the baton from Bergson. Moreover, it seems that the response has long been known: reminiscence . . . involuntary memory.[*]

Bergson defines the past as a memory-in-itself irreducible to any remembered present, but in so doing removes it altogether from human subjectivity. Proust, on the other hand, 'saves it for us' in the form of involuntary memory. An ambiguous rescue. If the only way the past-in-itself can still be for-us is in the form of memories which are not elicited by us, how is it ours? It is ours, Deleuze will argue, because it constitutes *our* horizon of questions. Involuntary memories, unable to be correlated with any intellectual activity on our part, assume the status of a *problem* for us. The past that has never been present is present as a sub- and ante-propositional problem without a definitive solution, and to which corresponds the non-signifying sign that provides this problem with its material form.

Kant's transcendental subject   It is in the philosophy of Immanuel Kant that Deleuze locates the first decisive investigation into the category of the future. Kant's goal in the first *Critique* is to elaborate the subjective conditions for the advent of experience and the

---

[*] Deleuze, *Difference and Repetition*, pp. 84–5.

objective knowledge claims that can arise from it (the famous synthetic *a priori*). For Kant, the answer to the question 'what makes objective knowledge claims possible?' is thus a theory of the subject. This subject is constituted by certain faculties (i.e., capacities in thought) and the unifying though empty unity of apperception. Regarding the former, Deleuze will focus his attention on the division between sensibility (the passive faculty that 'receives' sensations that arise from encounters) and the understanding (the active faculty that provides the categorical rules or categories that give structure to sensation). Now, as Kant says, the faculty of sensibility is the faculty that provides the general spatio-temporal character to experience: 'there are two pure forms of sensible intuition, serving as principles of *a priori* knowledge, namely, space and time'.[*] It is important to note that these are not for Kant conceptual determinations – time and space are not concepts, but pure forms that condition all intuitions. However, there is a key difference between the two. The form of space only applies to what Kant calls 'outer intuition',[†] that is, sensations that arise in contact with the empirical world. Time, however, is the form of all phenomena, all thought insofar as it arises only on the basis of the structure of the transcendental subject. This includes not just encounters with the material world of sensation, but everything:[‡] memories, images produced by the imagination, habitual associations, judgements of taste, and so on.

As such, the form of time is actually a split that runs through the entire edifice of the transcendental subject for Kant. On the one side, we have the encounter with sensations that is spatialised. But we also have thought in general (including the thought of spatialised sensible manifolds), which is absolutely subject to the empty form of time.

Kant's split subject   The identity of objects in Kant is provided by the coming together of the spatio-temporalised manifolds from sensibility (intuitions) with the categories of the understanding: the form of time divides objects of experience into two halves. However, the same is true for the subject. Kant notes in the

---

[*] Immanuel Kant, *The Critique of Pure Reason*, ed. and trans. Paul Guyer (Cambridge: Cambridge University Press, 2008), A22/B36.
[†] Kant, *Critique of Pure Reason*, A34/B50.
[‡] Notably, Kant excludes from this the form of objects in general and the ideas of reason, since both of these are transcendental fixtures. Deleuze, by modifying the theory of ideas and the doctrine of the faculties, and expelling concepts from the regime of the transcendental, will eliminate these exceptions.

Transcendental Deduction section of the *Critique* that there must be a means by which all of the different judgements or rule-bound objects of experience are provided with a unity that goes beyond them, not insofar as knowledge itself forms a unified whole (this will be the role of Reason in Kant), but as a coherent body of knowledge *for* me. If I am just the ensemble of my experiences, as Hume argues, then there is no 'I' at all. For Kant, on the contrary, representations (experiences) must be attributable to a subject in order to be experiences (synthesised representations) at all. However, this subject is not the clear-eyed Cartesian cogito, but a fixture of the transcendental subject, namely the transcendental unity of apperception. I am not, strictly speaking, this unity, but insofar as I am aware of anything at all, it must be a part of the transcendental structure that I suppose in being a self. But if I am not this unity of apperception itself, which does nothing, and insists in experience only to link together all of my experiences, then what am I exactly? At the level of conscious experience, I find myself in fact in the operation of sensibility in relation to the empirical world I encounter in the form of sensations. Running between the transcendental unity of apperception on the one hand (the empty form of the subject) and the empirical self on the other (the synthetic product of intuition) is of course the empty form of time: the Kantian subject is split.

The form of time and the future   Deleuze will generalise Kant's insight about the empty form of time and its consequences for subjectivity and objectivity in two steps, steps which correspond to the names of Freud and Nietzsche respectively. First, though, an initial answer to the question 'what has the form of time to do with the future?' For Deleuze, the answer lies in the fact that every *content* of thought in Kant is subordinate to this form. This holds for any present experience, but also any memory, and the significance any memory might have for us – *pace* Bergson – as the kernel of a problem. This means that the form of time not only sits between the two halves of the subject, but also constitutes the horizon towards which everything moves and from which everything new will come. In other words, the form of time is not *in* time, but marks the necessity of everything else being temporally bounded.

Deleuze's fidelity to the Freudian death drive   Despite the oft-repeated mantra – supportable if not necessarily supported by certain remarks in Deleuze's work with Guattari – that there is no death drive on

Deleuze's account, it is rather the case that Deleuze repeatedly returns to it, and in particular to the explication provided in 'the masterpiece which we know as *Beyond the Pleasure Principle*',[*] drawing a variety of consequences from Freud's speculation on the topic for the theory of time. In fact, the death drive provides the fulcrum for Deleuze's own 'return to Freud'. Deleuze's reading of this theme dovetails with the Proustian position elaborated above. However, instead of treating time as an enchained differential series of subjectivity-producing syntheses, his reading of Freud primarily works to expose the basic crevasse at the heart of time itself, one that falls between the present and the past on one side and the future on the other; or again, between the content of time and its form; or again, between the pleasure principle and the death drive.

Nothing is beyond the pleasure principle

The central question Deleuze poses here is as follows: what precisely does Freud identify as beyond the pleasure principle? Deleuze's surprising conclusion: *nothing*. 'There are no exceptions to the principle – though there would indeed seem to be some rather strange complications in the workings of pleasure.'[†] That is, on Deleuze's account, it is not what is beyond in the sense of being outside of the reach of the principle that Freud is concerned with, but what accounts for the subordination of pleasure to a principle in the first place: 'Freud's problem, we may say, is the very opposite of what it is often supposed to be, for he is concerned not with the exceptions to the principle but with its *foundation*. His problem is a transcendental one: the discovery of a transcendental principle – a problem, as Freud puts it, for "speculation".'[‡]

On Deleuze's account, the pleasure principle is an empirical principle, and has a constitutive function in a primary field of operation, namely the scattered state of local excitations and resolutions in the nascent psyche. What it constitutes is a systematisation of these resolutions engendered by the process of binding. That is, the pleasure principle is not a principle insofar as it characterises the diminution of the quantity of excitation – it is a principle because it does so in a *systematic fashion*. Binding is systematised by means of the

[*] Gilles Deleuze, *Masochism*, trans. Jean McNeil (New York: Zone Books, 1991), p. 111.
[†] Deleuze, *Masochism*, pp. 111–12.
[‡] Deleuze, *Masochism*, p. 113.

mechanism of repetition, which 'alone makes [excitation] "resolvable" into pleasure'.* The repetition of these resolutions gives rise not just to a rule-bound activity, but to a certain passive form of subjectivity attendant to this activity: the Id.

Put this way, however, it isn't yet clear what constitutes the foundation of the pleasure principle, and the ground for its synthetic role with respect to excitation – what provides it with its very *applicability* to the field of unresolved excitations. We are yet to account for 'its own particular status, the fact that it has dominance over the whole of psychic life'.† For Deleuze, the answer is that the death drive accounts for the global applicability of the pleasure principle. This assertion, which seems to border on nonsense, can be made sense of once we situate it on the terrain of repetition.

Repetition and
enjoyment   The activity of the pleasure principle is already a form of repetition. The systematisation of the resolutions of particular excitations involves the creation of an habitual connection that leads the ego, time and time again, to resolutions that have before been appropriate in these cases, in light of the situation as it in fact presents itself (this is why Deleuze will say in *Difference and Repetition* that the reality principle extends the pleasure principle rather than standing against it). The psyche is thus in its most basic sense a structure of repetitive habits: systems of repetitions of the past in the present. Deleuze's key question can then be rephrased as follows: what is it that grounds these habitual repetitions of the present-past complex? The answer is *the form of repetition itself*.

We need only recall Freud's discovery of the link between repetition and the death drive to see where Deleuze is heading here: the repetitive character of the death drive is without a goal at the level of the ego and the deployment of the pleasure principle. But rather than concluding that the death drive is thus the exception to the rule, Deleuze will insist that it is the rule itself. If I can repeat, it is because the ground of the pleasure principle, as the habitual organisation of repetition, is the form of repetition as such.

❖

* Deleuze, *Masochism*, p. 113.
† Deleuze, *Masochism*, p. 113.

Deleuze will make the same point in more directly temporal terms also: 'If it is possible to add the future (i.e., *after*) to the other two dimensions of repetition (i.e., *before* and *during*), it is because these two correlative structures cannot constitute the synthesis of time without immediately opening up to and making for the possibility of a future in time.'* In other words, there can be no present or past in time without their necessary opening onto a future. The question of foundations thus shifts again, since what is strictly at issue is not the grounding of the pleasure principle in something 'beyond' it, but the foundation of the present and the past – the past of the unbound excitations and the present of the coordinated Id and global ego – in the possibility of the opening to the future. The foundation of the pleasure principle, what allows it to function as a global rule for the resolution of excitation, is repetition itself, conceived as the irreducible opening of the past and present onto the future (i.e., the future is that opening that necessarily returns, repeats itself for every present-past nexus).†

Ego and superego   Deleuze will go on to note that this split between the *before* and *during* on the one hand and the *after* on the other corresponds in Freud to another decisive structural split, that which lies between the ego and the superego. Recall that the latter is made possible in a two step process on Freud's account. First, a desexualisation of libidinal energy takes place that corresponds to the formation of the reality principle, constituting a mobile, plastic, libidinal body. This libido is free to be invested in a variety of artificial goals, including that of the ego itself (via idealisation), or that of the superego (via identification). These two paths correspond to the trajectories traced out in their fullest extension by neurosis and sublimation, though a third also exists and is of primary importance to Deleuze in this context, namely perversion. Here, it is the split between ego and superego that becomes the object of investment. Since, though, the perverse investment is thus necessarily an investment in a form, it has an object in a quite different sense; perversion is literally an investment in nothing. The systematising function of the pleasure principle thus finds itself spinning around an empty centre insofar as its non-object choice continually ejects it

---

* Deleuze, *Masochism*, p. 115.
† It is worth remarking that the same line of argument is made by Lacan in his seminar on object-relations, where the death drive is described as a figure of the ephemerality of existence.

from the stomping grounds of neurosis. Unlike the neurotic claim 'I (guiltily) enjoy in the repetitive satisfaction of habit', the pervert says instead 'I enjoy repeating as such.' At the limit, this becomes indistinguishable from its obverse position: 'I repeat in order to enjoy.' The ground rises up to the surface.

If the split between ego and superego correlates to that between the before and during (the ego as the 'I was and am') and the after, or the future (the superego as the 'you should and will be'), to invest in the formal reality of this split is to invest in the form of time itself. In masochism, it is the superego which is made subordinate through disavowal – as we have already seen above in the discussion of Lacan – and suspension to a mythical (gynocratic) past. In sadism, by contrast, custom and the rule of law are smashed against the implacable advent of the future in order that its absolute violence with respect to the present might be unleashed at each moment. In both cases, it is repetition as such that is the 'object' of investment. The golden tonsils of hysterics should concern us less than the blind revolutions of the pervert, if we want access to the fundamental nature of subjectivity.

Thus, contrary to what a number of his otherwise astute readers will assert, the watchword of the mature Deleuzian theory of time is simply that there is nothing stronger than time. All strength dissipates before the 'hard law of being': the death drive.

Deleuze's eternal return   Deleuze will also find (or read into, some would say) the same theme in Nietzsche's doctrine of the eternal return. As we have said above, the name 'Nietzsche' marks one alternative point of departure where the relation of time and repetition is concerned, one that aims to avoid the Hegelian capture. On Deleuze's (well-known) account, the eternal return is and can only be the return of difference, which is to say the ejection at the ontological level of identity, similarity, essence, and so forth. We'll pass over here the question of Deleuze's fidelity to the letter of Nietzsche's text, since what really concerns us here (and matters as such) is the new conception of the future Deleuze's meditation on the theme engenders. In its briefest formulation, this new conception can be put as follows: *Deleuze will replace the empty form of the Kantian transcendental unity of apperception with the eternal return as the empty form of time.*

❖

Where Deleuze breaks with the apparent letter of the Nietzschean text is in insisting that the eternal return is not the return of the same but of difference. How though does time make difference return? It does so because it brooks no exceptions – since nothing, no existing state of affairs, is not subject to time. At the level of empirical change, that is, the passing present, not every state of affairs is necessarily overthrown, of course, and it may also be the case that nobody alive has any memory of certain things ever being any different (the passage of the seasons, for example). At the level of the *form* of time, however, the form of identity itself comes up against its absolute limit, or rather against the principle that undermines it in the order of reasons. If the form of time is prior to the form of identity – and such is the claim that Deleuze derives by passing with Nietzsche beyond Kant – then the form of identity is not supported by the form of time. Instead, difference, the advent of the new, finds in it an absolute guarantee.

It is even the case for Deleuze that this empty form of time constitutes a repetition. In this case, the repetition in question is static in nature, since what is repeated is the form of time as such. Alternatively, we can speak of the essence of repetition being revealed in the empty form of time, since what this form requires is the repetition of the advent of a new present, that is, time as such. To use this terminology, though, obviously subjects the notion of essence to a dramatic torsion.

The theory of time in *Difference and Repetition*   This strange menagerie of concepts and influences is brought together to powerful effect in *Difference and Repetition*, the capstone of Deleuze's early trajectory and a work that marks the advent of a thought prosecuted on its own terms. There, Deleuze presents time as a triple synthesis: the synthesis of habit or the present; the synthesis of memory, or the past; and the eternal return, the synthesis of the future. While these differ qualitatively in a variety of ways, they share the characteristic of being *(im)-passive*, that is, of being synthetic processes that have no need for a prior subjective agency beyond that of time itself. They are all also, for the same reason, unconscious syntheses, and therefore only thinkable critically, that is, via Kant's transcendental deduction and Freud's teratological deduction.

Habitus: first synthesis   In keeping with his reading of the pleasure principle, the first synthesis is constitutive-contractive.
Beings of all kinds are engendered by the binding of matter; the
'habits' (later, writing with Guattari, Deleuze will call them 'refrains',
ritournelles) in question are not activities preferred by subjects or
law-bound dispositions of objects, but the rhythmic coherence of
subjects and objects alike. The repetition of this binding, Deleuze
says, extracts a difference, but one that emerges on the side of the
contractile subject as a habit. As in Proust, the synthesis of habit
gives rise to modes of being in the world relative to the encounters at
the material-sensible level. However, for Deleuze this is also a
Freudian point in the case of the human being, for what the synthesis
of habit produces in the first instance is an elementary network of
bound investments, a primary, passive Id populated by a scattered
local egos (Deleuze notes that the French translation of Freud's *Es* –
Ça – is also an adverb that refers to the 'here and there' [*Ça et là*]
character of excitation in the *Id* that is bound by the ego), each functioning according to their own contractive rhythms.

Mnemosyne: second   The second synthesis, following Bergson and
synthesis   Proust, constitutes the memorial network or structural insistence of the past in the rhythms of the present. If habit
constitutes a kind of functional apparatus on the surface of reality,
the second synthesis gives it depth. This depth is not a new dimension
of habit, but an *a priori* depth that affects the surface not by replay-
ing it (as if the synthesis of memory was a task undertaken by the
subject, or by a second subject beneath habitual subjectivity) but by
marking it as always already replayed. It is only by conceiving
memory as this kind of *a priori* repetition that what Freud calls
Nachträglichkeit (the deferral characteristic of psychic life as such)
makes any sense, not to mention the characteristic doubled structure
of pathological symptomatology (the problematic return of the
repressed). Conversely, for Deleuze, this doubled structure is also
what grounds erotic investment, since the structure (past-present)
that it introduces provides the means for disguise and displacement
in psychic life. The play between present habits and sensations and
their complicated echoes with this structural conception of memory
provides the space for desire to come into being. In other words, it is
only when there are memorial-ideational objects of investment that
Eros develops. These objects are never the same as anything else (and
habit renders everything the same), not because they are experienced

as always new, but because they seem to reveal an immemorial or eternal depth to what was previously experienced as being entirely consumed in the present (thus Proust's madeleine gives rise to a memory of Combray that it cannot itself account for *qua* object of sensible experience). In more direct terms, it is the gap between what is given in sensible experience and its capacity to bear investment – this difference itself – which memory adds to the synthesis of the present: the undertow that makes the tides. These memorial 'objects' of investment Deleuze calls virtual objects, but his framework for discussing them is explicitly that of Lacan's *objet petit a* – thus the distinction between the first two syntheses repeats Lacan's famous distinction between need and desire. Habit gives rise to both the rhythmic satisfaction of needs and the nascent subject who needs, while memory intricates these primitive subjects-of-objects (in the sense of being 'subject to') within a differential framework that problematises them as objects and as subjects, handing them over into the regime of Eros.

It is also the synthesis of the *a priori* past that makes sense of the experience of involuntary memory. If memories can arise without being actively sought out, there must be a process in play that is beyond my means to dominate and direct. I am rather an inhabitant of memory, and my present experience is perpetually displaced by the past which inevitably accompanies it. The past, in other words, is that modality of time in which we *suffer differences* in order that we do not just consume the world habitually construed but become able to enjoy it. Again, we meet up with Lacan at this point: it is not that we desire objects which are consequently prohibited, from which suffering emerges. The institution of desire only takes place when the immemorial past gives to objects a depth which is at the same time an absolute distance – makes them desirable on the basis of an *a priori* disguise that marks *that* they are desirable without showing *what* they are, since memory is nothing but this difference itself.

Empty form of time: third synthesis The third synthesis, though, pays for all. Deleuze is keen to emphasise that habit and memory, however differential they are in function, function by excluding novelty. However, and for the same reason, they cannot account for the advent of the new materials upon which they as syntheses work. There must be a further dimension to time that accounts for the possibility of the new. Here the earlier work on the death drive and the eternal return comes into its own in Deleuze's architectonic. The third synthesis does not contract or embed subjects and objects, but forces them to confront new situations that they may or may not be able to contract. In essence, the time of the future is just an empty form, an inexorable requirement for another temporal moment in which something different might happen. *Might* happen: there is no necessity at the level of material cause and effect for Deleuze.

Back to the present   This is not at all Badiou's position. For Badiou, the category of time, so central a concern of philosophical 'materialists' of many stripes, is little more than a misrecognition. Rather, it is the confusion that a linguistic predication – avowed or obfuscated – presents as either its immanent ontology or operational logic. Already in the *Theory of the Subject*, Badiou was seeking the royal road (we use this term 'decisively') to the relegation of the question of time to its proper place as an adjunct of what happens (in situations), thus to the time of the subject. In this text he reconfigures Lacan's prisoners' dilemma, at once reducing its logical force and redirecting its analytical purpose. In *Being and Event* and the shorter texts that follow, time makes way for the production of truths whose formalisation is made possible by the axiomatising of the infinite, and in his *Deleuze*, under the same formal constraint, he offers a reading of Deleuze's relational or synthetic nexus, key to which is the latter's deposition of truth by his avowal of time as ontological function. In *Logics of Worlds,* Badiou condenses all this: 'We could also say that the event extracts from one time the possibility of another time. This other time, whose materiality envelops the consequences of the event, deserves the name of new present. The event is neither past nor future. It presents us with the present.'* Thus time does not do the splitting of anything; time is itself split by what is *not* being qua being. The subject keeps time and is unqualified.

Badiou ends his *Second Manifesto for Philosophy* affirming a desire, desired above all else: 'Truth, in a soul and in a body'. If we live or participate in this conviction, he says, 'then we will be stronger than Time'.† It's a compelling motif, drawn from a long engagement with Sylvain Lazarus, and one that accompanies Badiou's entire oeuvre.

---

* Alain Badiou, *Logics of Worlds*, trans. Alberto Toscano (London: Continuum, 2009), p. 384.
† Alain Badiou, *Second Manifesto for Philosophy*, trans. Louise Burchill (London: Polity, 2011), p. 130.

Its not that time is a concept of no importance for Badiou, it's that its not a concept at all. Following Lazarus, and tracing what he calls the romantic era's 'temporalisation of the concept' to Hegel's technical 'assiduousness', which, he notes, is nevertheless 'learned' with regard to mathematics (a learnedness, he notes in a key aside, Nietzsche and Heidegger 'dispensed with'), Badiou diagnoses the beginnings of the contemporary preference for the binding of the thought of the infinite to the philosophical determination of its concept. Mathematics as a singular discipline of thought is hereby reduced to an adjunct of philosophy, not only extrinsically but also intrinsically useless Badiou says, and as such 'dead for thought'.* If the concept of the infinite is philosophically given rather than mathematically produced (and thus as something *to be* thought), then, Badiou argues, the infinite is circumscribed by the motif of the One – there is, in effect one thought of the infinite, and as mathematics cannot think this thought itself, as philosophy contends, then philosophy determines the infinite fixed for all time – in the concept. Time becomes the transcendental for all thinking of the infinite. Hence its correlation to Being (as the ground of its 'strength') – the very form of a misrecognition up to and including it being 'recognised' as a form. The 'disentanglement' of philosophy from mathematics, Badiou argues, is key to this 'temporalisation of the concept', which becomes, as such, subject to the One of time. That is, the infinite is one thing for philosophy always. The link between temporalisation and place, the proper place for the thought of the infinite, is key to comprehending Badiou's aversion to the concept of time. Ultimately, this disentanglement of mathematics from philosophy which, after Hegel, becomes a disavowal and, as such, a repression, has consequences for thought in general, specifically for the thinking of situations of whatever denomination and so for politics in particular but love and art no less.

We get a first glimpse of this in *Theory of the Subject*, and it's no coincidence that Badiou here takes Lacan to task over the prisoner's dilemma or the question (or 'entanglement') of Logical Time. It occurs to us that Time is a concept for a philosophy that submits itself to the conditions of language up to and including conceiving of language as the expression ne plus ultra of being itself. Thus, as in

---

* Alain Badiou, *Theoretical Writings*, ed. and trans. Ray Brassier and Alberto Toscano (London: Continuum, 2004), pp. 34–5.

Lacan but no less in Deleuze – as Badiou recognises in his *Deleuze**
– the problem then becomes one not primarily of structure (though
that matters), but one of the correlation of distribution and place;
or as Badiou will call it, the 'space of placements'. Two things ensue
for Badiou: first, via a 'conditional'† re-entanglement of mathematics
and philosophy, the infinite can be unbound from its philosophical
finitude. Philosophy, as so conditioned, can set to recomposing the
space of thought appropriate to what mathematics demonstrates
concerning the infinite: that there are infinite infinities and not one
(thus to Deleuze's category of 'infinite speed', Badiou simply asks,
in exemplary Deleuzian fashion, 'which one is?'‡); secondly, Badiou
must philosophically intervene on the philosophies of Time and
place, of finitude and the One and do so by, effectively, submitting
this thinking of time and space to its proper place, which is not for
him the thought of being as such. The key to this latter move is the
re-composition, under the condition of mathematical axiomatisa-
tion, of the three philosophical questions par excellence: being, truth
and the subject.

Time submitted to
formalisation   Time, then, as we see with Badiou's conception of
                               the generic and its law of forcing – anticipation/
retroaction – is submitted to mathematical formalisation in a sort of
return of the repressed, whereby the subject, whose time this most
essentially is, works bit by bit or point by point (temporally, spatially
under condition of an evental rupturing of 'time' and 'place') to construct a true present whose conditions are presently lacking presentation, from the perspective of a future whose past is being determinedly
undone and, moreover, from the revealed insistence therein of an
inconsistency which the linguistic, knowing structure of the situation,
its 'state', could not know.

Thus the subjectivation of time as future anterior, a consequence of
the mathematical formalisation of the infinite, reveals the ignorance

---

* Alain Badiou, *Deleuze: The Clamor of Being*, trans. Louise Burchill (Minneapolis: University
  of Minnesota Press, 2000), cf. Ch. 5.
† Its worth noting that Jean Hippolyte gives this *conditional* formulation of philosophy in an
  interview with Badiou from January 1965, calling the non-philosophical 'the conditions of
  philosophy' and insisting on their conditional relation to philosophy, and, consequently,
  that the philosopher 'thinks his time'. Rejecting the 'end of metaphysics' Hippolyte also
  insists that philosophy must be declared to exist. See *Badiou and the Philosophers*, ed. and
  trans Tzuchien Tho and Giuseppe Bianco (London: Bloomsbury, 2013), pp. 6–8.
‡ Badiou, *Theoretical Writings*, p. 75.

of language in its encyclopaedic form. This ignorance, the knowledge of which being already precluded by the encyclopaedic structure of the state is, Badiou demonstrates, the consequence of this very encyclopaedic structuring of objects and beings within, ultimately, a framework of finitude in which every thing must be decidable.

> This poverty of knowledge [of a constructivist universes] – or this dignity of procedures, because the said poverty can only be seen from outside, and under risky hypotheses – results, in the final analysis, from its particular law being, besides the discernible, that of the decidable. Knowledge excludes ignorance. This tautology is profound: it designates that scholarly ascesis, and the universe which corresponds to it, is captivated by the desire of decision. We have seen how a positive decision was taken concerning the axiom of choice and the continuum hypothesis with the hypothesis of constructability . . . what patient knowledge desires, and seeks from the standpoint of a love of exact language, even at the price of a rarefaction of being, is that nothing be undecidable.[S]

Moreover, as he notes in the same passage already quoted from *Second Manifesto for Philosophy*, knowledge is concerned only with the preservation of bodies and languages and that such preservation must be at the expense of truths, which, for Badiou, are exceptions to it. Given such a condition, the exceptionality of their existence must be formally demonstrated such that truths can be thought. Within the framework of finitude, which is to say, the logical or sensible framework of the infinite, time guarantees that every thing be decidable: that the indiscernibility of what is undecidable be impossible. For Badiou, form is not spatial, so 'empty', but is the process by which the new in being comes to be thought. To wit:

> Why? What is a decision? A decision is always a point where, at a given moment, there is something concentrated or crystallised where one faces a cut. It is a point that cuts and on this point, I would not say that axioms are on the side of state or official politics.[¶]

Thus the general schema is that every event is an opening of a new possibility of formalization, carried forth by a new body. This new body always supports the formalization with respect to formal articulations. This is maintained for every truth procedure, and the

[S] Alain Badiou, *Being and Event*, trans. Oliver Feltham (London: Continuum, 2005), p. 314.
[¶] Alain Badiou and Tzuchien Tho, 'The Concept of Model, Forty Years Later', in *The Concept of Model: An Introduction to the Materialist Epistemology of Mathematics*, ed. and trans. Zachary Luke Frazer and Tzuchien Tho (Melbourne: re.press, 2007), p. 101.

study of particular formalizations will be the study of a regional world.[*]

Every creation of thought is in reality a creation of a new formalization and at the same time this new formalization establishes a relation or takes part in an interaction with the particularity of what we are trying to express. In this case, we determine the formalization as a universality, but it is ultimately a particularity that carries universality in the model.[†]

The time of no time There is no formalisation of Time. Effectively, Time exists for Badiou, philosophically speaking, as a philosopheme, a sophistic concept to be overcome, displaced and subjectivated. 'Coextensiveness with time', he notes 'engenders the lack of being'.[‡] Every reference to Time in Badiou's work is a negative one, along one of these lines. Its not even treated in *Logics of Worlds*. It has no affirmative force in his work whatsoever except, perhaps, insofar as it marks the incapacity of those theories submitted to the temporality of the concept to restrict the Ideal and so true effects of the time of the subject to its finite, situational or worldly manifestation. Against exactly the 'laws of the world' or 'the service of goods' or the pedagogies of subjective incapacity[§] Badiou asserts: 'Certainly, a truth is eternal in that it is never confined to a particular time – such a restriction being hardly tolerable for that which is a prisoner of no world, not even that in which it is born. Any given time is always the time of a world.'[¶] Time in this sense, according to *Logics of Worlds*, is simply an object of a world: An object being that which appears *for a world* and not *for any subject*. Put another way, the advent of the new requires no extrinsic guarantee and any such referent to a guarantee is a surrender to the One against the immanence of the subject. The Idea, manifest in any subject, in any world is, as Heidegger *rightly* noted vis-à-vis Plato, what resists temporalisation; whether the latter is claimed as concept or form.

We will now expand on this trajectory – looking first at Badiou's intervention in relation to Lacan in *Theory of the Subject* regarding its effect on the form and place of the subject and marking its

---

[*] Badiou and Tho, 'The Concept of Model, Forty Years Later', p. 89.
[†] Badiou and Tho, 'The Concept of Model, Forty Years Later', p. 91.
[‡] Alain Badiou, *Theory of the Subject*, trans. with intro. Bruno Bosteels (London and New York: Continuum, 2009), p. 26.
[§] A. J. Bartlett, 'Innovations in Incapacity: Education, Technique, Subject', *Digital Culture and Education*, Vol. 5, No. 1 (2013).
[¶] Badiou, *Second Manifesto for Philosophy*, p. 26.

consequences for the assignation of Time in *Being and Event* to that
of the subject alone and thus what a truth deposes, and finally at
his argument with Deleuze, and how this sets up the possibilities of
the displacement of place in *Logics of Worlds*, coincident with the
eternity of the Idea. We are not providing here an entire typology of
Badiou's engagement with Lacan in *Theory of the Subject*. Readers
can look elsewhere for this. What we will do is read the short section
of *Theory of the Subject* wherein the prisoner's dilemma is put to
the test by Badiou, for it provides a shortcut into his affirmative
and formal refusal of Time as the motive concept of all thought that
submits itself to the authority of language. We know the critical
importance of language for Lacan, for philosophy – especially in
Heidegger's wake – and for thought. But we need to see how time
is an essential component of philosophies of language. Badiou's
refusal to submit thought to language, let alone allow that language
expresses being as such, is intimately related to his materialist and
hence subjective lack of interest in time. Indeed, there is no better
place to start than with Lacan because it is where Badiou himself
restarts every time – in order finally to take his 'irreducible distance'.*

Let's note again that Badiou here is seeking after the materialist
subject and precisely 'to the side' of 'historical materialism' and
at the limit of the dialectic. He notes the affiliation of this engagement with Lacan to that of Marx's 1843 engagement with Hegel's
Philosophy of Right.† As such, what is at stake is a revamped conception of praxis: the singular universal (the proletariat having no
special rights is the universal class); critique, not of avatars and the
simulacrum but of the real (à la contra Feuerbach). In sum, however,
what is at stake is the subjective control of time. Here, this is in the
sense of the anticipation of certainty wherein the key to subjectivation is not certainty but the courage to anticipate, against the 'logic
of time', *what will have been certain*. In this way, the universal class
not only avoids the determinations of logical certainty (competitive
time)‡ in which it is hitherto inscribed as a particularity under the
constraint of others, but voids this logic entirely. In effect, the certainty of one's anticipation is only certain retroactively under condition of the anticipatory act. This passage from *Theory of the Subject*

* Badiou, *Theory of the Subject*, p. 248.
† Badiou, *Theory of the Subject*, p. 248.
‡ Badiou, *Theory of the Subject*, p. 250.

sums up the contiguity Badiou asserts between himself and Marx, and thematises the contiguity of time and *esplace*:

> We can see that this test amounts for an individual to complete the differential trait (black or white) that marks him, and thus to achieve, by the symbolic act of exiting, the status of free subject. It is important that this solution occurs from the point of the Other (the two others), who alone is in possession of every premise.[*]

'The prisoner meets the muppet hi-fi . . .'[†] Badiou details Lacan's five-point logic of subjectification, that is, the subjectification of the prisoner who walks out first, a so-called 'free' man, that we have already seen above. Logical time is broken into: 'the time to understand', thus that of deduction, calculation of the deductive time of the other; the time to conclude or to act as decided; representation of a possible haste – thus as other mover also the notion that the move is illogical and thus, as Badiou says, the retroactive discovery of a possibility to anticipate; scansion – the moment when all stop, when this act makes objective the reasoning of the others; lastly the walk against time – governed now by a certainty 'fully grounded'. This whole dilemma rendered here as a problem of time is governed, Badiou asserts, by the *esplace* – the rule of the warden and thus the state. The time to act is intimately linked to the logical constraint of the warden as the guardian of what takes place. The outplace (*horlieu*) – that which a-voids the space of placements (*esplace*) in any placing – is thus an 'outtime (*hortemps*), a time of possible advance, by which the act, the step forward, anticipates – perhaps! – the well-founded certainty'. The key distinction that this 'anticipated certainty' reveals is that between subjectivisation – which is essentially a-temporal or, as it will become later, evental – and the subjective process which this subjectivisation actually anticipates as its future. Thus the function of haste, its prematurity, becomes critical as the point at which *excess* – an excess of knowledge as such – opens onto a *decision* (with-out knowledge) and so onto an *unknown certainty*. Time, then, is an effect of the subject, effectively brought into being by the subjectivisation of the *hasty* – and thereby constituted – subject. Badiou: 'There is no subjectivisation without anticipation, which in turn can be measured by the subjective process.'[‡] As Badiou notes, however,

---

[*] Badiou, *Theory of the Subject*, p. 249.
[†] The Clash, 'The Prisoner', CBS (1978).
[‡] Badiou, *Theory of the Subject*, p. 251.

as true as this formulation might be, here in Lacan's rendering it relies on an algebra its own logic makes impossible, which is to say, since to assume all three prisoners reason alike, deductively, and thus in time or even harmony, means there is only one time and consequently the impossibility of there being anything other than the *esplace* (of the warden), the logic of competition and therefore an outcome which the logic itself prescribes.

Effectively, Badiou re-ontologises/topologises Lacan's five logical-time axioms into three possible operations of thought whereby a hierarchy of inclusions renders the noted harmony of deductions in such a way that this problematic symmetry between space and time can be re-read for the inconsistency it harbours as its very condition of possibility. This harmony is based on a certain effective duration – how *long* it takes to conclude (or not) – which every reasoner, being identified as such, will share.* This 'one time only' renders the 'periodisation' of subjectivisation and the subjective process (exact and existent as they may be in Lacan's formulation) 'jointly undone' since the event of the former which gives rise to the latter has no place in a schema whose logical or algebraic construction excludes what it presupposes – that is, the freedom of the subject or the conditional time (retroaction/anticipation) of the latter.

In other words, the key point is the formal consideration of the inexistent (as it will be again in *Logics of Worlds* thirty years later) whose excessive insistence the formulation of these logical identities necessarily represses. Thus Badiou seeks to *supplement* Lacan's reading based on what Lacan does not say. And this really is that 'the other might be stupid' and thus the haste of the 'subject', its certainty, is based on its non-identity with the others. It's clear the metaphorical work Lacan is doing here for Badiou, although we won't belabour the point by drawing the political conclusions or summarising Badiou's. At the heart of the problem is the identity of logic and time – that marvellous attempt 'to cross the asymptotic effects of time, anticipation, suspension, retroaction, and the reflection effects of pure logic'.† Instead, we will give a schematic summary of Badiou's reconfiguration that highlights the subjectivisation of time through the set or topological displacement of language or logic as mentioned

---

* Badiou, *Theory of the Subject*, p. 253.
† Badiou, *Theory of the Subject*, p. 252.

above, and prefigures the relative indifference to the concept of Time in *Being and Event 1 & 2*.

The key is the dis-identity of the 'prisoners' marked by the quality of 'haste'. A qualitative 'possibility' Lacan leaves unsaid, given, as he says, it has no 'logical function', and which effects time, the construction of time as the adjunct or even immanent expression of logic. Badiou argues there can be no temporal measure of this lack of identity; it's a pure contingency – 'knowing whether the supposed knucklehead may not be about to get lost in the most straight-forward premises'* – which is to say, an active part of the 'experiential field'.[†] Hence the lack of identity has to be included in the logic, averring that there are 'different speeds of reasoning'.[‡] In fact, Badiou says, this dis-identity is key to haste itself, the 'speed' on which Lacan's reading of the dilemma relies, because haste relies intrinsically on the fact that the other be actually other. One only hastens on the basis of this heterogeneity inscribed in the prisoner's dilemma, since if the prisoners' capacity to reason was identical there would not be a time differential which logic would capture as the essence of its own progression. Here we have, as Badiou contends, the topos entering as the displacement and re-composition of a finite logical or algebraic space, for if one starts to reason on the non-identity of self and other here then possible 'subjective neighbourhoods' arise for the reasoner 'through which [he] evaluates the other'.[§] Alluding to the larger structural make-up of the concept of the subject in this work, Badiou remarks that the reasoner under sway of this immanent qualitative difference, as soon as it's a matter of acting, must pay attention to this differentiation and thus to recognize it as a force in his reasoning. A force for Badiou is what a logic of placement cannot 'place', as such, what is purely indifferent to the former, and thus we have, retroactively speaking, the identification of an outplace or 'place of force' in the world of the prisoner's dilemma based only on the excessive presumption of the algebra of the place itself. Badiou's topological reconfiguration ('I read haste as the interference of a topology in an algebra'[¶]) demonstrates the immanent excess of a logical time – which is to say, that time and logic both include that

---

* Badiou, *Theory of the Subject*, p. 256.
† Badiou, *Theory of the Subject*, p. 254.
‡ Badiou, *Theory of the Subject*, p. 254.
§ Badiou, *Theory of the Subject*, p. 255.
¶ Badiou, *Theory of the Subject*, p. 256.

which they altogether exclude in the distribution of their discursive consequences and mark an inconsistency against all efforts to present them as well founded or beyond qualitative analysis. And it's this inconsistency – the 'force by which the place finds itself altered'* – that marks the anticipations of the subjectivisation of the subject and the retroactive force of its process. Its consistency as subject in other words, and importantly its exposure to the real.[†] 'The splace is always already the locus of the subjective.'[‡]

It is therefore not time but the subject that is the critical feature of the dilemma Lacan uses to cross 'Time and Logic' and thus attempt to solidify their conceptual contiguity by way of an example whose subjective image is crucial to Lacan's (larger) effort. Lacan is clearly intent on the subjective aspect of the dilemma but effectively subordinates the subject's subjectivity, the act of its thought, to the place in which the dilemma takes place, the better to reconcile the thought of the subject to the linguistic expression of its being as such. Such a being inscribed by language situated in time will become subject insofar as his act of thought will be that which accords with the rule of the *esplace*. It is not that Lacan has succumbed to the Althusserian conception of the subject, but that he has mistaken the 'locus of subjectivity'. To put it in terms Badiou will later deploy, in *Conditions* for example, Lacan puts the void on the side of the subject whereas the void is properly a matter of being and the subject is properly the matter of the event;[§] or, as here, the act of subjectivisation whose past will have been the subjective process it instigates. Lacan miscrosses the subjective strands, as it were: 'Lacan sides with Sophocles but points at Aeschylus, which is where we want to get.'[¶]

For Badiou, it's not simply that the act takes precedence over the calculation but that at a certain point there is nothing left to the subject but to decide: this puts the subject outside logic and out of time precisely because the matter of the subject is the 'recomposition of consequences in the light of the interruption' that it effectively is.

---

* Badiou, *Theory of the Subject*, p. 255.
† Badiou, *Theory of the Subject*, p. 256.
‡ Badiou, *Theory of the Subject*, p. 255.
§ Cf. 'I think the separation I maintain is the idea that the relation between the subject and formalism is on the side of formalism and not on the side of the subject. In the rigorous examination of formalization, one can dispose or place the subject, ultimately, as an effect and not as a cause.' Badiou and Tho, 'The Concept of Model, Forty Years Later', p. 88.
¶ Badiou, *Theory of the Subject*, p. 161.

It is not about 'pursuing the algorithm' which, after all, sutures Logic and Time, but, as noted, breaking this very law to which it owes its place.* Badiou concludes this reading by noting how haste, which is the force that escapes the logic of the place as such – even as its inclusion in the latter is what gives it its existence (in this place) – divides in two. Badiou retains this motif of division throughout his work, a motif Deleuze perceptively remarks in Plato as prior to dialectics.† Here, as a mark of the consistency Badiou demands of analysis, he remarks how haste is divisible in the terms of the subject's decision to conclude. The subject confronted with the real of the dilemma – that is, to get out 'free' – is split between the clear logic of the algorithm and the topology which requires the consideration of the 'neighbourhoods'. This undecidablity, which organises the entire dilemma, delivers the subject to anxiety. As such it is, in Badiou's analysis, on the side of and linked to the superego. To hasten under the condition of the algorithm alone is to run to the warden, the 'key to my very being', and beg release. Thus the subject is here inscribed in the anxiety/superego nexus, wherein the former is the subjectivisation and the latter is that which sustains the subjective process.

So we have, Badiou asserts, a subjective act: the prisoner decides at the point of the undecidable; but he mistakes his object so to speak, the warden or law for the real of the place. As he says, it is as a wager on the real that calculation itself must be broken with, and that 'I' (the prisoner) can 'complete the reasoning'.‡ The latter 'subjectivity' Badiou calls 'courage' – the (modified) typology of the subject will return in *Logics of Worlds* – and while these are two generic forms of subjectivisation, for which 'haste is their One', 'the subjective modes are opposed insofar as one blocks a rigid law under the effect of too-much-of-the-real, whereas the other bets on the real under the effect of an anticipated calculation'.§

From subjectivisation to being and event   In *Being and Event*, time is more rigorously subordinated to formalisation – or mathematicisation – on the one hand, and to the truth of the subject on the other. Let's not fail to remark that the very title of the text refers itself to Heidegger (more so than to Sartre) and as is well known Badiou sets

---

* Badiou, *Theory of the Subject*, p. 257.
† Deleuze, *Difference and Repetition*, p. 74.
‡ Badiou, *Theory of the Subject*, p. 258.
§ Badiou, *Theory of the Subject*, p. 258.

out his project in the introduction as explicitly opposed to Heidegger and, by extension, to the philosophical and philo-sophistical field Heidegger institutes and presupposes. The particularities of Heidegger as philosopher matter here. Badiou names Heidegger the 'last universally recognisable philosopher'.* For Badiou there are not many philosophers and certainly Heidegger is not ultimately one of the crucial philosophers for Badiou,† but we should also recall that, given the subjectivating force of anti-philosophy, this numeration is not really what matters! But let us note in passing that philosophers and anti-philosophers remains distinct in terms of what is expected of them.

Being and Event is therefore not critique but philosophy. Badiou agrees with Heidegger, the philosopher, that the ontological question is paramount.‡ For Badiou, however, ontology as mathematics ('the hard kernel of metaphysics for Heidegger'§) merely 'delimits the space of philosophy'.¶ Ontology is neither the site of the latter's forgetting nor the single kernel of its reconstitution as such. Thus, and this is paradoxically our point, the debate with Heidegger 'bears on ontology and the essence of mathematics on the one hand and then on what is signified by the site of philosophy being originally Greek'.**

As such, this ontological dissension is not about time. Time is rather the unsaid of the debate over the ontological paradigm and the site of philosophy, its condition and its act. Note that there is no chapter in *Being and Event* devoted explicitly to Heidegger, as there is to Plato, Hegel, Spinoza, Leibniz, Aristotle, Rousseau, Pascal, etc., even though he dominates 'contemporary philosophical ontology'.†† Instead, Badiou interrogates Heidegger through the notion of *physis* as the apparent of being and its discursive issuing in the poem as presence.‡‡ In essence, then, the latter is for Heidegger, ultimately, the language of the recuperation of the question of being, a question, of course, not only forgotten but whose forgetting is forgotten under cover of the 'metaphysics' of the idea – whose 'advent' is Plato. Badiou seeks not to oppose the poem per se (as we have seen) but

---

* Badiou, *Being and Event*, p. 1.
† These are: Plato, Descartes and Hegel. Badiou, *Logics of Worlds*, p. 571.
‡ Badiou, *Being and Event*, p. 2.
§ Badiou, *Being and Event*, p. 9.
¶ Badiou, *Being and Event*, p. 15.
** Badiou, *Being and Event*, p. 9.
†† Badiou, *Being and Event*, p. 9.
‡‡ Badiou, *Being and Event*, p. 123.

to insist on the mathematical foundations to the thought of being and thus to institute another disposition of these two orientations to being,* one that does not surrender the idea, to the 'ontologies of Presence'.[†]

We cannot go into an analysis of all that is at stake here between Badiou and Heidegger. What is key is that whereas temporality is critical to Heidegger's ontology and indeed to *Dasein* – 'temporality is the meaning of being of care' – and that concomitantly the force of temporality with regard to *Dasein* impacts upon the spatiality of *Dasein*, its 'being-there',[‡] the radical re-disposition Badiou proposes decouples the integral relation of these two. As we have already intimated vis-à-vis Lacan, Badiou puts in the place of the force of time the occurrence of the event 'beyond being'. Whereas Heidegger's recourse to the poem as the site of the unveiling requires that there be a conception of the 'whole' of ontology, discourse and Dasein articulated not only phenomenally but in terms of an issuing forth, emanating; the being whose whole ontology is, for Badiou, mathematics makes all this inconsistent and thus, paradoxically, One or not-multiple. Inconsistency, for Badiou, not only delimits the field of ontology – its own consistency relies upon the inconsistency that founds it. For Badiou, ontology is itself a situation, a situation of being wherein lacking all means of presence, presentation is presented. Thus the subject is convoked by ontology as the mark of what it is not, so to speak, rather than as a figure of the interior. 'Outside' being, then, and so without time, the subject is the veritable construction of its own time, the time of the event (of deciding) whose contingency ontology itself sets up as 'necessary', and, as such, the event, rather than issuing in time, or as some sort of temporal ecstasy of Dasein and thus related to the whole of presence itself, is both indifferent to time insofar as it occurs and dismissive of place insofar as it is what initiates the very taking place of the subject, who in turn guarantees that what takes place took place as distinct from place itself. Time and space are decoupled on one side by the indifference of the event to any force of time and, on the other, by the force of the event with regard to place. Again, Badiou's substitution of the foundationally rigorous categories of mathematical

---

* Badiou, *Being and Event*, p. 125.
† Badiou, *Being and Event*, p. 123.
‡ Martin Heidegger, *Being and Time*, trans. Joan Stambaugh (Albany: SUNY Press, 1996), pp. 335–6.

ontology for Heidegger's rigorously deployed yet poetically unstable and ecstatic categories of 'remaining-there-in-itself' and of 'opening forth', realises in retrospect that *physis* does not constitute the site of the reconstitution of being, but is merely 'what is most rigorously normal in being'.

This sideways re-ontologisation of Heidegger's ontology (science over the latter's metaphysics of the metaphysics of all science) – comparable in its 'necessity' to Deleuze's *Difference and Repetition* and not out of joint with Lacan's own taking leave of Heidegger* – is crucial to Badiou's own continued subjectivisation of time. In *Being and Event* the only sustained (and even this term is unsustainable) discussion of time occurs like an after-thought. There might be reason for doubt over Badiou's strategy, but as we will see more clearly when we discuss Deleuze's own full concept of time qua creativity, for Badiou the articulation of being and subjectivity passes through truths, where truths are an immanent construction in the present of that which an event renders possible for a situation. Against 'memory', thus, 'the becoming-truth of the subject, qua the becoming-subject of time', and the subsequent 'memorial injunction to recommence perpetually', and therefore against the concomitant 'abolition' of a present, Badiou declares truth to be 'the end of memory, the unfolding of a commencement'. In short, truth is a forgetting of time.[†]

Eternal truth   Nevertheless, as we know, truths are eternal insofar
                       as their situated procedure, of which a subject is
the finite and faithful 'embodiment' in a situation or world, may be exhausted but their trajectory can literally be taken up any time, being valid in an infinite number of situations outside the force of chronology and of spatial constraint. But again finite and infinite are quantifiable and not 'conceptual' or temporal in the Hegelian 'romantic' sense; nor in the sense of the virtual. In *Being and Event* the question of Time, in the sense that it requires capitalisation,

---

[*] Cf. Jacques Lacan, 'The Function and Field of Speech in Psychoanalysis', in *Ecrits*. Žižek notes that they part company at the point of their greatest similarity: Lacan still deploys being in the Heideggerian sense, even if the consequences he draws are nothing like Heidegger. See Slavoj Žižek, 'Why Lacan is not a Heideggerian', *Lacanian Ink*, Vol. 3, Fall (2008), pp. 134–49. Badiou notes that a comparison of the two has all the 'attractions of a rhetorical impasse'. See Alain Badiou, 'Lacan and the Pre-Socratics', in Slavoj Žižek (ed.), *Lacan: The Silent Partners* (London: Verso, 2006), p. 7.
[†] Badiou, *Deleuze: The Clamor of Being*, p. 65.

comes up only in the final section of meditation twenty on the Intervention. Already, we are in the time of the subject (of fidelity, to be more precise) and the realm of the event. As we speak of the event later in this book we won't here give too much of an exposition; suffice to say, what concerns Badiou is the splitting of the event as what happens from the intervention of the (becoming) subject such that the 'what happens' is established to 'have happened' independently of the intervention which, by giving the event the name of the event, is itself the single mark for the situation hosting this event that this 'aleatory figure of non-being' did in fact take (or is in fact what takes) place. The problem is that here we hit upon the curious fact that the implicative structure of the event and the intervention seems to become circular and thus the intervention is a function with no legitimacy outside the event whose existence it guarantees by its intervention.* What then is at stake is the form of the intervention. First, let's recount the problem as Badiou states it:

> Because the referent of the intervention is the void, such as is attested by the fracture of its border – the site – , and because its choice is illegal – representative without representation – , it cannot be grasped as a one-effect, or structure. Yet given that what is a-non-one is precisely the event itself, there appears to be a circle. It seems that the event, as interventional placement-in-circulation of its name, can only be authorised on the basis of that other event, equally void for structure, which is the intervention itself.†

Quite simply, Badiou says, 'the logic is in danger of being circular'.‡ Thus what he proposes is to 'split the circle' at the point where the intervention itself would become another event, an event for the first event, and thus we would have the problem all over again. Instead, he notes that any intervention presents one event for another.§ What does this mean? Here we should note that Badiou takes the very logic of intervention, whose singular function is to decide, from the axiom of choice.

Without going into detail, this 'occasional' axiom, determined by Cohen to not be inconsistent with a model theoretic conception of the axioms of set theory, works at the level of function or operation. Like the intervention, it operates on an existence, which it simultaneously

---

*   Badiou, *Being and Event*, p. 209.
†   Badiou, *Being and Event*, p. 231.
‡   Badiou, *Being and Event*, p. 231.
§   Badiou, *Being and Event*, p. 232.

guarantees. However, it is not the operation per se which can provide the guarantee of presentation. In the case of the intervention, nothing of the situation guarantees its existence beyond its function. It cannot ultimately secure the existence whose existence it has decided into being. It requires another existence beyond and consequent upon itself. Badiou puts it this way, 'an intervention is what presents an event for the occurrence of another. It is an evental 'between-two' (all existence is predicated on its belonging to or being presented by another).*

What Badiou is suggesting – and this really we draw from the subsequent presentation of what it is to 'live with Ideas' (these being 'eternal') in *Logics of Worlds* – is that the event (pre-its own intervention) is what is named by Idea. That is to say, it is the Idea of another event-site and thus of its truth that makes it possible to think the presentation of the intervention even as it is nowhere presented. The existence of the intervention as a presented multiple is subtended to the event to come qua presentation, not as a temporal effect. Infamously, Badiou provides a matheme for this event that provides an Idea of an Idea. The event is outside 'ontologisation', but, insofar as it happens, is within the realm of the Idea.

History as discontinuity   For Badiou, this 'evental recurrence' is essentially the name for history as discontinuity. There is no History, just as there is no Nature. At any given point 'in time' – thus in a world that is not atonal – there are interventions on events and the Idea (of the event), which will have presented the form of the intervention. In this way, Badiou says, intervention 'forms the kernel of any theory of time'. Intervention is Time itself. Time is 'thought as the gap between the two events'.† Between two events, intervention takes place; or, in other words, the subjective struggle produces this time of truth. While the subject itself might form a finite instance, as Badiou says, truth, understood, as post-evental, as the subjects constructive, consistent configuration of the pre-evental situation's void, has no such constraints. The 'measure' of this Time established by intervention is, 'if not coextensive with structure, if not the sensible form of the law',‡ between event and exhaustion. This measure is named fidelity by Badiou (ontologically, 'deduction'), and constitutes

---

* Badiou, *Being and Event*, p. 232.
† Badiou, *Being and Event*, p. 232.
‡ Badiou, *Being and Event*, p. 210.

in and through its organised control of this time between events what Badiou calls 'a discipline of time', or what, in *Logics of Worlds*, he calls the function of consequences.[*] Either way, it is the subject alone that temporalises an instant of truth, whether political, amorous, scientific or artistic. In summary, time itself is simply a matter of the subject, more accurately, of the fidelity that organises and sustains its trajectory. Moreover, it is the form of the subject not subject to time – phenomenal or transcendental – which serves to animate the eternity of a truth in the disparate worlds to which it may appear.

This assignment of the motif of time to the delimitations of structure and act, thus, presentation, is a consequence of Badiou's mathematical materialism, which is to say, the decision to affirm the mathematicisation of infinity as a condition of philosophical thought over and against the strong Romantic historicist conception: 'It was the newfound certainty that infinite or true being could only be apprehended through its own temporality that led the Romantic to depose mathematics from its localization as a condition for philosophy.'[†] Against Romanticism and its 'positivist and empiricist' variants' representation of the infinite in terms of horizon and finitude, as if the infinite is only properly manifest within the concept of the limit, mathematics 'presupposes the infinite as its site' and 'links the infinite to the bounded power of the letter'; its 'very act repeals the invocation of time'.[‡] We are back to one of the great themes of Badiou's work: the 'modern' deposition of mathematics by the suture to the poem, or in other words, contemporary anti-Platonism. Or, more urgently, the deposition of multiple being by the finitude of the One. Badiou's symmetry here hints at his invention.

Matheme, infinite   As Badiou asserts: 'The infinite must be submitted to the matheme's simple and transparent deductive chains, subtracted from all jurisdiction of the One, stripped of its horizonal function as the correlate of finitude and released from the metaphor of the Open.'[§] Mathematics deposes time with regard to the concept. What there is, is what is thinkable, the thematic of chaos is set aside, the thematic of the Whole is rendered inconsistent and consequently any perspective that ascribes the end of metaphysics to

---

[*] Badiou, *Logics of Worlds*, p. 211.
[†] Badiou, *Theoretical Writings*, p. 24.
[‡] Badiou, *Theoretical Writings*, p. 24.
[§] Badiou, *Theoretical Writings*, p. 27.

its incapacity to think the 'being in totality' or 'unicity' that it is said to occlude or repress. That a philosophy takes up the thesis that the One is not, disposes it to another trajectory whereby what is called metaphysics is revealed as inherently split between the thought of the one and the thought of the multiple, rendering the dismissive 'usage of the notion [of metaphysics] inconsistent'.* Both, Badiou contends, retain the idea that what there is can be thought. Insofar as one continues to decide either for the one or the multiple, one remains within metaphysics. To decide, then, as the matter of thought, the articulation between consistency and representation, existence and language, idea and concept, subjects and simulacrum: this is the essence of the 'return of philosophy to itself'.

To recover the *problem* of time (rather than the *question* of time), we will work through Badiou's engagement with Deleuze, specifically on Time, in *Deleuze: The Clamor of Being*.† Deleuze is a key figure in the first deposition given his calling in *The Logic of Sense* for the 'reversal of Platonism'.‡ Badiou usually treats Deleuze as one of the group who make up 'anti-Platonism' for today – a moniker which unites otherwise disparate figures and trajectories.§ However, in *Deleuze* Badiou refigures Deleuze as a Platonist of the One. This is a polemical determination with two inversions but, as always with Badiou, the *polemos* never goes into the world unaccompanied by rigorous demonstration. This determination both allies Deleuze as a philosopher and distances him by way of the most fundamental philosophical construction – the distinction between the one and multiplicity. Even if in 'One, Multiple, Multiplicity', Badiou qualifies this by pointing out, first, that philosophy is necessarily a diagonalising discourse and thus refuses to accept well-worn categories as its terms, and that Deleuze certainly approaches this distinction in this frame. However, the diagonal drawn by Deleuze remains, Badiou contends, 'subordinated to a renewed intuition of the One'. More notice should be taken of the analysis of this diagonal, Badiou says, than of the need to 'enforce textual orthodoxy'.¶

❖

---

* Badiou, *Theoretical Writings*, p. 178.
† The very title resonates with Aristotle's *De Caelo*.
‡ See, for example, Gilles Deleuze, *The Logic of Sense*, trans. Mark Lester with Charles Stivale (New York: Columbia University Press, 1990), p. 53.
§ Badiou, *Theoretical Writings*, p. 25.
¶ Badiou, *Theoretical Writings*, pp. 68–9.

Badiou's determination reverses Deleuze's own insistence and, more-over, this reversing of Deleuze stands Plato back on his feet. In *Logics of Worlds* Badiou states this flat-out with regard to what he deter-mines as Deleuze's four axioms of the event: 'It suffices', Badiou says, 'to reverse the axioms' and, he reminds us, 'the reverse is what makes negation appear'.* The latter is notoriously a concept that Deleuze wants no truck with – whatever the complexities of this negation. Nevertheless, Deleuze's own understanding of Plato – specifically his absolutely correct contention that division operates in Plato more fundamentally than even dialectic, and that it is on the basis of division as conceived in Plato that the latter must be overturned[†] – suggests to us a nascent Platonism in Deleuze's diverse philosophical interventions.

For Badiou, what this boils down to is the question of truth, that is, truth as that which, rather than being subject to or deposed by time to the realms of the eternally transcendental, 'joyously' suppresses time because truths are 'actual multiplicities': neither eternal verities, nor 'analogical' conceits, nor narratives in which the passivity of the past comes to the reality of virtual rest, and nor do they depend on the concept for their being thought.[‡] They begin, as it were, from nothing – from that which is both subtractive of the state and sub-tractive of being as such.

Badiou's central claim here as elsewhere is for the transtemporality of truths (as we mentioned in the chapter on the Contemporary). This transtemporality – in which time is displaced and deposed as a motive force and so does not determine either the power of thought, the designation of place, or the finitude of what there is – means 'that we really are the contemporaries of Archimedies, Newton, Spartacus...'.[§] The true is actual or manifest insofar as what Spartacus thought (as Badiou 'formalises' it in *Logics of Worlds*: 'we slaves we can and want to return home'[¶]) can be thought at any time and, under the force of the subject, will be. As a subject one participates in a truth, or better, it is this participation in the construction of a truth that exposes the certain existence of a subject

* Badiou, *Logics of Worlds*, p. 385.
† Deleuze, *Difference and Repetition*, p. 70.
‡ Badiou, *Deleuze: The Clamor of Being*, p. 60.
§ Badiou, *Deleuze: The Clamor of Being*, p. 60.
¶ Badiou, *Logics of Worlds*, p. 51.

and moreover the certain existence of the eternity of the Idea – the same for Spartacus as for the Sparticist, and not at all disregarding their extremely distinct circumstances – indeed this is what forces the consideration of their in-distinction or invariance as 'truth'. What remains critical in this, as we have said, is the possibility in any place and time, in any world, that is, of the real existence of the really new. The new marks time but is not a matter of time.

One of Badiou's conceits in this book, expressed in the chapter that concerns us, is that Deleuze and he share in the pursuit of a classical metaphysics concerned with Being and ground. Being 'classical' (albeit post-Cantor), truth should follow as primary concern. For Badiou, however, Deleuze seems to follow a road more travelled and resolves the question of truth on the side of time, as time itself, Badiou claims, and thus ultimately, on the side of the One. Badiou goes so far as to link Deleuze with Hegel on the latter and by extension then, to associate Deleuze with the regime of the temporalisation of the concept, even though Deleuze arrives at this by other paths – Nietzsche, Bergson and even Leibniz. Badiou's target here, as we have already pointed out, is Deleuze's 'inversion' of what we have to call the 'received wisdom' concerning the power or authority of the 'true' into the power of the false.[*]

Badiou asks 'whether the fact that beings are simulacra and that they therefore manifest, in the Nietzschean tradition, "the highest power of the false" prevents the virtual as ground from acting to secure a possible intuitive truth'.[†] Clearly this presentation of the question relies on it containing within its terms everything to which Badiou is opposed. Schematically: simulacrum (subject), Nietzsche (Plato), vitalism (mathematics), virtual (actual), intuition (generic). Quoting a letter from Deleuze dismissing the 'foregrounding of the question of truth', this division is expressed readily as 'the possibility of an actual' against 'the reality of a virtual'.

Badiou says that for Deleuze, truth is normative, abstract and mediatory (thus metaphysical), thus it is a category, if not the Category, and it sets up a schemata that is analogical, transcendent and referential. What we have, then, is a conception of truth as fixed,

[*] Badiou, *Theoretical Writings*, p. 120.
[†] Badiou, *Deleuze: The Clamor of Being*, p. 55.

self-reflexive, and verificational – this, Badiou claims, is merely the truth of a science or *techné* and so, as he continues, a limited conception; one that readily conforms to Deleuze's 'concocted' Platonism.* The nomination for this concocted conception of truth, 'power of the false', Badiou says, is not really what is problematic about Deleuze's construction. Rather, it is Deleuze's depiction of the 'model of truth' upon which his power of the false arises – not against but despite this model – that Badiou questions. That is to say, and this is important in that Deleuze wants to proceed against categorisations or at least despite them, that the power of the false is derivative of a category of truth – model and copy – one, moreover, that Badiou contends has never served other than as a 'mediatory image'. Effectively, Badiou is suggesting that Deleuze is misconceiving the problem (and indeed in conceptualising necessary problems rather than possible truths per se). Thus there are questions.

Is Deleuze's correspondence-cum-analogic conception of truth all there is to say about truth? If not, is there is another way to conceive of truth that avoids all the faults of the concept Deleuze aptly describes? Badiou certainly agrees that the model Deleuze presents is less than satisfactory. But, then, whither the power of the false? That is to say, what does it become? Finally, if the power of the false is another 'secret' name of the true for Deleuze, then it requires yet another articulation than the dialectical, analogical or judgemental. Badiou posits that this is *narration*, whose circularity conforms to a central demand in Deleuze concerning intuition, whose 'uncategorisable' form in turn is the basis of the link between Deleuze's original empiricism and his conception of the concept.

Badiou seeks textual support in an excerpt from *Cinema 2* – a text to which we return from Deleuze's point of view in the next chapter. Three things need to be noted. In the essay 'One, Multiple, Multiplicity', which begins as, but quickly surpasses, a response to critics of his *Deleuze* (surpasses because the criticisms don't amount to much more than orthodox ejaculations), Badiou notes the 'detailed philosophical' form of the texts on cinema. Second, cinema as time-image: time and the visible being key to the problematic explored here. Third, Badiou's method: discern a notion, concept, function, operation or deployment that consistently orients the thought under

---

* Badiou, *Deleuze: The Clamor of Being*, p. 56.

consideration (a key Deleuzian theme of reading!), of the work or philosopher (or whatever) under consideration; extract one usage from a context which is conceptually and/or problematically applicable to the current discursive context. Thus, textual orthodoxy misses the point – and it would appear in this strict sense is contra Deleuze's own prescriptions for reading.

The passage from *Cinema 2*, Badiou says, 'gives rise to five remarks', but we can further reduce it to a fundamental point: the power of the false/the form of the true; and thus power v. form. It is this very point that, in 'Deleuze's Vitalist Ontology', Badiou identifies as that of 'greatest proximity' which is also the point of 'pure difference' Ø {Ø}; or 'as such', 'as one'.* (Tellingly, Badiou will then use the example of 'grazing' to distinguish empiricism from mathematisation in regard to the 'richness' of their different productions.) Narration here serves to support what elsewhere Deleuze exposes as key to the question of being Univocal, that is to say, its indiscernibility, that it is that which always withdraws from that of which it is effective. This guards being from any actualisation as either number, category or ineffable, and effectively subtends the circularity of the thought of the return (the thought Deleuze's ontology authorises†) and the key to his conception of time, whereby narration supports the power of the false which indiscerns truth from itself 'in favour of a new narration'.‡ Badiou's five-fold response, as noted, devolves to that of the disjunction of power/form. Badiou is not opposing them, but marks the stages of their compatibility or reversibility up to a certain point of indiscernibility. Along the way – points 1, 2, 3 – he manages to note the false image of Platonism Deleuze abides; that the philosophical provenance of undecidability is Platonic, as is the taking up of narration and all its attendant powers of the false on the side of conceptual demonstration. It's just that narration is not all there is to it.

Indiscernibility, as noted above, is the fulcrum. In *Being and Event*, Badiou gave the formal deductive explanation contra Leibniz for the existence of the indiscernibles – ostensibly, that two identical elements cannot exist in the real (logically, it is another matter). This affirmation of existence is not contra Deleuze, who also affirms the

* Badiou, *Theoretical Writings*, p. 70.
† Alain Badiou, 'Of Life as a Name of Being, or, Deleuze's Vitalist Ontology', trans. Alberto Toscano, *Pli, Warwick Journal of Philosophy*, No. 10 (2000), pp. 191–9.
‡ Badiou, *Deleuze: The Clamor of Being*, p. 56.

existence of the indiscernible; rather, everything is staked in how to think indiscernibility, how indiscernibility is actualised rather than as that which maintains the mark of the virtual (real) as (really) present, so to speak. Ultimately, one way gives immanence a consistency, and being a univocity, and the other, insisting also on immanence and univocity, comes to lack – again, an affirmation of the formative power of negation that Deleuze's temporal structure seeks to substitute. The argument concerns what is actual and what virtual. The actuality of truths, that they can be isolated as such, as what immanently inscribes 'that share of being that founds being', is the matter of Badiou's concept of the generic: 'the formal isolation of truths in the infinite deployment of actual beings'.* Not only is it 'the same to think as to be' for Badiou, but any presented element of a situation can be equally presented in an entirely distinct situation which is the generic extension of the original presentitive situation. Notions such as presence, preservation, memory or duration are undercut by the singular universality of the generic.

On the other hand, for Badiou, Deleuze's 'power of the false' as 'the name for truth' is coextensive with the 'One-virtual' or Univocal-being, and as such there is no capacity to isolate actual instances of the true but rather to link instances of the power of the false – simulacra – to the machinery of immanent affirmation, which, Badiou argues, Deleuze inherits from Nietzsche. This linking and affirming, for which there is no isolation, no negation, is inherently circular – vital, as such – and so intuitive because no thought interrupts the narrative flow which unifies the 'One true' and the 'Multiple false'. What is left to thought, then, by this operation of the artistic or creative power of the false, is narration; for it is the case that any thought that seeks to either cut or formalise can be categorised as always already implicated in this power – reactively, for example, or falsely, thus truly conditioned by categorical predicates that cannot be authentically extended beyond the range of the discourses which specify their operations.

Time and narrative   Badiou links narration and time. The former allows for inveterate co-existences of pasts and presents whose truth or falsity or contradictions have no currency. The affirmative power of the false, having done with the 'form' of truth,

* Badiou, *Deleuze: The Clamor of Being*, p. 58.

and thus formal actualisation, reconciles narrative existences in and across time. Truth, as the power of the false, and time are synonymous as 'ground': time being that which puts 'the notion of truth [qua form] into crisis'.* Badiou returns here to the 'paradox of contingent futures' mentioned in the opening of the chapter and which, he says, gives Deleuze the means to show that the formal conception of truth that subtends philosophy hitherto prevents the proper configuration of the relation between truth and time or indeed its synthesis. 'It's the power of the false that lifts this immanent prohibition making possible the primacy of time and the deposition of truth', Badiou claims.[†] Badiou says this is a choice, ultimately. A decision to, as it were, sublate the possible thinking of truth (such that truth remains over in some indistinct sense) to time; for (non-chronological – thus narrative) 'time', Badiou quotes Deleuze as saying, is 'subjectivity itself' and, as such, foundational.

Badiou draws from this three summary points which will lead ultimately to a concept, Relation, and a practice, Memory, which taken together give the parameters of a thought of the virtual. These are: time is truth itself; as truth, time is not temporal: it is 'integral virtuality'; and the absolute being of the past is indiscernible from eternity.[‡]

We need to remind ourselves that in this work Badiou is claiming Deleuze's affinity not just to the One, but to a certain Platonism. Thus these three points serve to mark the process of synthesis between 'the temporal power of the false' and 'the eternity of the true' and this returns Deleuze to the Platonic depiction of time as the 'moving image of eternity'.[§] Badiou dismisses the immediate reaction that this depiction is the inversion of what Deleuze is affirming and argues that if we take the image as simulacrum (and not mimesis), and eternity as the One, and thus 'integrally virtual', then time for Deleuze is the expression of the eternal – just as Plato said. Moreover, situated in the 'creative power of the All', these images or 'volume-images' are beyond movement – the movement that is time liberated by the power (of the false) – and so immobile. This being the being or truth of time, Badiou contends.

* Badiou, *Deleuze: The Clamor of Being*, p. 60.
† Badiou, *Deleuze: The Clamor of Being*, p. 60.
‡ Badiou, *Deleuze: The Clamor of Being*, p. 61.
§ Badiou, *Deleuze: The Clamor of Being*, p. 61.

The problem arises, then, of thinking the immobilisation that founds the mobility of time. Two notions come together: productive or creative time and duration. The first is such that past and present are indiscernible. The present is not an aftermath in which the past is an absence. This, Badiou contends, would require being to be said in two senses at one and the same point, once according to its present and once according to its absence. Rather, the past is the positive production of time, of time as the opening of the present. This opening splits the present into the past and the future of which it is the creative expression. This very splitting of the present is what affirms the One qua duration ('the creative incorporation of the past, its virtualisation') and the immanent change of the One – thus 'double creation'.*
Recall that Badiou cites Deleuze speaking of 'volume images' as the expression of eternity and here we have something like a cumulative 'agglomeration' of the qualitative change in which the past is operative. Thus the incorporation and accumulation of all such differentiated pasts – the condition of the virtual after all – constitute 'duration'. The immanent circulations between presents and pasts 'trace' the actual.† Badiou asserts that 'duration', the 'great total past of time', is one with the virtual, and that as the being of time as truth cannot itself be temporal, as such, Deleuze requires an a-temporal determination of the One – Relation.

Ultimately, this does not break the structuring logic of the One, as is supposed, but dissimulates its effect under the condition of intuition and in the form of narration, such that the very idea of the actualisation of truth is impossible because the 'power of the false' reigns over every multiple in such a way that its exposure cannot not be simultaneous with any other – thus there is no form for declaring that one is true against any other. Badiou summarises the 'thread of the analysis of time':

> An object [a being] is never anything else than an immobile section of duration or instantaneous dimension of the present. It cannot therefore, in itself, bear a relation to other objects because no pure present can communicate directly with any other. Presents are simple, transient coexistences. Inasmuch as there are temporal relations, or something like time as such, it can only be in depth, in the differentiations that take place between singular pasts in the total

---

* Badiou, *Deleuze: The Clamor of Being*, p. 62.
† Badiou, *Deleuze: The Clamor of Being*, p. 62.

Past, in the 'large circuit' of virtualities. But these deep differentia-
tions are nothing other than qualitative changes of the whole, or the
being of the One as change. The result is, negatively, that 'Relation
is not a property of objects' and, positively, that '[r]elations . . .
belong to . . . the whole'.[*]

Movement in the space of objects is, as actuality or simulacrum,
the unbound contiguity of presents-objects. But, in its virtual depth,
in its truth, it is the internal change of the One, which is expressed
on the surface by temporal relations, such as the Simultaneous, the
Antecedent, Memory, Project, and so on – relations that are unintel-
ligible as long as one imagines that they are properties of the instan-
taneous dimension of the present. 'By movement in space, the objects
of a set change their respective positions. But, through relations,
the whole is transformed or changes qualitatively.'[†] This passage
sums up Badiou's contention. It is instructive, though, to go back to
a passage just prior to this which – alluding to the economy of the
notion that the ground always undoes what it founds, which is in
turn the 'thread' of the above passage – concludes with the italicized
classical conception of the work of truth: 'truth is the undoing, or
defection, of the object of which it is the truth'.[‡]

That time equates to truth for Deleuze, means then that his conception of time is effectively deposed by the function of truth itself. All
truths depose their 'objects'. Thus if truth is time, then time has to be
thought in a way consistent with Deleuze's conception of truth and
so effectively detemporalised, as Badiou suggests. Deleuze therefore
needs a concept for the whole that is strictly a-temporal yet supports
the divisive and recollective operation of time as such, and so both
the splitting of the present into past and future[§] and agglomeration
as the essence of duration. The regulation of this whole in terms of
its becoming and the One is Relation. It is, as Badiou remarks, a
quite Hegelian reconciliation even if the operations involved differ
between the two.[¶]

Let's end this critique with the essence of Badiou's final objection. If
truth is time for Deleuze it is also subject. As such it's a matter of how

[*] Badiou, *Deleuze: The Clamor of Being*, p. 62.
[†] Badiou, *Deleuze: The Clamor of Being*, p. 63.
[‡] Badiou, *Deleuze: The Clamor of Being*, p. 62
[§] Cf. Deleuze, *The Logic of Sense*.
[¶] Badiou, *Deleuze: The Clamor of Being*, p. 63.

this subject actualises its being in the world. For Badiou, given the time-image Deleuze effects, what is present as the past is actualised through memory: 'an incorporation within Being of its own actualized fecundity'.* For Deleuze, the structure of memory is Relation thus 'virtualisation and differentiation' and the modality by which the past/present is actualised as such in space and by time. Actualisation, what Badiou calls a truth procedure, results in Deleuze, he says, in memory or even 'absolute memory'. This again gives us a double effect – 'truth as time forces every present into forgetting, but preserves the whole of the past within memory'. Forgetting, then, bars the return to the past but memory sustains the possibility of recommencement. From separative injunction to begin, to the necessity of recommencing – this is the procedure of truth for whom the subject is time, Badiou contends, and so there is 'no commencement, but only an abolished present (undergoing virtualization) and a memory that rises to the surface (undergoing actualization)'.†

By contrast, for Badiou, time is a category 'derived from presentation' as such, and it is in itself multiple. Time is the 'being-not-there of the concept' and a truth is always the undoing of a time. It's the invention point by point of a new time, the time of truth and as such the time of the subject. Truth is that which sustains the locus of an interruption through which time is forgotten, as if time never existed – thus the a-temporal or even eternal time of the subject, subject to the truths of its time. Badiou, to end: 'It is the abolition of time which is engendered in the eternity of truths.'‡

---

* Badiou, *Deleuze: The Clamor of Being*, p. 64.
† Badiou, *Deleuze: The Clamor of Being*, p. 65.
‡ Badiou, *Deleuze: The Clamor of Being*, p. 65.

CHAPTER FOUR

Event

This chapter explores the thought of the event in our three thinkers. Notably, there is no question of the event's centrality to the work of both Deleuze and Badiou; whether Lacan has any comparable interest in the event has to date been under-considered. What this chapter therefore does first is examine Lacan's situation, and the places in which his thought touches on something that could be considered under this heading. On the basis of what we might call his fundamental pessimism regarding the chance of an event – which doesn't mean that there is no such thing for him – we then turn to an account of Deleuze's and Badiou's development of a concept of event as central to their thought.

Back to the event   Undoubtedly, a rethinking of 'the event' is considered an urgent requirement for the contemporaneousness of contemporary thought. As Justin Clemens and Oliver Feltham put it in an article titled 'The Thought of Stupefaction; or, Event and Decision as Non-ontological and Pre-political Factors in the Work of Gilles Deleuze and Alain Badiou':

> We will characterise the situation as a knot of legacies and opacities: Heidegger's thought of the event as *Ereignis* and language as the house of being; Hegel as delivering the problem of becoming considered in terms of negation; Saussure's conception of language as a diacritical system of differences which provides a scientific model for a systematic thought of systems; Freud's anti-philosophical theorisation of repression and repetition. We believe that the emergence of the contemporary French thought of the event – exemplified by Michel Foucault, J.-F. Lyotard, Jacques Derrida, Deleuze and Guattari, and Alain Badiou – is bound up with the struggle to escape the force-field of these legacies. All these thinkers find Heidegger overwhelming, and his elaboration of the destining of Being as rupture-and-continuity a crucial resource for a diagrammatic reconstruction of heterogeneous discourses. But they

also cannot be happy with his characterisation of Being, nor with his politics. They all recognise the crucial need to think *becoming*, to conceptualise how change can occur in situations à la Hegel, but outside of any dynamic provided by a logic of negation. They also recognise that Saussure has enabled a new and powerful thought of variant institutional structures, but that he also thereby confirms language *as* institution, as the very paradigm of institution and, in doing so, reduces difference to bundles of oppositions. They grapple with the Freudian aetiology of philosophical conceptuality as the dissimulating sublimation of phantasm and trauma, the atemporality and inconsistency of the unconscious as a power of undoing, but they cannot accept many of its presuppositions and consequences.[*]

One name, perhaps symptomatically, unmentioned in this paragraph is of course that of Jacques Lacan. But Lacan's name is not one among others in such a context, for he not only predates the other French thinkers mentioned here, but is already the thinker who deals immediately, directly, extensively and incisively with the legacies of Hegel, Heidegger, Saussure and Freud. As we have already indicated in the preceding chapters, Lacan is: *anhegelian*, in that his rejection of totality and teleology, the suture of truth to knowledge, and the subversion of the dialectic is coupled with a long-standing commitment to the uncircumventable theses of Hegel; *anheideggerean*, insofar as he agrees with the philosopher's theses regarding the absolute centrality of language in human being, the separation of truth and knowledge, and the crucial role played by art, but demurs regarding the fundamental problematic of being and time, as well as the analytics of technology in modernity; *asaussurean*, insofar as he picks up the signifier/signified distinction in order to emphasise the primacy of the bar of division in the establishment of signification as a system; and *hyperfreudian*, insofar as he machinates the most thoroughgoing 'return to Freud' yet envisaged.

A lost cause   What is peculiar about Lacan's situation – and that of psychoanalysis in general – is that the very idea of an event starts to look otiose. The difficulties begin with Freud, for whom there are indeed psychic events, which lead from the problems

* Justin Clemens and Oliver Feltham, 'The Thought of Stupefaction; or, Event and Decision as Non-ontological and Pre-political Factors in the Work of Gilles Deleuze and Alain Badiou', in R. Faber et al. (eds), *Event and Decision* (Newcastle: Cambridge Scholars Press, 2010), p. 20.

of neurology and path-breaching through the seduction hypothesis (the reality of a particular cause) to the official orificial phases (oral/anal/genital) and beyond (death drive and interminable analysis). Yet it is also the case that any account of Freud must acknowledge that, regarding the thinking of event, there are two abiding, connected issues.

The first issue is that these 'events' are considered more like programming demons than they are radically new or eventful; that is, at a particular developmental 'stage', the subject will constitute itself by means of a decision which involves whether to uptake or not a particular trait, if according to a number of possible different modalities, and which will thereafter be 'coloured' by the incomparable specificity of its content. These events therefore have a peculiar structure: on the one hand, they are absolutely singular for the subject, and can be almost anything (a particular interaction, a word, a shine on the nose, etc.); on the other, they trigger one or another subroutine from a well-defined range of generic processes (repression, identification, etc.). Contingency is imbricated with necessity in an unprecedented fashion.

The second issue is that, as Freud's work progresses, the ambiguities in his position constantly lead to new 'solutions' which create new ambiguities in turn. As Jean Laplanche and J.-B. Pontalis point out in their classic essay 'Fantasy and the Origins of Sexuality': 'we shall find a marked ambiguity of his conceptions as new avenues open out to him with each new stage in his ideas'.* Yet, and despite the constant post-Freudian innovations within psychoanalytic theory itself – as we can see very clearly in many of the most popular theories of trauma current today – the constitutive event *of* a subject continues to function as irretrievable *for* that subject, yet deposits spectral traces of its irreparable loss in such a way that the event itself can *never* be reconstructed from its remains and, indeed, becomes all the more forbidding in its essential irrelevance to its effects.† This is one

---

* Jean Laplanche and J.-B. Pontalis, 'Fantasy and the Origins of Sexuality', *IJP*, No. 49 (1968), pp. 1–18.
† On this issue, see the countervailing position of Catherine Malabou, whose extraordinary *The New Wounded: From Neurosis to Brain-Damage*, trans. S. Miller (New York: Fordham University Press, 2012), attempts, 'under the sign of cerebrality, *a thinking of destruction of the psyche different from that of psychoanalysis*' (p. 84). See also Slavoj Žižek's response, 'Descartes and the Post-Traumatic Subject', *Filosofski Vestnik*, Vol. XXIX, No. 2 (2008), pp. 9–29, and Malabou's response to Žižek's response, 'Post-Trauma: Towards a New

of the major reasons why Freud considers psychoanalytic therapy an 'impossible profession': treatment cannot target the cause, which is constitutively lost; nor can treatment target the effects, which are constitutionally epiphenomenal. Nor can it target the 'organism' itself, without simultaneously exacerbating and re-masking trauma through aggressive technical interventions into the biological substrate, interventions that must by definition produce uncontrolled and unknown effects. The neurological is as much at the mercy of the sexual as vice-versa, if the latter is reconstructed and understood as a form of extimate catastrophe-creation that short-circuits the onto- and the phylogenetic, the biological and the social. As Jacques-Alain Miller has put it, the body is effectively the 'first entry of an element foreign to analysis', that in Lacan the 'Imaginary is the Body', and that it falls under the structure of the signifier, which is to say it is the subject 'mortified'.* It is no wonder that institutional psychiatry, psychology and psychopharmacology continue to find Freud an abomination. The problem posed here therefore concerns the problematisation of the very notion of event in and by psychoanalysis itself.

Repetition demands novelty   One of the paradoxes of Freudian psychoanalysis, then, is that the problematic of the event is at once crucial and sidelined throughout. This peculiar conceptual ambivalence must also be understood as a positive phenomenon, not one to be corrected or lamented (e.g., it's not that Freud should have concentrated more or less on the event for one reason or another). Lacan is, as ever, entirely consumed with rethinking and thinking-through this Freudian path. As such, it is unsurprising that he himself undertakes several different accounts of what we might call an 'event'. The four examples we will give here are as follows: first, the mirror stage; second, the encounter; third, the analytic act; four, poetic creation. In each case, however, Lacan broaches his investigation with regard to the problem that the unconscious poses to philosophical concepts of the event, that is, that what appears as novelty or departure or divagation is itself rather the dissimulation of a constitutive generic

Definition?', in T. Cohen (ed.), *Telemorphosis: Theory in the Era of Climate Change, Vol. 1* (Ann Arbor: Open Humanities Press, 2012), pp. 226–38. Finally, see S. Tomsic, 'Three Notes on Science and Psychoanalysis', *Filosofski Vestnik*, Vol. XXXIII, No. 2 (2012), pp. 127–44.

* Jacques-Alain Miller, 'Mathemes', in Ellie Ragland and Dragan Milovanovic (eds), *Lacan: Topologically Speaking* (New York: Other Press, 2004), p. 38.

operation. This essential tendency of psychoanalysis to dissolve the import and grounding of (narcissistic) rhetorics of radicality, self-fashioning and free transformation is undoubtedly one of the reasons for the widespread spontaneous hostility to psychoanalysis, which, as we will discuss at greater length in the next chapter, has also a commitment to an unknowable anachrony that constantly repeats itself at a series of heterogeneous levels.

Smoke and mirrors   We can see this tendency operative in Lacan from his very earliest work onwards. In the famous 'The Mirror Stage as Formative of the I Function as Revealed in Psychoanalytic Experience', the Freudian paradox of the event as pre-programmed contingency is paramount. At some stage between the ages of six months and eighteen months, the otherwise mainly helpless infant catches sight of him- or herself in a mirror – and recognises the reflection as his or her own for the 'first' time. Considered as an event, this experience is the advent of *identification* for Lacan: 'namely, the transformation that takes place in the subject when he assumes an image – an image that is seemingly predestined to have an effect at this phase'.* This event has at least a six-fold import.† Above all, the 'recognition' is more satisfactorily denominated a misrecognition. First, the child misrecognises the image 'over-there' as 'over-here': a spatial confusion. Second, the child takes the form of its body as the form of its ego, a confusion-creation of inside-outside. Third, the image is recognised as a living thing, not as an inhuman trick done with mirrors. Fourth, the very formal unity that the child apprehends in its image is an apparition from the future: the child is in fact not-yet unified. Fifth, the image is not only misrecognised as actual, but as actualisable: no such formal unity will ever be available to the human subject. Sixth, the form is greeted with jubilation, and thus an affective misrecognition. In Lacan's words:

> For the total form of his body, by which the subject anticipates the maturation of his power in a mirage, is given to him only as a gestalt, that is, in an exteriority in which, to be sure, this form is more constitutive than constituted, but in which, above all, it appears to him as the contour of his stature that freezes it and in a

---

* Jacques Lacan, *Ecrits*, trans. Bruce Fink (New York: Norton, 2006), p. 76.
† See the chapter on Lacan in Justin Clemens, *The Romanticism of Contemporary Theory* (Aldershot: Ashgate, 2003), for a detailed exposition of this six-fold transformation, and its implicit links to the 'later Lacan'. These links show a divided 'seventh' negation to be already at work through the inverted time of the looking glass.

symmetry that reverses it, in opposition to the turbulent movements
with which the subject feels he animates it.*

The consequences of this 'event' are multiple. The imaginary form is
the bedrock of what will eventually become the 'I', the ego. This ego
is necessarily neither-one-nor-two and simultaneously one-and-two:
it is only itself through its image and its image through itself. As such,
it is simultaneously narcissistic, giving the joy of self, *and* aggressive,
jealous, establishing itself as its own double and rival. As Lacan adds,
in a phrase that is indicative of the conceptual peculiarity of psychoanalysis – whose fundamental concepts all target the paradoxical
intersection of nature and culture, reality and fantasy, without the
reduction of either to the same – this is the 'knot of imaginary servitude'. As Lacan will later constantly reiterate, psychoanalysis deals
with slaves who think they are masters. The transformative, 'evental'
nature of this experience that is the mirror-stage, then, establishes
the conditions, limits and operations of the vital evil of the ego
– but hardly constitutes a thought of an irreversible rupture with
unexpected consequences. On the contrary, if it is indeed an irreversible rupture, the consequences for certain subjective operations are
thereby also established. Lacan's conception is hence directed against
any creative optimism, which is thereby considered a typically low-
grade ruse of the imaginary itself.

Repetition demands
novelty
But to move from the imaginary to the symbolic,
and thus to the register of sexuality and the
symptom, hardly changes this fundamental psychoanalytic approach.
As we have already seen – and which is in any case widely known –
the Freudian revolution in thought tends towards the conservation of
primordial inexistence rather than the affirmation of experiments in
and with existence. A 'symptom' for Freud and for Lacan is an emer-
gent psychophysical phenomenon that ciphers as novelty the return of
the archaic: the once-again of the never-was. What is therefore
separated-out by psychoanalysis is the received equation: event =
novelty. On the contrary, the symptom is always new, but is not an
event in the sense of effecting a rupture: rather, the (real enough)
novelty is one of the ways in which expression must be considered
dissimulation. Furthermore, the novelty of the symptom is tied to a
failure of departure, to the presentation of an inexpressible as stymy-
ing a new beginning by seeming to participate in it. Finally, the

* Lacan, *Ecrits*, p. 76.

aetiology of this symptom is always contingent and singular, if the name that must be given to the 'activation' of the singular contingency in the organism is 'sexuality'. Yet that 'original' event is itself the consequence of another, later 'event', neither necessarily significant in itself: an essentially arbitrary experience during infancy is retroactively electrified by another essentially arbitrary later experience during, say, adolescence. A spark leaps the gap between two points, making a retrograde connection. And it is precisely this temporal dehiscence without presence that is the correlate of symptomatic presentation as dissimulation. This paradox, however, constantly shades into an ambiguity whose import we will return to below. Is an event constitutive of the subject, or is it rather co-constituted with the subject? Whatever answer one would like to give, the event remains a nugatory and divided contingency, correlated with a subject that is a doubled vacuity.

Contingency, yes – but at what price! The necessary contingency of sexuality in psychic life, a contingency that structures and is experienced as psychic necessity, is certainly also an essential conviction of Lacan's, and one which he continues to affirm – with many reservations and revisions – against post-Freudian revisionists, even to the extent of occasionally blurring the relation between erotic and death drives in his structural reconstruction of psychopathology. One can see this quite clearly in the complications of Lacan's theory of 'the encounter' perhaps most fully elaborated in *Seminar XI* (1964), but which is fundamentally continuous with his theory of the signifier. Here, the 'encounter' is linked to *tuché*, that is, to what, beyond the 'automaton' of the network of signifiers, is an 'encounter with the real'. As Lacan emphasises in regards to the Freudian unconscious:

> Impediment, failure, split. In a spoken or written sentence something stumbles. Freud is attracted by these phenomena, and it is there that he seeks the unconscious. There, something other demands to be realized – which appears as intentional, of course, but of a strange temporality. What occurs, what is *produced*, in this gap, is presented as *the discovery* . . . as soon as it is presented, this discovery becomes a rediscovery and, furthermore, it is always ready to steal away again, thus establishing the dimension of loss.[*]

---

[*] Jacques Lacan, *The Four Fundamental Concepts of Psychoanalysis: Seminar XI*, trans. A. Sheridan (London: Penguin, 1994), p. 25.

The symptom is an ever-reinvented invention that becomes a cease-less reforgetting of rediscovered loss. But this repetition of the uncon-scious, which, as we have been saying, is linked precisely to novelty as 'the vanity of repetition, its constitutive occultation', is precisely set up to avoid the encounter. In fact, 'the real is distinguished . . . by its separation from the field of the pleasure principle, by its desexualization'.* The real, thus redefined as the impossible, is pre-cisely 'impossible' in and for this or that subject alone, at the same time that it becomes the name for everything refractory for ontology in general. The subject *is* sexuation, separated from its own obliterat-ing enjoyment by an impossible encounter. And the impossible, as Lacan will later reconfirm in *Seminar XX, Encore*, is therefore that which 'doesn't stop not being written' – the sexual relationship as such.

As Malabou elucidates Lacan's position in *Seminar XI*: 'The Real knows no lack, it exceeds any horizon of anticipation and, for this reason, can never be encountered. But, for Lacan, *this lack of encoun-ter is always converted into a missed encounter*.'† In her reading, then, psychoanalysis must fail to conceptualise what contemporary neuroscience effects: for the subject of psychoanalysis, 'there would, once again, be one and only one principle: *trauma* [i.e., the event] *has always already happened*'.‡ But the 'post-traumatised subject' of neuroscience 'disconnects the structure of the always already. The post-traumatised subject is the never more of the always already.'§ Leaving aside the problem that, in order to discern the necessity of the contingency of disconnections without antecedent, neuroscience has to already take place on a presumption of developmentality, one might also respond that Lacan was already attentive to precisely this eventuality – and, precisely because of his fidelity to Freud, was in his late seminars finally able to pinpoint its aporia without any recourse to developmental psychology. If Malabou's account seeks to reintroduce a new thought of material causality – which makes post-traumatic subjects of neurological disorders *'living examples of the death drive'* in a way inaccessible to psychoanalysis – we have,

---

* Lacan, *The Four Fundamental Concepts*, p. 167.
† Malabou, *New Wounded*, p. 134.
‡ Malabou, 'Post-Trauma', p. 229; emphasis in original.
§ Malabou, 'Post-Trauma', p. 227.

on the contrary, to assert that this is precisely the stake of Lacan's late work.*

Novelty demands repetition

This is where Lacan's notorious 'real' makes its radical re-entry. Despite the apparent stability of the signifier, in his later work 'the real' changes its import for Lacan, according to precisely such exigencies. For it is here that a number of interlinked innovations are introduced, all concerned with a rethinking of the 'impossibility' of analysis on condition of the irruption of the real as contingent, inconsistent, irrecuperable materiality. On the one hand, Lacan seems to maintain his famous doctrine – 'The real, I will say, is the mystery of the speaking body, the mystery of the unconscious'† – an assertion which is absolutely continuous with his earlier positions. On the other hand, Lacan also reintroduces a different thesis, that of the *trait unaire* or unary trait (first broached in *Seminar VIII*) as a kind of material inscription prior to all signification, and which must be thought as originary repetition of a *jouissance* that is essentially dis-connection.‡ By *Seminar XXIII*, the real does not 'consist' at all, but ex-sists; it is without any meaning; it is 'in suspension'.§

The act as a cut

The 'end' of analysis had already been conceived by Lacan as the traversal of the fundamental fantasy (i.e., the relation between the barred subject and its co-originary object, *objet a*), and the psychoanalytic 'act' would then be that paradoxical moment at which praxis ('free association' between 'analysand' and 'analyst', and therefore already a *quadripartite* experimental 'space' of voids) encounters its limits in the suspension of the sense of existence delivered by a relationship to language. Lacan will even denominate the 'desire of the analyst' the 'desire for absolute difference': such absolute difference must by definition exceed the law of the subject, such that even the latter's appalling

---

* Note that Malabou's critique hinges above all on 'early' and 'middle' Lacan, especially Seminars VII (1959–60) and XI (1964). But it is only following Seminar XVII (1969–70) that Lacan really starts to up the stakes of the real in the materialist way that we discuss here.
† Jacques Lacan, *Encore: The Seminar of Jacques Lacan, Book XX: On Feminine Sexuality: The Limits of Love and Knowledge 1972–1973*, ed. J-A. Miller, trans. with notes B. Fink (New York: W. W. Norton, 1998) p. 131.
‡ See for example Jacques Lacan, *The Other Side of Psychoanalysis: Seminar XVII*, trans. R. Grigg (New York: Norton & Norton, 2006), p. 89.
§ See, for example, Jacques Lacan, *Le Séminaire XXIII: Le sinthome* (Paris: Seuil, 2005), p. 134.

manifestation as gold-shit proves a moment of narcissism. Absolute difference certainly cannot not avoid the consequences of the pure cut – 'castration' – delivered by the virtuality of the Other, whose insistence must be exposed as such, in its various modalities of obscenity, absence, lack, etc. This is the paradox of the act in psychoanalysis, which can shade into looking something like the exposure of a pure negativity, whether of the primal signifier or S1, through its negative limning in the course of an analysis. The analysand, having interminably-repeated-itself-with-differences, reaches the limits of its signification itself, the place at which the subject's inconsistency of utterance becomes _at once_ indiscriminable _and_ separable from the cut of primal repression. At such a (virtual) point, the suspension of reference with which the praxis of free association must begin comes to coincide with a suspension of the structure of reference itself. In slightly less abstract terms, the subject encounters its own limit in discourse as a non-negotiable cut, and that cut as itself contingent. This conception of 'the end' of analysis as an act of suspension of structure persists, if in an ambiguously radicalised form, in Lacan's late seminars, where the psychoanalytical problem of ethics is crystallised as the problem of act qua event that is one of a disconnection that at once constitutes a suspension (of the existing subjective organisation as meaningless contingency) and _may condition but does not entail_ a new beginning (of a new subjective organisation).

From suspension to striation

Leaving aside her propensity to reduce the _subject_ ('of the signifier') to the _individual_ ('brain'), this is another ambivalence in Lacanian psychoanalysis that Malabou misapprehends and reduces. Insofar as there is still any residual reference to the articulation of the drive with desire in Lacan, then there is certainly a presumption that the event has always already occurred. Yet the late Lacan identifies something else, in the process of inscription itself that is of a pre-sexual nature, and this is the materiality of 'the letter' that is itself the trace of a disconnection without precedent. This feature may be marked by an ambivalence that is crucial to psychoanalysis – that is, its therapeutic inspiration that always seeks out possibilities for real disconnections that are not irreparably destructive – but it is patent nonetheless. In the late Lacan, the real as irruption of pure materiality without precedent or sequent is the basis of what must be thought, and it must be thought as contingent discontinuity. Its consequences may be dissipatory – but not _neces-_

sarily so. Its consequences may not be internalised – but not *necessarily* so. Lacan likes to figure it by recourse to the image of flying in a plane over the striated geography of the vast Siberian wastes.

Materiality of the letter as impasse of the real

Hence the ambivalence of the materiality of the letter in late Lacan: it is no longer a signifier; it is originary repetition of a trait; it is that non-place in which the real comes to be inscribed as an impasse; it can become the material for poetry as the basis for re-creation; it can become the material for mathematical formalisation qua meaningless reference; it can become the material for matheme as the basis of pure, a-signifying transmissibility; it can take further, unprecedented directions. The key operation, in our opinion, is precisely that Lacan is revivifying one of his own most important early realisations about the discursive situation of psychoanalysis. Not only are there discourses that are irreducible to each other – for instance, to advert to the Platonic struggle, between poetry and philosophy, or between politics and mathematics – but that part of the singularity of the discourse of psychoanalysis is that it must stake its own position at the impossible crossing-place of these irreducibles. The most important aspect of psychoanalysis is its attempt to refuse the temptation to think – as philosophy allegedly does – that there is a universe for the taking-place of all these discourses. Rather, psychoanalysis has to affirm that subjects are produced as division, and that this division is absolutely irrecuperable with regard to a whole. Yet if no one discourse can be permitted to master another, the relation-of-their-non-relation must nonetheless still be rethought.

Psychoanalysis and philosophy as the inverted crossing of incommensurables

Hence, as Justin Clemens puts it in *Psychoanalysis is an Antiphilosophy*, elaborating on a fundamental doctrine of Badiou:

> Plato is properly the origin of philosophy insofar as he interrupted the claims of poetry (qua paradigm of mysterious unveiling) by the claims of the matheme (qua paradigm of rigorous knowledge). Rational knowledge (exemplified for Plato by geometry) curbs and supplants the irrational inspirations of literary effusion. For Freud, however, the situation is precisely the reverse. If philosophy interrupts the poem with the matheme, psychoanalysis interrupts the matheme with the poem. Psychoanalysis is therefore literally the inversion and other side of philosophy. As it happens, both discourses are centrally concerned with science and literature – which

is why they do indeed tend to share certain features – but they go in opposed directions. The ancient quarrel between philosophy and poetry of which Plato speaks in the *Republic* is here given an unprecedented twist. Philosophy interrupts literature with science, psychoanalysis science with literature.[*]

Why this matters in the study of the matter of the letter hinges upon the non-reducibility of the incommensurable limit discourses that simultaneously constitute the subject: mathematics and poetry are these limit discourses. Precisely because they cannot be reduced without falsification means that the subject itself must be formalised as a singular knotting of these incommensurables. Moreover, it means that, in Lacan's own vocabulary, 'the big Other does not exist'. Why not? Because there is no one, no all, no whole, no totality. There is no consistent environment in which difference can take place and be reconciled. Yet 'some of the One' persists or subsists regardless, both at the level of the subject and at the level of its study. The subject cannot go without a modicum of *unairation*, so to speak, the 'one-ning' of event. Philosophy, at least in Lacan's terms, is also obsessed with this stupidity or imbecility of the One, not least in its belief that it is capable of speaking being (that is, the One), without recognising that the being of speaking undermines this very project. But then philosophers are among the most stupid of all beings. As Lacan writes in *Encore*: 'It is precisely because he was a poet that Parmenides says what he has to say to us in the least stupid of manners. Otherwise, the idea that being is and that nonbeing is not, I don't know what that means to you, but personally I find that stupid. And you mustn't believe that it amuses me to say so.'[†] To put this in terms provided by Barbara Cassin, Lacan's is therefore a 'sophistic logology', which considers 'discourse in its rebellious rapport with sense, that passes through the signifier and performance, and distances itself from the truth of philosophy'.[‡] Or, in Badiou's terms, Lacan's is an anti-philosophy which saves truth at the cost of demeaning ontology.

But this approach has severe consequences for psychoanalytic discourse itself. By the mid-1970s, Lacan is becoming more and more hermetic in his utterances, precisely because a limit of analysis in regards to the presentation of its formalisation of the materiality of the

---

[*] Justin Clemens, *Psychoanalysis is an Antiphilosophy* (Edinburgh: Edinburgh University Press, 2013), pp. 12–13.
[†] Lacan, *Encore*, p. 22
[‡] Barbara Cassin, *Jacques le Sophist* (Paris: EPEL, 2012), p. 52.

letter – not to mention the consequences for treatment itself – seems to have been reached. To our mind, Lacan never finds a way to shift or transform this limit: either one reverts to the new Aristotelianism of the nascent neurosciences (plastic, developmental, technological) or to exhausted revelations of the primacy of communication (linguistic, communication and media theory). Lacan's final work leaves us at this limit, which cannot find a way to pass through the impasse of letter-being, or, as in the seminar on Joyce, beyond the litter of the letter. As Jean-Claude Milner puts it, in the work of the late Lacan the antagonistic poles of formalisation (technically, the Brunnian links) and creation (specifically, creative language-use exemplified by poetry) come to be counterbalanced and destructive of each other: 'On the one side, the taciturn knots; on the other, at once disjoint from itself and omnipresent, the poem, attested to and abolished by its own abundance.'* Hence concludes the most radical materialist programme of the twentieth century: in silence and self-cancellation. Or, in point of fact, in a finalising Act of Dissolution – thus a legislative declaration of disappearance – of one's own School.

The event in Deleuze   Such an outcome would have been not only otiose but impossible for Deleuze, whose very theory of the event makes such an act of dissolution incomprehensible. Deleuze sometimes claims that his philosophy as a whole should be thought of as a philosophy of the event, and that the event is his central category. A cursory examination of his work, however, makes such a global assessment seem implausible. Not only does the term itself only appear intermittently (with the exception of *The Logic of Sense*, as we will see), it does not seem to be given exactly the same status in each case.

Nonetheless, the generalisation can be rescued by noticing that two of the most common features that Deleuze will ascribe to the concept of the event can be found, under other names, throughout his work. The first of these is the general conception of the foundational status of change or becoming. We could say that Deleuze's philosophy is a philosophy of the event due to the fact that it privileges such change or becoming – the register of *events* – over any putative stable, foundational level of reality – the register of *essence*. That is,

* Jean-Claude Milner, *L'Oeuvre claire: Lacan, la science, la philosophie* (Paris: Seuil, 1995), p. 165.

what we consider to be fixed and unchanging, whether this be being itself (as in Parmenides, or Spinoza) or the form of subjectivity (as in Kant, say, or Heidegger, Badiou or Lacan), is not in fact fixed or essential in any fashion, but subject to an ongoing and fundamental ungrounding that necessitates change. At this level, Deleuze's work on the event is of a piece with his work on time. The second alibi for the notion of the event in Deleuze is the virtual-problem-concept-affect chain (one that could be extended even further). In each of these cases, we are presented with an instance of 'something' that is not reducible to the material existence of the here and now, but which nonetheless functions within it as a point of friction only able to be resolved by a change in this material situation.

When we find in Deleuze an explicit concept of event, it each time displays both of these tendencies in his thought. That is, the concept of the event in Deleuze is always allied with a fundamental break with the metaphysics of essence whose claim is that novelty is secondary in relation to identity. On the other hand, the concept of the event always appears as an ideal problematic element in contemporary situations that play an important role in the genesis of change in those situations. It is important to note, especially vis-à-vis Badiou, that events for Deleuze are ubiquitous rather than rare, and are not solely exposed to the subject.

Event, essence, accident This said, even insofar as the event is seen in Deleuze as an ideal problematic element that gives rise to change, it would be a mistake to consider the event as reducible to change itself. Consequently, the concept of the event is not just opposed to the concept of *essence*, it is also opposed to that of the *accident*, and has as its necessary correlate that of the *encounter*. Deleuze aligns the thematic of the event as accident with a certain simple empiricism, one that would tend to both reduce the significance of the role that the event plays in fomenting change and to reject out of hand its ideal modality. The event, that is, cannot be conceived simply as 'what happens', or as what is constitutive of 'states of affairs'. Instead, it is what gives reason and orientation to what happens, in a sense to be discussed in what follows. On the other hand, and more importantly, events in Deleuze only have effects insofar as they are expressed at the level of material encounters: the regime of bodies (of all kinds), the regime of sensations. In other words, insofar as something is an event for me, for a society, for a given species of animal and so on, it is so only insofar as it is *encountered* within the existing material regime.

Deleuze's account can thus be summarised as follows: events are ideal problematic features of reality that give rise to change, without however being of the same order as what itself changes or recuperable by it ('events escape from states of affairs'*). This account is a *transcendental* account, however, and does not involve any form of substantial dualism or split in being. For this reason, Deleuze will describe his project at one point, distinguishing it from Kant's while nonetheless indicating its general Kantian heritage, as a 'transcendental philosophy that bears on the event rather than the phenomenon'.† Crucial to this account is thus the notion that the empirical regime of bodies and sensation does not by itself illuminate the nature of the event. Indeed, the simple empiricist account that treats events as 'what happens' is mistaken exactly because it decides *a priori* – according to a kind of abortive single-step transcendental thought – that the sensible-empirical order accounts for all that there is. This is why, in *The Logic of Sense*, Deleuze describes the same project for a philosophy of the event in the following terms: 'We seek to determine an impersonal and pre-individual transcendental field that does not resemble the corresponding empirical fields.'‡ Finally, then, Deleuze will insist upon the exclusive opposition between the order of the event and that of representation, where the latter is understood as a prior conceptual investment in the categories of identity, analogy, resemblance and opposition, which for Deleuze undermines any adequate attempt to think multiplicity and difference, prejudging being in terms of identity instead. The event, that is to say, cannot be the object of either theoretical or 'natural' representation without being mistaken by this very act.

Five characteristics of the event in Deleuze   In order to pass beyond these general points, it is necessary to turn to the more detailed account provided in *The Logic of Sense*.§ As Badiou himself notes, this the

---

* Gilles Deleuze, *Essays Critical and Clinical*, ed. and trans. Daniel W. Smith and Michael Greco (New York: Verso, 1998), p. 21.
† Gilles Deleuze, *The Fold: Leibniz and the Baroque*, trans. Tom Conley (London: Athlone, 1993), p. 163.
‡ Gilles Deleuze, *The Logic of Sense*, trans. Mark Lester with Charles Stivale, ed. Constantin V. Boundas (London: Athlone, 1990), p. 102.
§ For an encyclopaedic treatment of this book's theory of the event, see Sean Bowden's *The Priority of Events* (Edinburgh: Edinburgh University Press, 2011).

central text in Deleuze's work that considers the concept of the event. There are fundamentally five characteristics of this account that speak, respectively, to: the relation between events and their situational precedents; the relationship between events and the situations for which they are events; the relationship that holds between events themselves; the relationship between events and language; and the ethical relationship that events and their actualisation makes possible.

First characteristic: the event as effect Deleuze holds, first of all and contrary to Badiou, that events have antecedent causes. However, following the Stoics, he will assert that the order of events differs from that of the causes in question. In other words, events, as effects of a cause, differ in kind from the causes which give rise to them. In *A Thousand Plateaus*, the point is put like this:

> When knife cuts flesh, when food or poison spreads through the body, when a drop of wine falls into water, there is an *intermingling of bodies*; but the statements, 'The knife is cutting the flesh,' 'I am eating,' 'The water is turning red,' express *incorporeal transformations* of an entirely different nature (events).*

On the one side, then, we have a network of causal relations which on the Stoic account and at the limit, includes all bodies, which co-exist in a complex of generalised interpenetration. Effects, however, belong to a second register proper to them, the register of what Deleuze calls here *incorporeals*. Events are thus the incorporeal effects of the network of corporeal causes – where corporeal is taken in a very broad sense, and includes linguistic representations, manifestations of personal thoughts and feelings, and even concepts that signify generalities.

Later, in his work with Guattari, Deleuze will term this corporeal aspect of reality that of the machinic assemblage, 'an intermingling of bodies reacting to one another'†; elsewhere, he will speak of a generalised regime of *alliage*, bodies as alloys of bodies.‡ Correlatively, the side proper to events will be termed the 'collective assemblage of enunciation',§ for reasons that will become clear shortly and concern

---

* Gilles Deleuze and Félix Guattari, *A Thousand Plateaus*, trans. Brian Massumi (Minneapolis: University of Minnesota Press, 1987), p. 86.
† Deleuze and Guattari, *A Thousand Plateaus*, p. 88.
‡ Gilles Deleuze, *Deux régimes de fou et autres textes* (Paris: Minuit, 2003), p. 164
§ Deleuze and Guattari, *A Thousand Plateaus*, p. 88.

the relationship between the event and language. What is first of all crucial to see is that, on Deleuze's account, events are effects and consequences that nonetheless differ in kind from their causes.

The tedious point must be made again here: to say that there is a difference in kind between causes and effects, bodies and events, is not to induce an ontological distinction that would raise events up to the level of a transcendent order. Such should already be evident on the basis of the fact that events are the impassive, causally inert effects of the interactions of bodies rather than eternal governing features of reality. Rather, bodies and events are the two facets of a common reality: 'the highest term therefore is not Being, but *Something* (*aliquid*), insofar as it subsumes being and non-being, existence and inherence',* that is, corporeal causes and incorporeal effects.

Second characteristic: event as structure From the point of view of bodies, events are thus subsequent in nature to the activities and passivities of bodies as such. However, this is only part of the story. For Deleuze, when we adopt the point of view of events rather than bodies, the properly evental perspective, a second feature of events with respect to bodies, becomes clear. While any given event is the effect of causal interactions between bodies, the regime of events as such constitutes the evental surface, populated with 'impersonal and preindividual nomadic singularities [which] constitute the real transcendental field'.† That is, the regime of events provides the ideal structure according to which the causal relations of bodies are arrayed.

Here, Deleuze's precursor is Leibniz, for whom the world, qua differential network of events-singularities, is expressed in each monad in such a way as to determine the particularity of the monad in question. The term 'expression' here (what is involved in the phrase 'according to which' above) is far from inconsequential, since it marks the precise form of relation that holds between implicit events and their explication in the relations between bodies. In Leibniz, an expressive relationship is one according to which what is expressed does not exist in any radical exteriority to that through which it is expressed. The concept of expression is thus another way of fending

---

* Deleuze, *The Logic of Sense*, p. 7.
† Deleuze, *The Logic of Sense*, p. 109.

off the return of substantialist dualism, such as that which plagues both Plato and Descartes. Deleuze's pithy definition runs as follows: 'By "expression" we mean, as always, that relation which involves a torsion between an expressor [here, a certain alloy of bodies] and an expressed [an event] such that the expressed does not exist apart from the expressor, even though the expressor relates to it as though to something completely different.'* Formally distinct but ontologically co-constitutive – such is the situation of bodies and events.

The role of events in the genesis of certain intrications of bodies is characterised by Deleuze in great detail, and according to a number of requirements that go beyond what interests us here. We have already seen, though, that Deleuze will refer to the surface of events as a *real transcendental field*. Here the term 'real' is significant, since he holds, along with a great number of post-Kantian thinkers, that the Kantian conception of the transcendental fails to attain the conditions of the genesis of reality, and remains (despite Kant's own best efforts) hypothetical in character. As transcendental features of reality, then, events for Deleuze constitute *genetic conditions* for the advent of reality. In the context of what has been said already, this is to say that events provide the ideal loci or focal point around which the causal processes of bodies are organised.

Being a structural feature of situations while lacking the causal efficacy of bodies is what leads Deleuze to assert of events, and the evental surface as such, that it is *quasi-causal*, 'the locus of a quasi-cause'.[†] Events, that is, possess an 'expressive quasi-causality, and not at all a necessitating causality'.[‡]

Event and structure not opposed in Deleuze   We might note, as Deleuze himself does, that in certain quarters (in, for example, Badiou's metaontology), the terms structure and event are mutually exclusive. But this is only one view of structure, and Deleuze, invoking not only Lacan but a whole panoply of other structuralist thinkers including Althusser, considers this opposition misplaced: 'There is no more opposition between event and structure or sense and structure than there is between structure and genesis. Structures include as many

---

* Gilles Deleuze, *Difference and Repetition*, trans. Paul Patton (New York: Columbia University Press, 1995), p. 260.
† Deleuze, *The Logic of Sense*, p. 124.
‡ Deleuze, *The Logic of Sense*, p. 170.

ideal events as they do varieties of relations and singular points, which intersect with the real events [i.e., the alloying of particular bodies, in our terminology] they determine.'*

Event as the virtual Finally, we should note that Deleuze's term for this transcendental quasi-causal structure, this 'transcendental topology',† is the virtual. In this regard, he will often make the following claim, frequently in all but an identical fashion:

> Perhaps the word virtuality would precisely designate the mode of the structure or the object of theory, on the condition that we eliminate any vagueness about the word. For the virtual has a reality which is proper to it, but which does not merge with any actual reality, any present or past actuality. The virtual has an ideality that is proper to it, but which does not merge with any possible image, any abstract idea. We will say of structure: *real without being actual, ideal without being abstract.*‡

It is worth recalling this – essentially terminological – point here in order to correct a frequent bias in certain readings of Deleuze, according to which the virtual is the name for the vital flux of being. If the virtual is structure, is it also impassive, the effect of the alloyance of bodies and 'effective' only as structure. If there is any vitalism in Deleuze – and certainly there is – it should not be invoked in terms of the virtual, since, in it, nothing lives, nor moves, nor has any form of being that could generate movement as such. It is tempting to speak of the virtual as 'stellar', possessing the function of orientation the stars provided to early sailors, and putting just as little force into the motion of the boat.

Third characteristic:
events as co-existent A crucial point – one that sets Deleuze apart from both Lacan and Badiou, and which arises because of the ontological status of events – follows from this, namely that Deleuze requires a theory of the co-existence of events. That is to say that the theory of the event in Deleuze must involve a theory of the relations between events, or, conversely, that an event can only be properly understood if it is understood in its relation to other events.

---

* Deleuze, *Difference and Repetition*, p. 191.
† Gilles Deleuze, *L'île déserte et autres texts* (Paris: Minuit, 2002), p. 242.
‡ Deleuze, *L'île déserte*, p. 250; see also Deleuze, *Difference and Repetition*, p. 208.

The first thing to say is that this account cannot involve the contention that events are engaged in causal interactions. This is because events, as effects of the interactions of bodies and possessing no causal capacity of their own as we have seen, and more generally the evental surface – the transcendental structure proper to the alloying of bodies – are in themselves causally inert. Any thinker who holds to the tenets of structuralism, such as Lacan, would find nothing unusual here (and for this reason, *The Logic of Sense* constitutes for certain partisans of Lacan – such as Žižek – the *locus classicus* of the true Deleuze).

The logic lying behind this point determines Deleuze's general approach to the characterisation of the relations that hold between events. Following the immanent method of transcendental philosophy, inaugurated by Kant, he will insist that the characteristics of the transcendental field must not be deduced from beyond the field, and that what pertains to the regime of bodies and representations has no capacity on its own terms to illuminate the evental structure.

It is for this reason that Deleuze departs from the Stoics and Leibniz both: neither approaches manage to develop a thought of the event adequate to the co-existence of events on their own terms, but instead import criteria from elsewhere. In both cases, Deleuze will argue that logical criteria oriented by a certain desire for harmony between events is invoked – one rooted in 'simple physical causality or . . . logical contradiction'* on the part of the Stoics, despite their advances, and in certain 'theological exigencies'† on Leibniz's part. However, what is characteristic about events for Deleuze is that, on their own terms, they do not exclude each other, even if, from the point of view of the logic of propositions, they might be considered to be contradictory or incompossible. Here, he has (as is well known) recourse to Lewis Carroll, and to poor Alice's various predicaments. It is true that Alice cannot both shrink and grow at the same time, that is, in the order of time constituted by the present. However, 'it is at the same moment that one becomes larger than one was and smaller than one becomes'.‡ In other words, while we can at any

---

* Deleuze, *The Logic of Sense*, p. 171.
† Deleuze, *The Logic of Sense*, p. 172.
‡ Deleuze, *The Logic of Sense*, p. 1.

given moment say how tall Alice is, and compare her to her previous height, two events are being actualised at the same time. To borrow (as Deleuze himself does) from Plato, Alice is participating in two events at once, even though at the conceptual-propositional level, these two events are incompatible. This is to say that the events 'to grow' and 'to shrink' *qua* incorporeal attributes of bodies co-exist on their own terms, as singularities in the transcendental structure. To pass to a consideration of events on their own terms is thus to pass to a level paradoxical with respect to the logic of propositions, of bodies and the passing present. However, from the point of view of events themselves, the very notion of good sense, and the definition of paradox that arises because of it, is irrelevant.

Affirmative synthetic disjunction   If events co-exist, then, they do so in their differences from one another without these differences being thereby cancelled out. This form of relation Deleuze – in part on the basis of an evolution of Leibniz's conceptual apparatus – describes as expressive disjunctive synthesis or 'affirmative synthetic disjunction'.[*] It is a disjunctive relationship because events are not made subordinate to one another nor to any higher principle (excluded on the grounds that we seek an immanent account of events that does not suppose anything beyond what is proper to them in order to account for them). It is an expressive relationship insofar as no causal capacity is proper to events, and thus their sole mode of being is to insist as immaterial effects of causes. There is, insofar as they co-exist and inter-express, a 'communication of events'.[†] There is no event then for Deleuze that does not co-implicate all other events.[‡] It is an affirmative relationship because – as when Deleuze insists upon the absolute affirmative character of something (cf. intensity as it is theorised in *Difference and Repetition*), he means this same point – there are no native ontological divisions such that events could be partitioned up, thereby allowing for their ranking. Insofar as they subsist as events and differ from one another they are necessarily affirmed.

---

[*] Deleuze, *The Logic of Sense*, p. 174.
[†] Deleuze, *The Logic of Sense*, p. 174.
[‡] Recall Zarathustra: 'Did you ever say Yes to one joy? O my friends, then you said Yes to all woe as well. All things are chained and entwined together.' Friedrich Nietzsche, *Thus Spoke Zarathustra*, trans. R. J. Hollingdale (Harmondsworth: Penguin, 1961), 'The Intoxicated Song', §10.

The relationship is synthetic. This is the most difficult of the claims since, as Deleuze notes, the notion of synthesis routinely signifies the attainment of an homogeneity, in relation to which disjunction can only play the role of a gate-keeper, engaged solely in 'a procedure of analysis which is satisfied with the exclusion of predicates from one thing in virtue of the identity of its concept (the negative, limitative, or exclusive use of disjunction)'.* For Deleuze, such a position once more maps onto events the exclusive disjunctions that exist at the level of propositions and bodies (Alice can only be growing or shrinking, not both at once). The synthetic character of the relations between events is in fact accounted for by the affirmation or absolute nature of the field of events as such – that is, the very fact of the absence of unifying criteria is what constitutes the mode of synthesis proper to events.

For Deleuze, in contradistinction to both Badiou and Lacan, if for different reasons, singularities enter into inclusive, inter-expressive relations of disjunction. For the latter pair, events in their plurality have no relationship (even if the form of the event has a self-relation of a certain conceptual kind for both, namely that of identity).

Fourth characteristic: the event as sense-event *The Logic of Sense* is also Deleuze's most extended consideration of language, and his treatment of this theme is closely tied to his elaboration of a philosophy of the event. In fact, as the title indicates, *The Logic of Sense* is concerned with the term 'sense' at greater length than with 'event'. Beyond this, however, Deleuze will treat the two terms as conceptually co-implicated: the event is always the sense-event.

Deleuze demonstrates the need for the concept of sense by considering what he calls the 'three distinct relations within the proposition',† namely *denotation*, *manifestation* and *signification*. A proposition first of all *denotes* some reality beyond itself (she is crying). This is to say that language has a first representational function, that of representing in language a certain state of affairs. Second, a proposition *manifests* a reality internal to the speaker of the proposition in question (I am crying because of what happened on Friday). Here, what is being represented in language is a set of desires and beliefs that

---

* Deleuze, *The Logic of Sense*, p. 174.
† Deleuze, *The Logic of Sense*, p. 12.

belong to the utterer of the propositions. Third, a proposition signifies insofar as it deploys certain conceptual generalities, embodied in
particular forms in the proposition (the concept of unhappiness, of
Friday, etc.).

However, as Deleuze shows early in *The Logic of Sense*, these
modalities of the proposition are engaged in a vicious circle. One
can argue that any one of them is primary, but the means by which
this can be done always begs the question, and assumes one of the
other two. At the level of the logical foundations of the philosophy of
language, then, we are required to pass beyond these three to a fourth
dimension. In other words, what is required is a way to ground language beyond the speaking subject (manifestation), the object spoken
of (denotation) or the network of general concepts implied by the
proposition (signification). This fourth dimension of the proposition is *sense*. The task seems formidable, though, precisely because
this fourth dimension must be able to be accounted for without any
reference to these other instances.

The infinitive form and   The concept of sense is provided by the Stoic
the event   theory of events as *incorporeal attributes of bodies*.
Events, first of all, are not objects, that is to say, constituted bodies
engaged in relations of causality. Instead, they are effects, registered
at their own level as subsistent features attributable to bodies.
Neither do events require a position of enunciation to give rise to
them, since their subsistence is *real*; they do not require a subjective
grounding. Finally, events are not generalities, even absolute generalities of the kind found in the Platonic or Kantian Ideas, but are
singular in nature. Moreover, nothing at the level of the structure of
events itself would allow for any one event to be radically isolated
from or purified of the other events with which it is engaged in
complex relations of co-existence.

Notice, however, that despite lacking the generality belonging to
concepts the singularity of sense-events is not a simple particularity.
This can easily be seen by considering one of Deleuze's examples
of an event, 'to cut'. If I cut you, we are dealing with the actualisation of the event from two points of view. From my point of view,
the event is actualised in the active position, while from yours, we
ought to speak of 'He cut me'. This indicates that events can be and
are actualised in a number of different ways – to the plurality and

disjunctive co-existence of events as such corresponds the plurality and mutually exclusive manners in which a given event is actualised. The co-existence is translated, Deleuze will say, into a distribution among bodies according to their position in the situation vis-à-vis the event 'to be cut'. In itself, then, the sense-event 'to be cut' has a certain neutrality – it is, in itself, neither active nor passive, neither individual nor collective. The singularity of the event as such is thus neither general (conceptual) nor particular, but structurally and genetically prior to both.

In sum, for Deleuze the proper being of events qua incorporeal expressed is to be thought in terms of the infinitive form of the verb (to cut, to grow, to cry), because this is what takes into account the singularity of an event (to grow is not to shrink) without attributing to it features that only properly belong to the regime of bodies (which include, to repeat, representations qua material images).

Moreover, the fact that events are sense-events has as its consequence the fact that the capacity for language – taken in a very general sense, and motivated by Kleinian and Lacanian conceptions of the relationship between subjectivity and language – that human beings mobilise is what allows us a particular access to the regime of events.

Fifth characteristic: the event as the locus of ethics

Deleuze will insist on an essential relationship between the event and ethics; in fact the chapter or 'series' entitled 'the Event' in *The Logic of Sense* is devoted to the ethical relationship made possible by events. This ethic, unlike Badiou's conception of an ethic of truths, is not constituted by the demand to continue the process of actualisation, but involves engaging in what Deleuze calls 'counter-actualisation'. This is so, in the first instance, because the actualisation or effectuation of the event at the level of bodies, involving a general ontological process, neither relies upon the support of a subject nor is subordinate to subjective decisions. For Deleuze, events invoke an ethical relation not because their consequences are only drawn by subjective fidelity, but because of the fact that no event is fully expressed in any one corporeal set-up. The event is always in excess of the manner in which it is actualised. This is so in two senses. On the one hand, it makes no sense to say that an event, being an ideal genetic condition, can be used up or exhausted in a process of actualisation. On the other, and more importantly for Deleuze, the interrelation of all events (the properly evental character of events) means that the actualisation of any one event implies the local actualisation of the network of relations in which the event in question is implicated. This is all classically Leibnizian: what is actualised is the whole of the network of events, but only a select locality is actualised or expressed clearly. What keeps the event as such in reserve is precisely its evental character, the mode of being proper to it, and this mode of being is essentially a mode of co-existence with other events – this is what makes the event structural in character. Consequently, the ethical relation to the event concerns its withdrawn character, its excess with respect to what is actualised in response to it.

Better death than the health we are given

If Deleuze is widely known as elaborating an ethics, the one that 'everybody knows' is his, it is Spinozist and Nietzschean, an ethics of *more capacity, more connections*. The problem with this view – along with the, frankly baffling, insistence of some commentators on conceiving of Deleuze's work as if it lacked any significant account of suffering, exhaustion and death, not to mention the death drive – is that it accords not at all with central elements in this work. It is to overlook the fact that Deleuze repeatedly presents the event of death as paradigmatic of events ('Every event is like death'*), that Deleuze selects the suffering body of Joe Bousquet as the one that engages in an ethical embrace with the event, and so on: the list could be extended at length. Worst of all, such a view involves overlooking the following magnificent text:

> If one asks why health does not suffice, why the crack [the rupture in the body left by an event that is too much for it] is desirable, it is perhaps because only by means of the crack and at its edges thought occurs, that anything that is good and great in humanity enters and exits through it, in people ready to destroy themselves – better death than the health we are given.†

Whether or not these two modes of ethical thinking are compatible is not what concerns us here – though if they are, it is on the basis of the view in *The Logic of Sense*, and not any hallucinatory experience of pleasure arising from some general activity of experimental connection, which would be the implicit acceptance of the ethical outcome

---

* Deleuze, *The Logic of Sense*, p. 152.
† Deleuze, *The Logic of Sense*, p. 160; translation modified.

that certain rhizome-smokers would seem to imply. Instead we seek to locate the link between ethics and the event.

Here is this ethic's most powerful formulation; note the normative, imperative tonality Deleuze uses:

> The eternal truth of the event is grasped only if the event is also inscribed in the flesh. But each time we must double this painful actualization by a counter-actualisation which limits, moves, and transfigures it. We must accompany ourselves – first, in order to survive, but then even when we die. Counter-actualisation … [gives] us the chance to go farther than we would have believed possible. To the extent that the pure event is each time imprisoned forever in its actualization, counter-actualisation liberates it, always for other times.*

Two determinations of the ethics of the event in Deleuze   The first positive determination of this ethics thus involves recognising our passive situation with respect to what is actualised, which is to say, what happens to us: 'Either ethics makes no sense at all, or this is what it means and has nothing else to say: not to be unworthy of what happens to us.'† This is what constitutes our situation with respect to the reserve of events, and in turn the specifically ethical location of the human being, for in fact there are only two ways in which to respond to what happens to us. Either we resent it, embodying in its nascent but also its most fundamental form the *ressentiment* diagnosed by Nietzsche (and, Deleuze says, this is the 'veritable *ressentiment*'‡), or we strive to be equal to it.

In turn, secondly, this striving does not consist in identifying with the position of the passive sufferer of what happens, but in adopting a certain positive orientation towards, not the event in question (to have been wounded, to be unable to breathe, to be crushed by anxiety), but to events more generally. We have seen that all events are co-implicated for Deleuze, and that as a result the actualisation of any one event expresses them all. The ethical act, which he terms counter-actualisation, consists in affirming those other events implicit in the event that is currently actualised in my body and in the bodies with which I am alloyed. This act is an act of the will for

---

* Deleuze, *The Logic of Sense*, p. 161.
† Deleuze, *The Logic of Sense*, p. 149.
‡ Deleuze, *The Logic of Sense*, p. 149.

Deleuze: 'it wills now not exactly what occurs, but something *in* that which occurs, something yet to come which would be consistent with what occurs'.*

What precisely is willed? It is the advent of other events that, while following on from this event from which I suffer, nonetheless mitigate its significance in a key respect, namely the seemingly absolute power of *this* event to determine my existence. Put another way, as I pass from the way in which the event is actualised, by an act of the will, towards that which in the event was not actualised, my relationship with the event is shifted, since what was *not* actualised now becomes the point of view from which I think and feel what has been actualised. This is why, reflecting on the case of Nietzsche, Deleuze will write: 'Health affirms sickness when it makes its distance from sickness an object of affirmation. Distance is, at arm's length, the affirmation of that which it distances.'†

Counter-actualisation as absolute, universal   Third and *a fortiori*, the act of counter-actualisation is necessarily of universal compass. This is again because of the implication of all events, the entire virtual transcendental structure, in every event, such that what happens to me necessarily involves everything (and everyone) else, for the most part in an obscure fashion. Insofar as I affirm the event that gives rise to my current situation, and in a perverse repetition of Sartre's maligned universalist claim in 'Existentialism is a Humanism', I affirm all events for all people. 'This is why', Deleuze asserts, 'there are no private or collective events . . . Everything is singular, and thus both collective and private, particular and general, neither individual nor universal. Which war, for example, is not a private affair? Conversely, which wound is not inflicted by war and derived from society as a whole.'‡ This 'all events' is what Deleuze will give the name Event, the single event that includes all of the others: 'Nothing other than the Event subsists, the Event alone, *Eventum tantum* for all contraries, which communicates with itself through its own distance and resonates across all of its disjuncts.'§ Clearly, given the differential

* Deleuze, *The Logic of Sense*, p. 149.
† Deleuze, *The Logic of Sense*, p. 173. A similar sentiment is advanced with respect to the case of Nietzsche – see Gilles Deleuze, *Pure Immanence: Essays on a Life*, trans. Anne Boyman (New York: Zone Books, 2001), pp. 57–60.
‡ Deleuze, *The Logic of Sense*, p. 152.
§ Deleuze, *The Logic of Sense*, p. 176.

and structural nature of the regime of events, it would be a mistake to conclude, as some have done, that Deleuze is speaking of an ontological unity of some kind.

At the limit then, acts of counter-actualisation are for everyone, but this is not because (*pace* Badiou) there is no extant State category capable of subtending them. Rather, and to the contrary, it is because everyone and everything is necessarily included in the ongoing process of actualisation. Conversely, what is willed in the act of counter-actualisation is not any particular event, but the ongoing expression of events in general, the affirmation of the fact that the actualisation of the next event will reveal the limited determining character of the event from which I suffer in the present – all of which can also be spoken of as an affirmation of the advent of the future as the guarantor of the advent of new events, and this is the point at which the analysis of time and the role of the eternal return as the empty form of time comes into contact with the theory of the event in *The Logic of Sense*.

At the limit then, ethics is concerned with the correlation between a generic body and the pure Event as such, *Eventum tantum*, and concerns the univocal affirmation of the partiality of what happens. It is at this extreme point that the final word on death appears in Deleuze's philosophy: while my death is an event which will end me as a coherent alloy of bodies, the very fact that this event is an event, and thus wedded to all events, it is necessarily partial. If, for Deleuze (as Badiou asserts), 'all is grace, even dying',[*] this is because death itself reveals its partiality as an event, and thus once more reveals the crack through which the future guarantees other configurations of bodies, other lives, to which correspond other events:

> dying is the negation [interesting choice!] of death, and the impersonality of dying no longer indicates only the moment when I disappear outside of myself, but rather the moment when death loses itself in itself, and also the figure which the most singular life takes on in order to substitute itself for me.[†]

---

[*] Alain Badiou, *Deleuze: The Clamor of Being*, trans. Louise Burchill (Minneapolis: University of Minnesota Press, 2000), p. 116.
[†] Deleuze, *The Logic of Sense*, p. 153.

The event in Deleuze
after *The Logic of Sense*   In the wake of *The Logic of Sense*, Deleuze rarely addresses himself to the theme of the event as such – even the monstrous *A Thousand Plateaus* only brushes past the concept, equates it with other concepts (such as haecceity), or recapitulates the thesis of *The Logic of Sense* in an extremely compact form. On the one hand, where we find it dealt with, he will insist on the same points again. This is what he does, for example, with Guattari in *What is Philosophy?*: speaking of the category of the virtual in relation to science, they characterise the event as 'the part that eludes its own actualization in everything that happens', concluding (as Deleuze does throughout) that 'The event is not the state of affairs. It is actualised in a state of affairs, in a body, in a lived, but it has a shadowy and secret part that is continually subtracted from or added to its actualization . . . The event is immaterial, incorporeal, unlivable: pure *reserve*.'* A similar note is sounded in the – strange, ineffectual – discussion of Badiou in *What is Philosophy?*, where Deleuze and Guattari write that:

> actual states of affairs and virtual events . . . are two types of multiplicities that are not [contrary to the reading of Badiou presented] distributed on an errant line but related to two vectors that intersect, one according to which states of affairs actualize events and the other according to which events absorb (or rather, adsorb) states of affairs.[†]

We find here all of the elements characteristic of the structural account presented by *The Logic of Sense*.

Ubiquity of the concept
of singularity in
Deleuze's work   On the other hand, Deleuze will frequently redeploy features of the theory of the event in other ways, most prominently with the category of singularity. In a sense, this takes us back to the account proffered in *Difference and Repetition*, in which the event is another name for the singularity proper to the differential transcendental structure of the virtual. In *The Logic of Sense*, this is signalled on a number of occasions with the use of the term 'singularities-events'. Likewise, the concept of potential, already closely connected to the event in both *Difference and Repetition* and *The Logic of Sense*, plays an important role at many other points.

---

* Gilles Deleuze and Félix Guattari, *What is Philosophy?*, trans. Hugh Tomlinson and Graham Burchill (New York: Columbia University Press, 1994), p. 156.
[†] Deleuze and Guattari, *What is Philosophy?*, pp. 152–3.

In his final text, the striking, gnomic 'Immanence: A Life . . .', both of these features are met with again. Invoking the singularity of the indefinite article, Deleuze will write once again of death (which opens onto this singularity) that

> The life of the individual gives way to an impersonal and yet singular life that releases a pure event freed from the accidents of internal and external life, that is, from the subjectivity and objectivity of what happens . . . it is a haecceity no longer of individuation but of singularization.*

The same holds more generally, beyond the case of the event of death: '*A* life is everywhere, in all the moments that a given living subject goes through and that are measured by given lived objects: an immanent life carrying with it the events or singularities that are merely actualized in subjects and objects.'†

It is worth remarking that this modal distinction between events and their actualisation is not reducible to that between being and event for Deleuze, since both facets are equally real: events having the full reality proper to them as virtual singularities, and likewise the actual in its own way (contrary to certain readings of Deleuze that make of the actual mere ephemera). To use some familiar terminology, both events and states of affairs express the univocity of being. The fact that they remain nonetheless distinct, however, means that, while events have being, it is not the case that being = event for Deleuze.

That Badiou arrays these three terms – being, event, actuality – very differently constitutes a major loci of disjunction between his position and Deleuze's.

Event irreducible to being   For Badiou, event and being are irreducible to each other and irreconcilable. They have no immediate relation; which is to say, their relation is void. However, this void can be thought or, in other words, be foundationally inscribed in a discourse that formalises its existence and accords it a consistency within a theory of multiple being or inconsistent multiplicity. To think the form of the non-relation between being and event, which is, as ontology itself prescribes, 'undecideable', requires precisely a decision. This decision is itself inscribed within the thought it thinks. That is to say,

---

* Deleuze, *Pure Immanence*, p. 28.
† Deleuze, *Pure Immanence*, p. 29.

it founds rather than is realised, is subjective – but not 'actualised' (in a way we will explicate) – is subtracted therefore from all linguistic norms (and so is not the knowledge of a subject) and marks the point of an 'absolute beginning' (for a situation but not for all time, as the event has no relation to totality), the consequences of which remark it as exactly this. The atemporal mode of the future anterior subtends the formal, thinkable trajectory of what an event makes possible.

An event 'happens' at that point in any situation, or any world, which is a site. In the later theory of appearing, the site as apparent to a world undergoes the maximal change in the intensity of its appearing or 'being there' under the force of an event. From the perspective of a world – the set of relations that it is, from those which appear most intensely correlated to the transcendental of that world, its rules of appearing, that is to say, that which condition any declared existent such that is can be said to be-there – the event, neither being as such or transcendentally marked, is thought 'in its site'. The site, then, is thought as the apparent of the event insofar as the intensity of the appearing of the site undergoes the maximal available change in its intensity of appearing in that world – from nothing to everything: which is simply to say from a point that marks only what inexists to that world, to a point which if 'subjectively' held, will be that point from which a reconfiguration of the transcendental order of that world might begin – point by point, as Badiou seeks to demonstrate in the course of the Greater Logic given in *Logics of Worlds*.

Back to the site   Let's turn back, if that's even the right metaphor given that *Logics of Worlds* makes no claims to reconfigure or renege on the ontology of worlds, even if Badiou leaves open to others the work of discerning whether the greater mathematised logic has the capacity to interfere in the being of any existent. With recourse to a theory of being multiple we say that the elements that a site presents are void for the situation in which this site is presented. These 'void' elements are those an event will 'mobilise' as itself under its 'own' name. A site is one presented element of a situation. A situation is a 'structured presentation'. Whatever is is presented as a situation. Every presented element is immediately represented in terms of its parts – this operation has the metaontological name 'state' in Badiou. The singularity of the site is that none of its elements are re-presented. They are, such that they belong to the site but not the situation, void. The void is that which can be thought and as such is the minimal consistency of that which is pure inconsistency or infinite multiplicity. It's the name of being for any situation.

In any non-ordinary (non-ordinal) infinite situation, for any world, this site 'exists' 'minimally'. Minimally, because its elements are not presented by the situation which presents the site. A site is formally demonstrable but locally 'unknown', if not exactly unknowable. The locality of the site, if not its existence, is presented by the event. The singularity of the site – that it is presented but not represented, belongs but is not included – is also its universality. Since every element, and every element is also a set, includes the void, thus every element has the (void) 'capacity' to not be represented by the state.* A part of every element remains unrepresentable vis-à-vis its situation. The void is a 'hazard' of representation. It is upon this hazardous capacity to not be counted as a part – its indiscernibility – that the 'evental' subject relies, so to speak. It is the subject that makes the universality of this singular site exposed in and by an event 'manifest'. It does this step by step or point by point linking what 'inappears' to the state, the void capacity of every element or 'inhabitant' of said situation, to what happened, the event. The event 'merely' violates the incapacity (that nothing not included exists) determined by the state; or it localises the void or indiscernible capacity generic to every presented element at a place or a point within any such situation. Every subjective manifestation or forcing of this generic capacity to be connected to an event, or to being incorporated into a new body of what is true of that world, is relative to this singular site/point immanent to any historical situation or the transcendental of any world. It is an immanent unfolding of the capacity inherent to all, but, crucially, it takes place in a situation or a world, and marks that which is other than, void to or despite the knowledge of this situation's 'state', this world's 'transcendental schema', its rule of appearing.

The event happens at a site
The event is what happens at a site: the storming of the Bastille, the invention of a new proof in mathematics, an encounter with a sexed other, a well-placed urinal, and so on. But the event is originally double so to speak. It is manifest insofar as it happens in the world: a proof is a proof, a urinal is placed, etc.

---

* The use of the term capacity here is merely a retroactive determination, marking what is an effect of structure or formal consistency. It should not be mistaken as a 'potential' or an empirical or experiential marker.

But the event's 'eventality' – its power of rupture over and beyond its happening as the immanent consequences of its happening – *depends* on its being taken up as what takes place. This is in the full sense of the event as set out above: happening at a site, mobilising what is nothing to the state, orienting the 'subject' to the situation under a condition of fidelity to the event and not as an expression of 'state' knowledge, etc. A new, thus, generic configuration is possible – what Paul Cohen's theory of indiscernibles (contra Leibniz) makes 'thinkable' – on the basis of an event qua rupture and not qua empirical or *a priori*. What inexists or exists minimally pursuant to the transcendental or state order, under the force of an evental rupture with that order (its rule, knowledge, logic, etc.), can come to exist forcefully point by point and ultimately maximally in that world or for that situation. Note though that this subjective reconfiguration, despite its unique orientation to its world, its avoidance of state knowledge, must be formalisable or thinkable: it is not some expression of an ineffable presence and is not reducible to the essential matter of some I or me.

The event being evanescent is 'what is not being qua being', but everything that is insofar as it is has a form and is formalisable. This means it must be thought under the constraints or liberations of the laws of being qua being. And indeed the very radicality of the event and its subject, and the generic reconfiguration of a world it effects, also has form, such that on the basis of the incommensurability of the event and being ontology is not incommensurate with real, evental change. That is to say, using an older language, that the 'incommensurability' between structure and subject can be thought. It's the event that marks the non-impossibility of thinking this incommensurability in Badiou's work – from the 1970s onwards, we suggest.

The generic set   It is possible, and this is where Badiou's decision for Cohen over Gödel at the point of their rational undecidability matters, to determine coincident with the laws of set theory, a generic set: one that inserts itself, or rather forces itself, at the level of its greatest extension between the first infinite set and its nominal power set or between presentation and representation, situation and state (to move into metaontology).* We need to affirm that

---

* For the best critique of this move see Ray Brassier, 'Presentation as Anti-phenomenon in Alain Badiou's *Being and Event*', *Continental Philosophy Review*, Vol. 39, No. 1 (March 2006), pp. 59–77.

decision inscribes itself as a demonstrable feature of the most rigorous form of formalisation. Certainly the forcing or generic construction of this second infinite set will follow all the rules of deduction as set out in the theory of set and so on. But the point here is that ontology itself prescribes, at the height of its rigour, a void site of undecidability and prescribes that a decision be made with regard to that which it formally deduces to be beyond its formal capacity. In short, ontology nominates the site for an event, an event which, occurring 'in' the void of formalisation, is not being qua being. That is to say, ontology prescribes the point of its own impasse and as such the point at which the laws of being qua being as articulated by mathematical ontology: the most consistent, rational and transmissible discourse available to beings such as us (one that renders 'us' eradicable) and thus the most suited to thinking what is essentially the thought of all. In other words, the univocity of being is registered in the one discourse that rejects equivocation at all turns.* And what is not being qua being, marks no equivocation on this point. It is the in-separation of being from event at the void point of the rationality of ontology itself that guarantees the univocity of multiple being – which *is not all*. 'What we have here is a subtraction of ontology as a whole from philosophy, which is now simply the language situation in which truths in the plurality of their procedures become pronounceable as Truth in the singularity of its inscription.'† Nevertheless any subject and any truth – both owing the chance of their existence to the evental break with situational order – have being and must be formalised as such.

Referring to Deleuze explicitly, but to a more general and essentially constructivist tendency – and so to an organicism Badiou sees as consequent on choosing the animal over number, Aristotle (ultimately) over Plato, life (total and divergent) and the fold over sets or situations,‡ but also to a philosophical trajectory that treats of ontology as inseparable from if not integral to philosophy§ (and of mathematics as a regional discipline), and indeed of philosophical (dialectical) discourse as the privileged representation of being

---

*   Alain Badiou, *Theoretical Writings*, trans. Ray Brassier and Alberto Toscano (London and New York: Continuum, 2004), p. 173.
†   Badiou, *Theoretical Writings*, p. 110.
‡   Alain Badiou, 'Gilles Deleuze, The Fold: Leibniz and the Baroque', in Constantin Boundas and Dorethea Olkowski (ed.), *Deleuze and Theatre of Philosophy*, trans. Thelma Sowley, New York, Columbia, 1994, pp. 51–69; 55.
§   Deleuze, *The Logic of Sense*, passim.

insofar as it can be said, expressed, known or thought – Badiou sum-marises the void relation between events and mathematical ontology: 'This is why I conceptualise absolute beginnings (which requires a theory of the void) and singularities of thought that are incomparable in their constitutive gestures (which requires a theory – Cantorian, to be precise – of the plurality of the types of infinity).'*

At last, a concept of the infinite

What the mathematician Cantor discovers or invents (discovery and invention being indiscerni-ble in terms of the 'movement of thought'[†]), what Cantor is the name of – the plurality of the types of infinity – has implications beyond mathematics, where it was not, anyway, universally well received. As Badiou remarks, 'events' are that which 'do not enter into the imme-diate order of things' (nor do they issue from being or, in terms of their capacity to not be, as becoming either).[‡] Like the geometric method in Plato's time, Cantor's 'transfinite numbers' strike not only at the current state of mathematical knowledge (as noted) but at the heart of a classical and eternal philosophical (and theological) conceit – the infinite. Cantor says something, indeed demonstrates some-thing, that changes the determination of the infinite absolutely. That there is a plurality of infinities is an invention that intervenes upon 'the entire history of philosophy, from its Greek origins on'.[§]

Two striking things occur when, as Badiou insists, this discovery – this event *in* mathematics or ontology – is taken to condition any possible thought or conception of the infinite. The (classical) infinite can no longer be conceived (or for that matter 'judged') as limit. That is to say, the single infinite, or the infinite as totality, which is the supposed and proposed limit or horizon of all thought, being itself 'inexpressible', is no longer tenable, no longer all that can be thought. The infinite is no longer the province of the concept, designated, for example, good or bad, or whatever, but can be 'actualised', or better (which is to say, contra Aristotle) 'completed', formally and rigorously. Mathematics thinks the infinite not only in its own terms, but its thinking of the infinite can neither be surpassed by nor sublated into a philosophical determination or be considered

* Badiou, *Deleuze: The Clamor of Being*, p. 91.
† Badiou, Deleuze, p. 91.
‡ Alain Badiou, *In Praise of Love*, trans. Nicolas Truong (London: Serpent's Tail, 2012), p. 28.
§ Alain Badiou, *Being and Event*, trans. Oliver Feltham (London: Continuum, 2005), p. 435.

as a regional specialty. Any such reduction, ostensibly carried out on the basis of the refusal to traverse the mathematical universe itself, puts itself in the place of knowing what mathematics is and what it can (or cannot) do. This is a fraught assumption to say the least, more accurately a sophistic conceit. The actualisation of the infinite, more correctly the formalisation of a complete infinite, means that any classical-style appropriation of the infinite (and correspondingly the deployment of the finite) by philosophy can only be, frankly, a falsification, a retreat to an idealism, logicism, romanticism or linguistic constructivism that cannot be sustained at the limit. Certainly the effort to renege on the Cantor event is alive and well, but at the limit the repressed returns to haunt the renegade concept. In Badiou's words: 'In the order of the matheme, the route [*trajet*] leading from Cantor to Paul Cohen constitutes this [mathematical] event. It founds the central paradoxes of the theory of the multiple, fully and demonstratively articulating for the first time in a discernible concept what is an indiscernible [generic] multiplicity.'[*]

Moreover, and this is the key result for Badiou, the integral consistency of the complete infinite, its thinkability, is to lose the One: precisely the 'being of the one' (the 'ontological impasse proper to Hegel').[†] There are infinite infinites, all the way up and all the way down as it were, but as actual or complete each infinite is structured in relation to its foundation and its limit, which is to say also its succession. Both foundation (or limit) and succession are immanently generated by the 'theory of the pure multiple' and together effect the consequence that the One appears as a result. 'Insofar as the one is a result', writes Badiou, 'by necessity "something" of the multiple does not absolutely coincide with the result.'[‡] 'Inconsistency, then, is not presented as such; it is rather presented as the presupposition that prior to the count the one is not.'[§]

There is no One   If the One is not, then, by implication, what is cannot be (qua being) One. What can be said of what is, if it is not One, is that it is pure multiplicity. But, as Badiou points out, there is no way to 'know' what Being (as opposed to Being qua Being) is, and in fact the most rational deductive operations

---

[*] Alain Badiou, *Manifesto for Philosophy*, trans. N. Madarasz (Albany: SUNY, 1999), p. 80.
[†] Badiou, *Being and Event*, p. 161.
[‡] Badiou, *Being and Event*, p. 53.
[§] Badiou, *Being and Event*, p. 52.

which demonstrate to us that the One is not can only mark what is not One as Ø. Void, as noted, is the name of being. Consequently, and this should not be overlooked, the infinite, given its capacity for formalisation and circumscription, up to the point of its own excess, becomes conceptually 'banal'. What is exceptional, rare, militant is the finite composition of a generic set, cut out of the infinite on the one side, thus a formal unbinding of the subject from being as such, and its excessive encyclopaedic re-presentation on the other. This is not a paean for human finitude of course, so much as a declaration against the desuetude of the subject effected by any thought which poses the reduction of man to his finite nature as the ruled capacity of what it is to think and to be. The so-called inexpressible infinite is precisely what mathematics' letters materialise: which coherently composed is the discourse on being qua being; the world is turned upside down – there is no One from which everything issues, no ineffable infinite unavailable to thought – but not, for all that, merely inverted in the manner of an egg timer.

Set theory as formalisation of pure presentation   In the wake of Cantor (who as 'mathematician' could not draw all the '(meta)ontological' consequences), and for philosophy as Badiou determines it, axiomatised set theory is the mathematical discourse within which every instance of being – regardless of how it appears in the world, what it appears as, what it is known as and so on – can be rewritten in terms of its pure presentation, its belonging to a set or situation. What exists is thus what is presented in its being, at its most formal, in all clarity and rigour, as little marks and letters, that start with the (existence of the) void, Ø. The Ø, as the name of being, is therefore the foundational term-multiple of any set or situation. In any given set or situation (every situation thought in its being is a set) the void marks the limit of its decomposition – which is to say it founds every set/situation. It is upon the prescribed existence of the void that all thinking (counting, etc.) takes place. The theory of the void thus gives us this doubling insofar as the void qua name of being presents being as the empty set, meaning that what the void Ø presents is precisely the nothing that is Being qua Being or pure multiplicity without One, of which presentation is the presentation. The one mark of the void, then, is the mark of the not-One of being.

The being not-One or multiple of any existing element, set or situation is the fundamental ontological lesson Badiou draws from the theory of the pure multiple or set theory. It's a lesson carried on into his re-configuration of the 'being there' or 'appearing' to a world and it's a theorem to which even 'that which is not being qua being', ostensibly the event, is also subject insofar as what is not being qua being participates in being given that, as event(al), it takes place and has effect. Moreover, the consequences that issue from this 'minimal' participation in being – whose matheme or scripted Idea (and thus an 'Idea of an Idea') Badiou doesn't hesitate to provide – are also subject to being-multiple.

The unmeasure of excess

Thus we return to our earlier elaboration of the unmeasure of excess and how this excess harbours the void as unmeasure. Representation has its own consequences, which in these terms amounts to saying 'what is included in a situation belongs to its state'.* Or the state is always in excess of its situation and really because it is an attempt to reconstruct presentation as One – without what marks it as not-One thus its non-totality. It is critical to remark the distinction between belonging and inclusion, or situation and state, or presentation and representation insofar as a) we are speaking of the same elements but under a different count or relation and b) because this relational or operational 'disjunction' vis-à-vis the elemental structure of situations produces the site of real change – change in the disposition of elements by the addition of generic and yet immanently situated multiples which reconfigure the structure and the topology of situations fundamentally – thus an-historically, a-naturally and yet as absolutely consistent with the integrity of situations and thus the theory of the pure multiple.

In order to show the rationality of the concept of undecidability and the consequent legitimacy of decision we need to briefly return to the problem of excess in its ontological form. That there must be a set that succeeds the initial infinite set – this is a law of the theory of the pure multiple, of multiple being as such. Cantor tried to show that the successor of the first cardinal ω_0 was its power set which would be ω_1, but Easton showed that the cardinality of the initial cardinal could not be definitively proved to be ω_1. While the rules of succession and differentiation are the same for infinite and finite sets, as we said, the former, obviously, cannot be counted, ordinally. What we do know is: there is an excess; that we do not know by how much it

---

* Badiou, *Being and Event*, p. 97.

is in excess; that its cardinality or power must be superior to the cardinality of ω_0. We also know, then, that to decide this measure 'that
we do not know' is rational. To reiterate: the state is in immeasurable
excess over the situation (representation over presentation) and this
immeasurable excess is really the reinstatement of the void – that
which cannot be 'known' or counted but is nevertheless marked as
such – by representation. In other words, 'the ontological situation
originally names the void as an existent multiple, whilst every other
situation consists only insofar as it ensures the non-belonging of
the void, a non-belonging controlled, moreover, by the state of the
situation'.* And, given that we 'know' that the 'state' is quantitatively
larger than the initial set (situation) and that its power is superior to
that of the initial set, it is not illegitimate to decide on its measure and
to determine its superiority. In other words, to decide is not to break
any law of being.

No all of being   Mathematics, then, at the extreme limits of its own
                   consistency, fails to know the All of being, a failure
– perhaps the better failure Beckett was supposing at the end of *The
Unnameable* – absolutely consistent with its own discoveries. It is for
this consistency alone that Badiou decides and, as such, for its consequences. In essence, no other discourse (but this discourse on being
qua being) can consistently and coherently furnish the point of its
own inconsistency, its own impasse, it own void. That every presentation presents an element whose elements are void is the rule of situational being. To decide, to take the measure of this void, is entirely
valid. However, as noted, the resources of the situation itself, that is
to say its ordinary rule, its knowledge, cannot provide the means for
this intervention. Something has to happen: the void at the heart of
presentation must be exposed, such that upon its existence – an existence which marks the not-all of the knowledge of its situation – the
truth of the situation can be staked. In other words, mathematics
prepares the way for the thought of that which it is not – the event
(and its consequences).

What happens, then, plainly, is that which is of the order of that
which is not. Effectively, that unpresentation will have taken
place. Nevertheless we need to keep in mind the fact that consistency demands that whatever happens, happens in a situation or in

* Badiou, *Being and Event*, p. 188.

presentation at a site – an always-presented and thus immanent point of a situation – and that whatever it is that comes to orient itself on the basis of that which is not – a generic construction – will come to be coherent with the laws of being qua being, the theory of the pure multiple. Which is to say, as not-One. To decide, then, the impasse of ontology (or that the revolution has begun, or that R. Mutt's urinal is art, or that 'I love you') is truly an effect of non-knowledge; it's a leap, a wager on the consistency of inconsistency. To decide is to wager that what took place at the site of an impasse – the consistency of inconsistency – will have been an event, and to wager is to imply the set of its consequences. For Badiou, the wager 'ontology is mathematics' is, as Oliver Feltham puts it, a philosophical idea, a decision on being, a decision forced on the philosopher by ontology itself which, to riff on Heidegger, is that which clears the ground for the disclosure of being like no other – infinity by infinity.

The decision shifts the ground   So, this decision, that mathematics is ontology, whose legitimacy we have explored, changes everything in terms of the philosophical orientation to the major philosophical questions – being, truth and the subject. It changes too, by consequence, the ground upon which the anti-philosopher accuses the philosopher of absolute knowledge or of inhabiting the discourse of the university. None of this can be thought as it has been hitherto, is the implication. If mathematics makes being intelligible, intelligible not apparent, interpretable, mystical or transcendental, then that intelligibility under condition of the Cantor event has consequences that it is for philosophy to draw. That mathematics, today, in our epoch, completes the infinite, and thinks the rationality of the new, thus making it impossible that Being (as such) be One, is a radically new development in thought that the philosopher cannot ignore. This is Badiou's neo-Platonist challenge. Not only to think what mathematics thinks but moreover to elaborate the consequences of the fact *that* 'mathematics' thinks – that it rigorously and consistently thinks its own limit on the basis of its very own delimitation of the infinite (and the finite).

Presenting the unpresentable   Two things are irreducible in this ontological configuration: the being multiple of whatever comes to be and, absolutely related to this, that ontology itself formalises the situated impasse at which an event should it take place will have taken place. In other words, the event can always be 'localised within presentation' despite being neither 'presented nor presentable'.* The event as occurrence, and so as not-being, thus not being countable, not being an effect of structure, being unpresentable, is not thinkable in ontology, that is to say, within the discourse of ontology. But as ontology is the discourse on being as such, as it formalises every form of presentation, the event must, insofar as it participates in that share of being which is not being, also be multiple – even though it 'presents itself' as that unpresentable multiple. After all, if its coming to be referred back to some originary One, if it were as one with the being which it is not, which is to say, if its not-being were merely a category of being as such (albeit a temporal hiccup or the constitution of a destiny), or if it were this One's effect or emanation or whatever, then the ontology of the multiple would be ruined. The point being that the event itself (which is not) is in accord with the discourse of ontology insofar as the (ultra)one or 'supernumerary' that it is, is originally Two (and not one, itself and the multiples of the site). 'Why "ultra-one"? Because the sole and unique term of the event which guarantees that it is not-unlike its site-on the edge of the void, is the-one-that-it-is. And it is one, because we are supposing that the situation presents it; thus that it falls under the count-as-one.'† For Badiou, ontology proves the irreducibility of being and event.

Despite its marking the impossible of (set-theory) ontology (that it delimits its own consistency) the event is not a miracle, specific or global, but situated at a site or oriented in its appearing by a point whose existence is minimal for the transcendental of that world. It is, then, unknown in terms of its being, and yet local and addressed to all (universal) in terms of its 'effect' or its capacity to 'be-there'. Suffice to say for now that being local precludes it having a relation to totality – which anyway is 'inconsistent'. To stress again: there are situations or worlds founded in their being on the void and thus on non-relation (that can only be traversed relative to the event) and there are infinite situations that cannot be rejoined, as Hegel imagined, resulting in a one presentation of all situations. There is a formal construction of the event in Badiou's work, which, in fact as we are arguing, precludes that the one Event is the same and single event resonant in all events. For Badiou, every event is relative to its

* Badiou, *Being and Event*, p. 178.
† Badiou, *Being and Event*, p. 182.

situation, its site, to the situated multiples which make it up, to that for which it is an event, to the truth of the situation it exposes, to the subject for whom it forms the orientation of a new and perilous trajectory.

It is not an ontological emanation, univocal (once and for all) of which every instance is its repetition, and nor, on the other side of being so to speak, is it what happens experientially, psychologically, traumatically or pathologically to or for a subject, and nor finally is it an act of a subject. Rather, as subtractive of being (rather than a filling), it opens a space for the subject (the subject, for Badiou, having no constitutive being whatsoever) to come to be as support of a truth. The event is in no sense the meaning of being. It neither carries nor is the support of any sense at all, 'appearing only to disappear'.[*] It supplements in the situation of presentation that element whose own presentation goes unpresented there. If you like, it exposes this unpresentation to be there – contra to all knowledge qua the logic of parts – and supports its existence against the statist regime of representation that counts it as nothing. The event is thereby situated and so singular – not being presented but presenting its elements and itself – and thus both separate from the All of being and any count-as-one in as much as it breaks this count, affirming in and by its very evanescence that the One is not – that every situation is immanently divisible and thus that there is no being of the One. Moreover, it has no relation to time as such and is resolutely not that which relates the future to the past as the occlusion of the present. If anything it 'unfolds', marks time as once again having begun, and opens the situation to the founding of a new present. It is not the place itself that takes place, as in Deleuze; the taking place or 'act' does not annul the relation of being to thought, as in Lacan. Ontology provides the rationality of the impasse – void and excess – and the legitimacy of the decision to intervene on that situated impasse on the side of what supplements it, such that it can be thought. Ontology cannot think (that is, again, make consistent within the terms of its own discourse) this eventual supplement. The thought, then, of this event that supplements the impasse of being and opens it to thought by way of its 'evanescence' must be that of a discourse other than ontology. This discourse for Badiou is that of the poem, insofar as it is a condition for philosophy.

---

[*] Badiou, *Being and Event*, p. 191 and *passim*.

Poem   Let's schematise the function the poem serves in
                        terms of its unique form of inscription. The dis-
course of the poem (Badiou has Mallarmé in mind) at the limits of
sense, at the limit of ordinary language, at the limit of discourse itself,
is that which attests, *avant la lettre,* to the evanescence of what takes
place such that it actually takes place. Slightly paraphrasing Badiou:
'In short, what is at stake is the opening of thought to the principle
of the thinkable, that thought must be absorbed in the grasp of what
establishes it as thought.'* This means that the poem thinks that
which is not, or rather, thinks the thought which ontology qua mathematics cannot think. It institutes this thought, marks the existence
of that which is to be thought beyond the impasse of ontology, by
providing what happens with a name, thus capturing in the act of
nomination the trace of what disappears. The discourse of the poem
is not the discourse of being, and at the limit of language it in no way
makes meaning or gives sense to what happens. As ever, citing
Mallarmé as exemplary (but no less Celan, Pessoa, Stevenson,
Beckett et al.), Badiou says, 'It subordinates sensible desire to the
aleatory advent of the Idea. The poem is a duty of thought.'† Its
thought, ultimately, is the thought of the trace. 'A poem by Mallarmé
always fixes the place of an aleatory event; an event to be interpreted
on the basis of the traces it leaves behind.'‡

For Badiou, then, Mallarmé's poem inscribes this trace such that
it may be thought, such that this thought may be practised, such
that something other than the ordinary rule (the transcendental)
of the ordinary state of the situation or world (representation and
repetition) comes to be inscribed therein. The poem – the set of
operations whereby this thought comes to think itself – thinks the
trace as capture of the advent of the Idea, the event as it exposes the
rational 'inconsistency' upon which all thought or any truth (formal
and subjective) 'must lean'. Thus the poem, Badiou says, surpasses
in power what the sensible is capable of itself – it is not mimesis –
for 'in its operation it exhibits an Idea of that which the object and
objectivity are nothing but pale copies'.§ In other words, the disjunction of the poem, which thinks 'what is not being qua being', and

---

* Alain Badiou, *Handbook of Inaesthetics,* trans. Alberto Toscano (Stanford: Stanford
  University Press, 2004), pp. 19–20.
† Badiou, *Handbook of Inaesthetics,* p. 20.
‡ Badiou, *Being and Event,* p. 191.
§ Badiou, *Handbook of Inaesthetics,* p. 21.

the matheme, which thinks what is, is situated for Badiou not in an opposition between intelligibility and sense but in the variation of their respective truth procedures. The former thinks the pure multiple qua inconsistency. The poem 'makes truth out of the multiple, conceived as a presence that has come to the limits of language'. It makes present the 'pure notion of the "there is"'.* Let's note that it is not for nothing that Badiou will address both Deleuze and Lacan via the relation both have to the poetry of Mallarmé, 'the poet thinker of the event and its undecideability'.† However we will leave poetry aside and consider the event 'in its own terms'.

The event in its own terms
In order that we have a set of reference points for the supposed encounter with the thought of Deleuze and Lacan over the event, we will elaborate to conclude with something like the schemata of the event by working through Badiou's short essay, 'The Event as Trans-being'. It is unavoidable that some of this is a reiteration of what has already been said, but as with any reiteration the essential aspect is its minimal difference to the initial iteration. It is in that (unconscious?) elaboration of this difference that all the difference is made – as Deleuze might say.‡

The virtue of this essay is twofold: on the one hand it concerns itself only with the rudiments of the event, rather than requiring us to delineate the post-evental (and retroactively crucial) notions of decision, names, intervention, truth, fidelity, subject, generic, and so on (some of which we have seen in their 'ontological' formulation). Secondly, it forms a sort of cusp between the strictly (extra)ontological conception of the event elaborated in *Being and Event*, and the (intra)categorial reconfiguration in *Logics of Worlds*. Thirdly, it actually works to cut across both the Lacanian conception of the passage to the act, whose 'subjectivism' Badiou avoids, and it prefigures what Badiou considers to be his reversal of Deleuze vis-à-vis the event in *Logics of Worlds*.

Critically, what remains the same in both *Being and Event* and *Logics of Worlds*, and forms a key component of Badiou's distance from Deleuze, is the status of the 'multiple' to which an event

---

* Badiou, *Handbook of Inaesthetics*, p. 22.
† Alain Badiou, *Conditions*, trans. S. Corcoran (London and New York: Continuum, 2008), p. 87.
‡ See Deleuze, *Difference and Repetition*, esp. Chapter 4.

ultimately belongs. For Badiou, there is not a two-fold theory of multiplicity – extensive and intensive – but an 'axiomatically homogenous' conception of multiplicity which, as he says, means he must account for the 'being of the event both as rupture of the law of segmented multiplicities and as homogenous to this law'.* (Let's note in passing the Pauline resonance of the undoing of the law as law.) What's at stake here (and we saw something of this above with the notion of differentiation and succession), Badiou says, and this is key to the 'dispute' with Deleuze, is that there where the law of the multiple 'fails' lies the greatest danger of the return of the One. And this is registered in Heidegger, Lacan, Nietzsche and Wittgenstein, he says (and in Deleuze is manifest in the concept of the fold, which for Badiou is to return the power of the One by way of a three-fold essentially anti-void 'series' of operations: anti-extensionality, anti-dialectical, anti-Cartesian, i.e., anti-Lacanian and thus anti-subject).[†] To break with the jurisdiction of the multiple and to remain faithful, demonstrably so, to multiplicity qua being (and appearing) is the challenge of thinking the event for Badiou. In Badiou's formula the question becomes, 'what subtracts the sheer "what happens" from the general determination of what is?'[‡]

This is the core of the event: 'what happens'. What happens, then, cannot be a matter of structure but at the same time, given that whatever there-is is multiple, and insofar as an event happens it must happen somewhere, this somewhere must be structured by the thought of multiple being. Again, 'a situation-being is historical if it contains at least one evental, foundational, on-the-edge-of-the-void site'.[§] A site is an abnormal multiple. Of course, 'it is not because the site exists in the situation that there is an event'.[¶] 'The site is only ever a condition of being for the event.'[**] Or in the terms of *Logics of Worlds*, 'if the inexistent of the site must finally attain maximal intensity in the order of appearing, it is only to the extent that it now stands in the place of what has disappeared; its maximality is the subsisting mark of the event itself in the world'.[††]

⚜

* Badiou, *Theoretical Writings*, p. 99.
† Badiou, *Theoretical Writings*, p. 99, and Badiou, 'Gilles Deleuze, The Fold', p. 52.
‡ Badiou, *Theoretical Writings*, p. 98.
§ Badiou, *Being and Event*, p. 190.
¶ Badiou, *Being and Event*, p. 179.
** Badiou, *Being and Event*, p. 179.
†† Badiou, *Logics of Worlds*, p. 378.

The event, then, is what exposes these unpresented multiples to the chance of this new order, to their appearing maximally for that world. Such elements are 'on the edge of the void' – on the edge of what separates [X], as a singular multiple situation, from its pure indistinct being, its pure multiplicity, etc.[*] Recall that what is not presented is counted as nothing by the meta-structure, the count for one of parts. The elements of the site are included as nothing precisely because their intersection with the situation is void. This reminds us that the state of a situation is just that. The state is thoroughly dependent on the situation, on the elements it presents. Indeed, the state is a constructible set. It presents elements whose existence as such is already determined, that is to say, elements whose conformity to law is the very basis of their being counted or included as such. The constructible universe does not admit the existence of indiscernibility, the existence of two elements whose intersection – thus their difference – is void. Hence 'the peril of the void' and the 'irony' that it returns in and by the operation of metastructure or representation, the operation whose *raison d'être* is the foreclosing of this peril; that there exists a self-multiple whose relation to the situation is unknown.

Badiou maintains therefore an ontology of the pure multiple with the advent of that which this ontology cannot count as such, the event, and without recourse to the 'power of the One'. In other words, given that it falls to philosophy to be the 'theory of the event', what philosophy (or what form does a philosophy take that can recognise the 'jurisdiction of the one' *and* be subtractively conditioned without retreating in some way to a proposition or guarantee situated behind 'what happens' and as that from which it issues, or that to which any act or occurrence returns.[†] And given that philosophy thinks the truths of its conditions, those that an event convokes in and for 'situations', the theory of the event is also the theory of the possibility of truths, the coming to be of an immanent truth of a situation.

This be the verse   So the framework is the following:

- Ontology formalises its own impasse. Or: for any transcendental there exists an element whose degree of appearing is the minimum.

---

[*] Badiou, *Theoretical Writings*, p. 99.
[†] Badiou, *Theoretical Writings*, pp. 101–2.

– The event is that which is not being qua being. Or: 'it is under its own law of appearance that the multiple comes to be counted'.*
– The event is a multiple made up of itself and the elements of the site. It is an illegal multiple. Or: if the inexistent acquires a maximal existential value, the multiple will be said to be an event.
– The event is trans-being: the genericity of a situation opened onto to its truthful construction: 'the supernumerary connection of chance to eternity'.†
– It is neither being nor subject but that by which a multiple comes to appear in an entirely new way (maximally).
– Decisively: 'a truth can only originate in an event' and the universality of a truth is bound to the contingency of the event.‡

* Badiou, *Second Manifesto for Philosophy*, p. 79
† Badiou, *Second Manifesto for Philosophy*, p. 81.
‡ Badiou, *Second Manifesto for Philosophy*, p. 81.

CHAPTER FIVE

Truth

If Alain Badiou is well-known for insisting on the integral role of the category of truth in philosophy, this is also the case for Gilles Deleuze and Jacques Lacan – a point often underestimated or overlooked. This chapter will establish the divergences, consequences, and, we will show, surprising convergences between Badiou's generic formalisation, Deleuze's problematic conception of truth, and the Lacanian insistence on the centrality of truth in analysis, its relationship with the unconscious, and its disjunction from knowledge (a theme decisive for Badiou's own later formalisations). Of course, truth is in none of these cases considered to be adequation, coherence or revelation; into the bargain, our thinkers' respective revisionings of truth are articulated with a systematic reworking of the a-historical relationship of different discourses in their 'geological', 'topological' or 'eternal' presentations. If, then, the very progression this book has already effected from the problematic of the contemporary through time to the event is vitally at stake, this chapter functions as a kind of knotting, suturing or folding of such progression to the concept.

Truth, yes, but as inconsistency, incompletion and unrepresentability   Despite the still-common prejudice that Lacan, as one of the great promulgators of the linguistic turn in psychoanalysis and philosophy, is therefore a sceptic if not a downright relativist with respect to a doctrine of truth, the case is quite the opposite. From the very beginning of his published work in his encounter with Alexandre Kojève to his final Act of Dissolution, Lacan emphasised that truth is always at stake when it is a question of the subject. Just as certainly, Lacan was concerned to emphasise that this is not a truth bound to consistency, coherence, or adequation, but to inconsistency, incompletion and unrepresentability. If Lacan's general position on these matters seems to have been established very early – possibly even from the moment he heard Kojève's lectures, and realised the extraordinary implications that the Freudian revolution had for the future of philosophy itself – his take on truth received different inflections throughout his long career. Yet the fundamental song remained the same: truth bores holes in knowledge, perhaps like a concrete drill or a nest of worms into wood.

Lacan contra Hegel   In an extraordinary discussion regarding the convoluted destiny of twentieth-century French philosophy, Jean-Claude Milner announces that:

> I accord a major importance to the emergence of what I will call dialectical language. If you take a writer-philosopher like Bergson, his language bears no trace of dialectics. Then, from a certain moment, philosophy in the French language adopts a dialectical language. Next, in its school, literary critique and literature itself do the same. We can obviously evoke the translations of Hegel; Henri Lefebvre, then Hyppolite. We can note the influence of Kojève. We can recall that, in the years 1950 and 1960, Hegelo-Marxism passed, outside our borders, for the obligatory thought of intellectuals of the French language.*

For Milner, this emergence is evidently a symptom as well as a phenomenon in its own right, one which marks a period which is today effectively closed. However, from a linguistic point of view, it marks an influence – 'Hegelian', 'Marxist' – which, to the extent that it came to be inscribed in the language itself, was uncircumventable even for those who explicitly repudiated both Hegel and Marx. Moreover, such dialectical inscription in a language necessarily has effects upon the thinking and expression of truth itself. A base of Cartesianised French can't receive a substantial squirt of Hegelianism without getting a little high. Where the impossibility of negation meets the necessity of contradiction in such a way that irresolvable division must be rearticulated with the vicissitudes of becoming – there is an encounter which clearly puts (in fact, *actually put*) the subject, language, history and being in question.

It remains the case, therefore, and despite the various reservations that we have been outlining throughout this book, that the fundamental Lacanian intervention in regards to the status of truth is established, illuminated and elaborated with respect to Hegel. As Elisabeth Roudinesco has shown, from the mid-1930s, Lacan

---

* Alain Badiou, Jean-Claude Milner and Philippe Petit, *Controverses* (Paris: Seuil, 2012), p. 174.

immediately committed himself to a 'comparative interpretation' of Hegel and Freud in collaboration with Kojève. Roudinesco notes:

> In the end, the study was never written. But in the fifteen pages that survive in Kojève's handwriting we find three of the major concepts used by Lacan in 1936: the I as subject of desire; desire as a revelation of the truth of being; and the ego as site of illusion and source of error.*

In previous chapters, we have shown that Lacan cannot be simply said to have been 'influenced by' Hegel. Rather, what Kojève's Hegel essentially enabled Lacan to do was to force out, quite immediately, the points at which the Freudian revolution immediately *falsified* the philosophical enterprise, exposed its constitutive prejudices and countermanded its methods. If Hegel functions as the strongest available representative of the philosophical tradition – a position which Lacan undoubtedly subscribes to, at least in a certain way – then emblematically philosophical concepts are inscribed in the Hegelian corpus *in extremis* (a view also adopted by Deleuze and Guattari in *What is Philosophy?*). For Lacan, these clearly include being, becoming, negation, totality, subject and truth; at least, these are the concepts that he recurrently adverts to throughout his own work. From the first, then, and despite some of the differences that we are about to discuss, we can affirm that Lacan: contests the priority of being within the philosophical enterprise; reconsiders becoming as tragic contingency; engages psychoanalytical negation as a process that is never sublated according to the 'negation of the negation'; concomitantly denies the possibility of totality, in subject and in substance, in favour of the irreparable asymmetrical division exposed by psychoanalytic inquiry. Nonetheless, and in contradistinction to many of his contemporaries, Lacan retains the priority of the subject and its integral relationship to truth. In doing so, of course, he utterly revises the status of both.

Psychoanalysis is neither philosophy nor science
In 'The Subversion of the Subject and the Dialectic of Desire', first presented at a 1960 conference on Hegel and the dialectic, Lacan opens by separating the psychoanalytic project from Hegel's philosophical one. For Lacan, in this

---

* Elisabeth Roudinesco, 'The Mirror Stage: An Obliterated Archive', in J.-M. Rabaté (ed.), *The Cambridge Companion to Lacan* (Cambridge: Cambridge University Press, 2003), p. 28.

specific context at least, psychoanalysis must be delimited by a double negation: not philosophy, not science. Throughout his work, in fact, he will continually return to the differences between these disciplines in his attempts to determine the specific difference of analysis *per se*. In these attempts, it becomes clear that neither psychoanalysis nor philosophy are sciences, and precisely because the 'knowledge' (or 'non-knowledge') that they (allegedly) deliver is and must be of another order than the knowledge of the latter. Yet psychoanalysis, unlike philosophy, is integrally linked to the rise of modern science as one of its preconditions. Whereas post-seventeenth-century philosophy constitutes for the most part a vast work of impotent reabsorption of the division inflicted upon human being by the sciences – one might even suggest from a broader psychoanalytic perspective that subsequent philosophy is structurally crippled by a kind of melancholia for the One – psychoanalysis is precisely born of this modern division. It, moreover, takes the divisive effects of this division upon subjects as its primary subject. Psychoanalysis is a child of modern science, not of ancient philosophy.

Something old, something new, something weird, something true For Lacan, as for the authorities upon whom he relies, the paradigmatic instance of modern science is the mathematised physics of the early-modern period. In this, Lacan is neither simply historicist nor relativist, nor simply in the grip of received idealisations regarding the supposed triumph of such a science. Rather, Lacan is sensitive to the unintended consequences of discursive transformations, in a sense that is essentially psychoanalytic: in Lacan's revisions, the unconscious, the Other, is a contingent-but-absolute virtual structure susceptible to symbolic interventions that make incisions into synchrony. Psychoanalysis itself is a praxis of cuts: as we saw in previous chapters, psychoanalysis simultaneously affirms the necessity of cuts, as it gives one of the most astringent critiques available of the diverse affirmations of events widely purveyed and available in the intellectual marketplace. In this regard, however, psychoanalysis isn't merely a hermeneutics of suspicion regarding the possibility of events or a method of interrogating discourses that affirm the possibility of events, so much as a goad to rethink what an event might be, how it and its implications might be inflicted, inscribed, inflected and redirected. Lacan himself constantly returns to non-linear series of exemplary phenomena in order to rethink their status and abiding import: Judaism, classical tragedy, Greek philosophy, Christianity, medieval theology, courtly love, modern physics, Marxism, and so on, all of which make new *kinds* of cut into the topology of language.

Literalisation-experiment   Whence, then, the significance of science qua mathematised physics? In a very simple sense, it is only when knowledge becomes subject to the double blow of (textual) literalisation *and* (physical) experiment – as it does with the exemplary figure of Galileo, as well as in different ways with Francis Bacon and René Descartes – that the alleged inherited 'knowledge' of scholars comes into question as in need of a support that goes beyond any tradition or adherence. As is well known, 'Aristotelianism' becomes one of the primary polemical codewords for all that the new sciences are against. For if empirical presentations cannot be formalised, then they cannot become part of the new philosophy; in order to be formalised, evidence has to be provided; for that evidence to be provided, then it must be of another order than that which has been inherited. 'Experiment' here is no longer the simple observation of natural phenomena, familiar to scholars from antiquity. Rather, an experiment now means the technological establishment of an artificial environment – that is, an explicitly non-natural, local space – in order to isolate a particular trait to be investigated. This renders every experiment a fiction, but a fiction of a particular kind, a fiction which is a *material space of purified repetition*. That these spaces can potentially and in principle be set up anywhere, presumes that the laws they are directed to investigating are everywhere: 'space' in general is no longer hierarchised or striated, regionalised in one way or another (as was the Aristotelian cosmos), but genuinely universal, and precisely insofar as it is susceptible to the fictional exceptions of experiment. As for the issue of mathematical writing, it is repurposed to link spatial fiction to abstract demonstration. As such, mathematics is detached from any human inheritance in order that it might become a referential inscription of inhuman necessity. Even more paradoxically, such necessity is linked to a new contingency of the universe: everything that happens may also be able not to have happened. The universe is infinite; there is nothing outside it; whatever happens is contingent, but governed necessarily by universal laws; matter can be experimented upon because it is not out to fool us.*

---

* Although this is not the place to discuss this development in detail, Lacan's own take on this particular issue was definitively inflected by the work of Alexandre Koyré, Kojève's brother-in-law. The key works of Koyré here include *Etudes d'histoire de la pensée philosophique* (Paris: Gallimard, 1971); *From the Closed World to the Infinite Universe* (Baltimore and

Novelty-in-knowledge or knowledge-as-novelty is the watchword of the day, as can be verified from the extraordinary titles of Bacon's books alone: *The New Organum*, *The Advancement of Learning*, *The Great Instauration*. Their content will only confirm the radical avant-gardism of the corrupt Lord Chancellor and *buccinator* for the *new sciences*.

Bonjour, Monsieur Cogito! Yet some sort of subject must be at hand to provide a support and articulation between the new evidentiary requirements and their formalisation in mathematics. This subject, however, cannot simply bring its inheritances with it, for such a subject is precisely what is brought into question by the new sciences. But how can those inherited prejudices be identified and neutralised in and by a subject itself? Impurity of thinking threatens the very foundations of knowing. Any long-term hangovers *a priori* compromise the integrity of knowledge. Having been poisoned by Aristotelianism, what sort of treatment must one undergo to recover? Is there an appropriate therapeutics of thought? What sort of practice, if any, can provide such novel support for such novel requirements? The answer? The Cartesian *cogito*!

Descartes is a staple reference for Lacan precisely because the former is the thinker who provides the concept of a new subject able to *rebind* without reduction a new *division* of matter and mathematics. The method of doubt is directed towards eradicating residual fantasms, purging the subject of all and any substantive beliefs; it comes to rest upon the pure fact of the impossibility of doubting thought itself; in doing so, it exposes the sole indubitability that cannot be vitiated or contradicted, for the act of contradicting must itself be inscribed in the definition of thinking. Doubt as a method is not sceptical; rather, Descartes' ethics engages the pursuit of doubt to the very end, such that he never gives way on his doubt. Yet it's because he doesn't give way that the doubt runs out. And it runs out, as is well known, into self-certainty.

Absolutely anybody anywhere For the first time in human history – at least on this interpretation – we have a recipe that *absolutely anybody anywhere* can repeat for themselves in the privacy of their

London: The Johns Hopkins University Press, 1957); *Galileo Studies*, trans. J. Mepham (Sussex: The Harvester Press, 1978).

own stoves as a fantasm-therapy, and which concludes upon the grounds of an exclusion of all particularities. Yet such a subject – preposterously impersonal and essentially un-individuated despite its first-person form – doesn't for all that succumb to the problems that stem from the Aristotelian *hypokemeinon*. The Cartesian subject, by contrast, can support accidents because it is itself neither really first- nor third-person, as Lacan himself (among many others) has shown in his commentaries on the cogito. The violence of the Cartesian dualism also immediately entails that thought can and must indeed go on in the absence of a body; or, at least, in the absence of any particular body. The Cartesian universe is also one that is replete with fantasmatic accidents, a universe emptied of the essence of mind that must nonetheless make a return there, to its other and double, to the regime of extension.

What Lacan pinpoints then, as we might expect, is that the Cartesian subject is a subject *in act*: it appears when thinking, as thinking, only to disappear at once. The cogito achieves its status of certitude by taking place at the level of enunciation itself. This renders it punctual, necessarily repetitive and evacuated, an ascesis of being.* Moreover, Lacan notes that the link Descartes attempts to forge between the 'I think' and the 'I am' aims at the real, but can only achieve this by being forced to give truth back to God. Certainty, in thinking, of thinking, can only be achieved by, at least foundationally, separating certainty from knowledge (what 'I' am certain of is not any kind of knowledge), and knowledge from truth (it is God as the infinite place of truth that enables the reconstruction of any positive knowledge at all following the deluge of doubt).

---

* It's finally time for Hadotians and Foucauldians to admit the inadmissible: the turn to 'philosophy as a way of life', to analyses of 'care for the self', and associated doctrines re-emerges in France due primarily to the influence of Lacan, and indeed psychoanalysis more generally. As such, and despite whatever Nietzscho-Heideggerean legacy they may claim for themselves, the very form of their researches continues to cipher limit-expressions of the Cartesian ego, mostly without knowing it. Lacan, as an analyst, and from the very first, made this a principle of what he would only later explicitly nominate as 'anti-philosophy': that modern academic philosophy remained, like ancient philosophy, a tool of the master, while it thoroughly misrepresented itself and its own history as a love-quest for knowledge. Yet, in its putatively radical attempts to overturn or displace this self-image, philosophy was forced to retain something *like* the priority of consciousness (even if a merely technical or pragmatic one, or an auto-care-without-subject) to the extent that it failed to uptake the consequences of the Freudian revolution. Yet another reason why Lacan must be considered as always already anti-Hegelian.

As Lacan consistently emphasises, Descartes thereby unsuspectingly institutes the *'vel* of alienation' for modern subjects. The 'I think, I am' will quickly find itself rearranged such that I am not where I think, and I do not think where I am. As subject, I am constitutively confronted by a forced choice, such as 'freedom or death!' or 'your money or your life!' or 'penis envy or castration anxiety!' Note the punctuation of the little exclamation – not question! – marks! The question is not really a question, but a demand, and a demand that issues from an inhuman other. The choice, then, is of course no choice at all, and for a number of reasons. First of all, you cannot not make the choice. Second, you cannot not make this choice *now*. The highwayman is not going to wait on your decision forever. Third, you cannot alter the options it delivers you ('man' or 'woman'); you can't negotiate with the other. Fourth, there is no principle or external position to enable a real choice to be made. In fact, fifth, you cannot not have made the choice already, even though, precisely, *you* did not make it. You, after all, are the outcome of the choice you therefore didn't make and couldn't not have made. A choice that was and was not a choice. A choice that happened immemorially yet forever repeats interminably as (if for) the first (or second) time. Welcome to the logic of the signifier . . . and have a nice day.

True freedom is the freedom not to have to choose [margin note]

God is unconscious [margin note] The paradoxes of this situation of non-choice are correlated with Lacan's famous 'anti-humanism'. For 'there is no such thing as a science of man because science's man does not exist, only its subject does'.[*] Psychoanalysis, in other words, would be unthinkable without the subjective-loss-of-man. Yet if the global enforcement of the cogito in the reign if science is a condition of analysis, analysis does something pretty funny to this subject too: as Lacan jokes, if the Cartesian God is incapable of deception, psychoanalysis shows that the danger is rather that God is Himself now liable to be deceived. To be even blunter: science serves us to hoodwink the God that we can nevertheless never live without. As Lacan will later put it, the true atheist statement is not that God is dead, but that God is unconscious.

Science is the continuation of Christianity by other means [margin note] This extraordinary new situation is itself the emblem of another extraordinary paradox. Modern science, for Kojève, Koyré and Lacan, is no longer, and despite

---

[*] Jacques Lacan, *Ecrits*, trans. Bruce Fink (New York: Norton, 2006), p. 730.

appearances, founded on the philosophical inquiries of the ancients, but on a feature drawn from another tradition entirely: the Christian conviction of the reliability of God. And it is precisely such a reference that enables Descartes to rebuild his house on the basis of only a single certainty, a certainty that no longer bears any relation to any inherited acceptations regarding knowledge. Instead, we are now confronted with the incontrovertible act and fact of thinking itself. When I think I'm thinking, I'm certain that I know I am; but this knowing is not knowing anything outside its own thinking; for thinking to be true, indeed, for truth to be true, it needs an outside that guarantees the validity of the contents of the inside; that outside can therefore itself never be known as such; it remains as an infinite guarantee of the veracity of the rather motley populations of the ego. So the certain truth of this certainty is certainly eccentric. As Lacan puts it, with reference to Descartes:

> The reference to a nondeceiving god, the one accepted principle, is based on results obtained by science ... It need hardly be said that matter does not cheat, that it has no intention of crushing our experiments or blowing up our machines. This sometimes happens, but only when we have made a mistake. It's out of the question that it, matter, should deceive us. This step is not at all obvious. Nothing less than the Judaeo-Christian tradition was required for it to be taken with such assurance.[*]

'God is tricky, but he isn't mean', as Albert Einstein would later hilariously put it: we now have a fundamental reliability inscribed within matter that we can trust or, at least, are unable not to trust without succumbing immediately to an ancestral irrationality. And we cannot not trust it because we are no longer substantial but essentially thinking beings that even the most extreme powers of a malign demon are incapable of spiriting-away, even if such thinking itself requires a further guarantee of the possibility of knowledge through the acquisition of renovated content. For such content has to be guaranteed by another agency: the infinity of God.

With Descartes, God becomes a cosmic underwriter. Yet the qualities He underwrites – if He still deserves a capital letter, not to mention a residual prosopopeia, which is hardly certain – are no longer of a *sexual* nature. The universe is not driven by sexual principles, but

---

[*] Jacques Lacan, *The Psychoses: The Seminar of Jacques Lacan, Book III 1955–1956*, trans. R. Grigg (New York: Norton, 1993), pp. 64–5.

regulated by desexuated laws. As such, *even* women become thinking beings (we can now know this on rational grounds), and our new
scientists – once again, paradigmatically Descartes and Bacon – start
to write in the vernacular so that *even* women and manservants might
understand. Condemn this position all you like, whether on the basis
of its lack of a proper gender or class analysis, or on the basis of some
other trait that it is allegedly miserably lacking or failing to lack –
such a condemnation itself remains inherently Cartesian insofar as its
elaboration contributes to the furtherance of doubts about the ultimate doubtingness of its doubt. In any case, since Descartes' medita-
tions had already dispensed with the malign demon which might have
functioned as a principle of the abyssal inconsistency of matter, we
can now happily find rest in our restless activity of thought. The cease-
less motion of thought itself will provide the firm ground upon which
the New Atlantis can be satisfactorily rebuilt – as long as we keep an
infinite-yet-irrelevant Other as the absentee guarantor of such a mix.

Knowledge ≠ truth   But this paradox – Christianity is the basis of the
modern science that thereafter comes to destroy
the former's claims to speak authoritatively of the fallen world – is
given a further torsion by the necessity for experimental confirmation, and hence the possibility that such confirmation can always also
be disconfirmed. Knowledge changes its status: no longer for all time,
but only for a short time, on notice until it is disproven or falsified or,
at best, established to be extended. Such knowledge is at once more
absolute and more transient than before, ever-ready to be *modified*
by *discoveries* but no longer *contested* by the *debates* of scholars.
Error is no longer false knowledge; it is not even knowledge at all.
Moreover, and Lacan himself never ceases to underline this feature,
the Cartesian subject of science *de facto* and *de jure* has come to
separate truth from knowledge from thinking. It's not that Descartes
was such a hot scientist himself – indeed, he scorned Galileo's pre-
posterous experiments – but he was the thinker to formalise the
subject that that science requires as its foreclosed support. Yet
another bizarre Lacanian formulation of the status of modern science
emerges here. Modern science is not distinguished by its objectivity at
all; it is, quite to the contrary, distinguished by the fact that it is an
entirely *subjective* enterprise. That is, if we understand, as we must,
'subjective' here in an absolutely non-humanistic and impersonal
sense. Moreover, if we understand 'subjective' as precisely what that
science cannot abide in its practices.

'Unpurged images of day recede'   Hence, as Russell Grigg has emphasised, on Lacan's description science can only take place through a suture of the subject that supports it* – the subject being excluded from the universe of science in both subjective and objective senses of the genitive – but it therefore leaves something behind, a remainder in the form of fantasms that the corrosive of radical, rational doubt cannot entirely purge from the 'experience' of individuals. These fantasms can be universally agreed to be *fantasms* for the first time, precisely because we now have a practice which functions on the basis of a necessary externalisation ('formalisation') of knowledge: science. Fantasms are residues of the subject which the subject may itself doubt, but without such presentations simply being able to be expelled by an act of consciousness. Or, if they are, they immediately return as a difference from themselves, that is, as another unrecognisable fantasmatic inflection of consciousness itself. Qua fantasms, they have no consistency; in fact, they dispel at daybreak only to reform in another disguise at dark (if they do not confuse the very difference between dawn and dusk!). Disguised, such fantasms 'advance masked', as Descartes' own motto has it – indeed, are mask itself. If they cannot always be truffled out in actuality, we now at least have a principle that compels us to shove the pig's snout of doubt into the dark forests of our minds. Yet these magical truffles somehow do not disappear even though eaten by doubt. On the contrary, they only inspire further illusions and delusions.

Note that Lacan's position does not mean that we have to 'agree' in any way with any of the historical presuppositions, methods, or results of the new scientists themselves; certainly, they did not agree with each other. Rather, all that is required for Lacan's thesis to be plausible and effective is the acknowledgement that, in its very foundations, science must differentiate itself as a knowledge-practice by seeking its foundations externally to all or any ancestral knowledge. In fact, one would expect that the *difficulties* concerning the establishment or verification or confirmation or externality of knowledge would immediately become a crucial problem for scientists. It is not that any particular method needs to be agreed on for science to be true science; on the contrary, and despite the best efforts of its ideologues, science itself isn't so simple-minded in its practice, theory or

* See Russell Grigg, *Lacan, Language and Philosophy* (Albany: SUNY, 2008), esp. Chapter 10: Descartes and the Subject of Science.

history. Rather, what is crucial for the instauration and advancement of modern science is that everyone agrees *that* a method must be agreed upon, even if they cannot agree upon any such method.

This is, indeed, what happens empirically: all the polemics of the period, whether between Kepler and his antagonists, Descartes and Galileo, Hobbes and Boyle, expressly hinge on the problem of establishing a link between formalisation and the world that eludes the typology of idolisation endemic to humanity. Yet these struggles for credibility, authority, dominance, and so on, are not simply the ineluctable political struggles that accompany any human interaction whatsoever; paradoxically, they are now absolutely central to the practice of the sciences themselves *due to the new reliability of matter.* Modern science institutes cuts within knowledge, exposing what previously looked like rival forms of knowledge as precisely forms of non-knowledge; yet, in doing so, it makes it impossible ever to return a sense (i.e., clear decisions about meaning, status or grounding) to these cuts. Moreover, and perhaps unlike more familiar struggles for social and political domination, the scientific injunction to novelty makes this struggle central, patent, impersonal and irreversible insofar as it enjoins the incessant, corrosive externalisation of the logic of all knowing-doing. Truth has disappeared from the field of knowledge that it guarantees; it subsists, nonetheless, as a hole that entails the constitutive incompletion of the whole.

The subject of science and the subject of psychoanalysis are the same subject   In the present context, what really matters for our discussion is why Lacan holds that the subject of science and the subject of psychoanalysis are the same subject, but also why science and psychoanalysis are not the same enterprise. Science forecloses the subject that founds it; psychoanalysis picks up on the irreducibility of the fantasmal residue left behind in each subject, the ancestral content that a subject cannot junk but which can have no place among the things of knowledge. The establishment of this 'scientific' division of the subject – torn between knowledge and fantasm by a revolutionary process in which the former is to be purged of the latter – is therefore the historical precondition for the emergence of psychoanalysis as a praxis of self. Psychoanalysis treats this irreconcilable division as such, a division that is installed as constitutive trauma for the subject, and which analysis nominates as 'sex' or, in its tormenting

unpresentability for the subject, as the unconscious. Unlike traditional forms of therapeutics, then – one could invoke here all sorts
of cultic, meditative and curative practices, such as Yoga, shaman-
ism or pedagogy, or indeed those that Pierre Hadot and Michel
Foucault reinterrogate as modes of life or technologies of care with
respect to the history of philosophy itself – psychoanalysis never had
to *adapt* itself to science. Rather, it belatedly had to *emerge* from it,
as a reaction to the unintended subjective consequences of the scientific revolution. Yet, in doing so, psychoanalysis, just as the very
subject that it treats, thereafter finds itself caught between science
and feeling, experiment and experience, knowledge and fantasm,
universality and singularity.

Post-scientific but no
longer religious
This does not make psychoanalysis a philosophy or
religion. But it does render psychoanalysis a strictly
impossible practice insofar as it must locate itself between knowledge
and fantasm, the new and the archaic, matter and memory. But this
impossibility is also the source of its feeble power. As a supplement
and parasite of modern science, psychoanalysis will survive as long as
such science does. But it won't ever survive all that well. As Lacan
very clearly puts it: psychoanalysis can never triumph, given it is itself
a *symptom* of science.* If it begins to do rather well, then something
has gone truly wrong. Indeed, one might suspect that certain philos-
ophemes or mythemes have reinfiltrated the process. After all, from
Lacan's perspective, both philosophy and religion share a fantasy of
the whole to which they give the key, whereas psychoanalysis and
science are *stricto sensu* practices of incompletion and inconsistency.
Yet since psychoanalysis has to deal with fantasms too, it requires
something else to support it, to give it a power of formalisation that,
though expressly and necessarily non-scientific, exceeds the religious
or philosophical closures. For, as Lacan puts it in several characteristically crystalline passages:

> Magic involves the truth as cause in its guise as efficient cause.
> Knowledge is characterized in magic not only as remaining veiled
> for the subject of science, but as dissimulating itself as such, as
> much in the operative tradition as in its action. This is one of
> magic's conditions.†

---

* See Jacques Lacan, *Le triomphe de la religion* (Paris: Seuil, 2005).
† Lacan, *Ecrits*, p. 740.

And:

> Truth in religion is relegated to so-called 'eschatological' ends, which is to say that truth appears only as final cause, in the sense that it is deferred to an end-of-the-world judgement.*

Yet such remarks only make sense in the context of an abiding difficulty. If psychoanalysis and science share the same subject, yet psychoanalysis is not a science, what prevents psychoanalysis from resorting to the placing of truth according to the practices of magic or religion? The risk of efficient and final causes is ever-present, perhaps even inexpungible from the realm of non-scientific practice. Lacan is again clear: 'Need it be said that in science, as opposed to magic and religion, knowledge is communicated?'† Knowledge, too, needs to be *communicated* in psychoanalysis; at any point, its practice and principles must be able to be publicly presented, just as in any significant scientific process. Yet, given that science 'sutures the subject it implies', and psychoanalysis takes it upon itself to analyse *that* subject, some other support for the transmission of knowledge must be sought than science itself can accept.‡ The relation between experiment and formalisation must be of a different character in psychoanalysis vis-à-vis science.

Another, supplementary support must be found. That support is literature. As Michel de Certeau brilliantly phrases the analytic recourse to the literary:

> literature is the theoretic discourse of the historical process. It creates the non-topos where the effective operations of a society attain a formalization. Far from envisioning literature as the expression of a referential, it would be necessary to recognize here the analogue of that which for a long time mathematics has been for the exact sciences: a 'logical' discourse of history, the 'fiction' which allows it to be thought.§

Psychoanalysis, positioned between science and literature, is therefore committed to an anti-philosophical project in its essence. That the status of its specific 'non-topos' is so consistently denied in the assaults upon psychoanalysis is evidently of interest. In not taking

---

* Lacan, *Ecrits*, p. 741.
† Lacan, *Ecrits*, p. 744.
‡ Lacan, *Ecrits*, p. 744.
§ Michel de Certeau, *Heterologies*, trans. B. Massumi (Minneapolis: University of Minnesota Press, 1987), p. 18.

psychoanalysis's peculiar literary interlocution with the seriousness that it deserves, psychoanalysis can only appear not scientific/too scientific, too religious/too atheistic, not literary/too literary, and so on and on. Moreover – and this is an immanent, irresolvable problem to which psychoanalysis dedicates much of its attention – psychoanalysis theorises transmission as going necessarily awry. What else is the Oedipus complex, for example, except an inter- and intra-psychological account of how transmission takes place unconsciously, that is, through misrecognition, antagonism, misfires and failures? Is not literature essentially a mistransmission of its own analyses of mistransmission? Moreover, what psychoanalysis therefore must commit to is a formalisation of its analysis of forms of address, whereby what they presume about themselves and the bodies that bear them must be reintroduced into the forms themselves. But how to formalise what will be misrepresented in and by that formalisation? Hence – as if they were needed – still more reasons as to why psychoanalysis must think of itself as impossible. Even more strongly: psychoanalysis is the first impossible practice to know itself impossible, the first ever really impossible practice.

Yet it is also immediately possible to see the scintillating ingenuity of Lacan's complex a-dialectical position: psychoanalysis formalises its own conditions of possibility as a symptom of modern science, yet it is not itself a science; rather, science, which emerged at a particular historical conjuncture, was itself an enterprise split between mathematics and experiment, and founded on a unique element drawn from Christianity, which it itself repressed and displaced; moreover, in order to take place, science required a subject that it forecloses, whose formalisation is given in and by the contemporaneous philosophy that science will also thoroughly sideline; this subject is itself constitutively split, and its routines can only be discerned by a new discourse, psychoanalysis, which, to do so, draws on literature as an indispensable resource of analytic effects. Psychoanalysis therefore sustains a notion of truth that exceeds knowledge and *a fortiori* the knowledge of science (which is, let's be frank, the only 'true knowledge' we can now have), but without such truth being able to be given any particular content or consistency – otherwise it would immediately contravene the 'necessity' that founds the volatile questioning of further scientific inquiry. In doing so, psychoanalysis finds its crucial topics in the vicissitudes of transmission effected by the truth that it lacks.

Back to the future . . .
of truth This position is worked out through Lacan's intimate assault on Hegel:

> In Hegel's work is it desire (*Begierde*) that is given responsibility for the minimal link the subject must retain to Antiquity's knowledge if truth is to be immanent in the realization of knowledge. The 'cunning of reason' means that, from the outset and right to the end, the subject knows what he wants.
>
> It is here that Freud reopens the junction between truth and knowledge to the mobility out of which revolutions arise.
>
> In this respect: that desire becomes bound up at that junction with the Other's desire, but that the desire to know lies in this loop.*

As Lacan notes, Freud separates truth from knowledge in a fundamental way. This way is compatible with the consequences of the scientific revolution, but it runs precisely counter to the ambitions of philosophy. As Lorenzo Chiesa points out, 'from this standpoint, an anti-philosopher is ultimately more "scientific" than a philosopher', insofar as the latter is unable to bear incompleteness.† For the truth of a subject – the arrhythmic process of its own becoming – is bound to the desire-to-know only at the subject's insertion point into the Other. The 'knowledge' thus established by the subject is never quite of the subject: the desire-to-know has its genesis in the Other; the terms of knowledge derive from the Other; the circulation of knowledge is confined to the loop between subject and Other. Genesis, structure, localisation: knowledge is at every level separated from the truth which it chases, like a brain-damaged dog its tail.

This sorry state of affairs doesn't mean that truth and knowledge are altogether without relation. Rather, truth is the name for the haphazard trajectory of the subject that hollows out established knowledges as it exceeds them. It's not simply that there's never a totality because you can always add another unit – that is, the bad infinite can only be sublated by wish-fulfilment – but that there's never a totality because the exchange with the Other is assured only through the constituting absence of a key element. You and the Other are (and are not) only because It isn't. Nor is there anything particularly liberating about

---

* Lacan, *Ecrits*, p. 655.
† Lorenzo Chiesa, *Subjectivity and Otherness: A Philosophical Reading of Lacan* (Cambridge, MA: MIT, 2007), p. 4.

this situation of non-totalisation; on the contrary, it founds the work of freedom that is the brand of human servitude.

In the end, it's this that's determining. For psychoanalysis is ultimately a treatment – not a cure! – for animals suffering from signification, that is, from unconscious desire, and the vast revolutionary project of psychoanalysis is directed by this very specific therapeutic situation. The analysand lies on his or her back on a couch and 'free associates', the analyst seated behind, both listening or, rather, doing their best to attend to their own incapacity to listen to the truth that withdraws behind the deranging words that bear it. Truth is always only half-said, a half-saying, for Lacan, corroding any and all knowledge we cannot help but erect on its sluggish drift. As we have seen, Lacan's aetiology of totality, his diagnosis of its appeal as irreducible and imaginary, goes all the way down. Other discourses exist to help out with this default fault, but they're not much help either, actually. But at least Freud and Lacan show us how far humans must have come to get to this weird place, this weird room of one's un-own, this divided and simple practice of analysis that nobody can really bear and have tried – keep trying – to shut down, in one way or another, from the moment of its emergence. The voice of reason is low, mumbled Freud, but it demands a hearing; the operations of truth are self-silencing, intimated Lacan, so it's never going to get much of a hearing. But, with or without it, we will all remain what we cannot help but be: cruel, stupid animals that take pleasure in calling our evil good. Strangely enough, we will find that evil, stupidity and malevolence also come to play their indispensable transcendental role in the Deleuzian theory of truth – if, unsurprisingly, in an inverted and displaced form.

There is a positive Deleuzian theory of truth
There is a certain orthodoxy surrounding Deleuze's project, according to which the category of truth has no place in it. It would seem that the basis of this supposition lies in Deleuze's 'well-known' rejection of classical metaphysics and distaste for concepts that bear even the slightest taint of morality. Like many orthodoxies, this one is rooted in fact, while at the same time grotesquely distorting the features of the position it purports to represent, often animated by a barely disguised morality of its own. Just as we get the problems we deserve, we also – it would seem – get the caricatures proper to our relationship to the texts of great thinkers.

A first observation: Deleuze himself never rejects the category of philosopher or metaphysician – to the contrary. We have recently even been told by a well-meaning gentleman that Deleuze is, after all, an anti-philosopher. Even the recollection of Deleuze's claim 'I consider myself to be a pure metaphysician'* was not enough to repel his friendly advisory advances. Indeed, we regularly encounter a comparable if inverted situation with Lacan: the man who consistently dismisses philosophy and philosophers, so often ends up being celebrated as one.

A second observation, then: Deleuze never shies away from taking up concepts from what could be considered to be the traditional canon (though it does not look this way from his point of view) that bear the moral stain and, with a characteristic lack of concern for critique (this is the philosophical 'innocence' noted by Derrida), elaborate the concept in a new way. Like the supposed materialist Nietzsche, he feels no reticence using terms like 'spiritual' or 'God', or invoking the semi-divine capacity of human beings to choose. The proto-orthodox responses to such usage – either to ignore such terms or to take them as the mark of ultimate worthlessness – overlook the fact that these terms are being *redeployed* in a philosophical register charged with new sense.† Of course we may wish to remain critical, this point granted, but can do so legitimately only once we work through the concept in question on its own terms.

Truth is just such a concept in Deleuze. It bears an immense charge in the history of philosophy, and has, at least since Parmenides (Detienne writes the history of what lies before this moment‡), been affiliated with representation, with the notion of a correspondence or correlation with what is – despite Badiou's assertion that such a view of truth has 'never been advanced by any philosopher other

* Gilles Deleuze, 'Réponse à une série de questions', in Arnaud Villani, *La Guêpe et l'Orchidée. Essais sur Gilles Deleuze* (Paris: Éditions Belin, 1999), p. 130.
† Perhaps the paradigm of this kind of error of partial omission can be found in the translator's preface to *A Thousand Plateaus*. Deleuze's own claim to the philosophical provenance of the book is cited ('Philosophy, nothing but philosophy'), to which the comment is added 'Of a bastard line'. However, the full text of the former passage reads as follows: 'Philosophy, nothing but philosophy, in the traditional sense of the word.' Deleuze is not helped here by the Lebowskiesque posture of the translator of this interview, who renders this passage 'It's just plain old philosophy . . .' Dude!
‡ See in particular his magisterial text *The Masters of Truth in Archaic Greece*, trans. Janet Lloyd (New York: Zone Books, 1996).

than as a mediatory image that the philosopher's entire thought will subsequently be devoted to dismantling'.*

Deleuze's approach to the concept is, at least at certain moments, to provide a critique of this image and an account of its genesis. However, for the most part, the concept of truth is the object of a renovation that is entirely disengaged from its previous investments. In what follows, these two moments will be treated in this order. Deleuze's points of reference in the course of this elaboration may surprise: Proust and Nietzsche, but also Plato and Descartes, these latter supposedly philosophers Deleuze could 'never manage to love'.† More surprising again may be the fact that the Nietzschean moment is only a preliminary one, and that Deleuze's account of truth ends up closer to a certain Platonism than to any mundane relativism.

The four postulates of the dogmatic image of truth   Truth, for Deleuze, is subject to four fundamental misunderstandings. The first is that truth is the immediate and natural goal of thought, and that thinking is primarily to be characterised as having a love of truth. This can be called the *spontanaeist* misunderstanding. The second is that truth is the truth of a *proposition* ('The apple is red' is either true or false). We can call this the *logical* misunderstanding of truth. The third is that truths are *universal*, in the sense that should a proposition be true, it is necessarily true for everyone. We can call this the *catholic* misunderstanding of truth. The fourth, finally, is that truth is *a-temporal* or *eternal*, according to which time makes no difference to truth (if 'The apple is red' is true, then nothing that can happen can undermine this). We can call this the *metaphysical* misunderstanding of truth. Conversely, for Deleuze, truths are intimately tied to the violence of an *encounter*, truths are an issue of *sense*, truths are *differential*, and truths are *temporal*.

The dogmatic image and its remedy   To understand the Deleuzian theory of truth, we must pass beyond these misconceptions. It is under the moniker 'the dogmatic image of thought' – that is, of an implicit set of unreconstructed postulates that bear on the nature of thought

---

* Alain Badiou, *Deleuze: The Clamor of Being*, trans. Louise Burchill (Minneapolis: Minnesota University Press, 2000), p. 57.
† Alain Badiou, *Logics of Worlds*, trans. Alberto Toscano (London: Continuum, 2009), p. 552.

– that Deleuze most directly and almost exclusively addresses these misunderstandings of truth.

Now, the dogmatic image of thought is not, or not only, a set of mistaken claims that sometimes contingently arise about the nature of thinking. While Deleuze sometimes puts the point this way, he has bigger fish to fry. The dogmatic image is in fact a complex of what Kant called transcendental illusions, an internally generated misprision of thinking proper to thinking itself. To misunderstand thinking is thus an inevitability due to the situation of thinking itself. We won't go into the reasons why Deleuze thinks this is the case here, but what is of importance is to see that we are dealing with a certain kind of fundamental stupidity, even a transcendental Stupidity, rather than any kind of simple error on the part of the distracted, the tired or the hung-over: 'stupidity is a structure of thought as such'.[*] Because this stupidity that is the degree zero of thinking is a proper element of thought itself, it can never be gotten rid of, but, once again from within thinking, it must be subject to an absolute critique, one which is endless and must be endlessly renewed.

As it happens, though, the dogmatic image is also undermined from an entirely different site altogether. It is not just the endless labour of the transcendental critic that *represses* (this is the word Deleuze uses with regard to the same general problematic in his book on Bergson) the dogmatic image, because it is also shattered at the level of encounters in sensation, by shocks that cannot be thought, its placidity become plasticity in the presence of a *sign*. This leads us to the first point and Deleuzian counter-point.

First postulate: there is a natal pact between thought and truth

The first, basic, claim that is made on behalf of truth from the point of view of the dogmatic image of thought is that truth is its natural object and orientation: 'We are told that the thinker *as* thinker wants and loves *truth* (truthfulness of the thinker); that thought as thought possesses or formally contains truth';[†] 'The mistake of philosophy is to presuppose within us a benevolence of thought, a natural love of truth';[‡] 'According to this

---

[*] Gilles Deleuze, *Nietzsche and Philosophy*, trans. Hugh Tomlinson (London: Continuum, 20067), p. 98.
[†] Deleuze, *Nietzsche and Philosophy*, p. 96.
[‡] Gilles Deleuze, *Proust and Signs*, trans. Richard Howard (Minneapolis: University of Minnesota Press, 2000), p. 11.

image, thought has an affinity with the true; it formally possesses the true and materially wants the true.'* Another, correlative, way to assert this affiliation, Deleuze notes, is to presuppose that thought has a natural method that leads from ignorance to the possession of truth. There is a natural inclination or means of passage that leads us to the truth, and here truth is conceived in precisely a representational fashion, as an image in thought of reality, that is, as a true proposition – this is the second fallacy, to which we will turn in a moment.

Contrary to this image of the relationship between truth and thought, Deleuze will always insist on breaking the compact between a supposed intrinsic capacity of thinking and the natural goal of truth. The essential point is that an encounter is required to engender thought at all: 'Thought never thinks alone [but] depends on forces which take hold of thought.'† We have already seen this in our consideration of the relationship between time and the sign in *Proust and Signs*. The encounter is a shock at the level of sensation, and this is what Deleuze calls a sign. The sign in turn expresses an event, a problematic instance that opens up thinking to a future in which it will have had to have changed in order to continue to exist.

Typological account of truth   This is how Deleuze will in the final analysis understand the entirety of the Nietzschean doctrine of truth. It is not that Nietzsche is a simple relativist, expounding on the subjective nature of point of view; nor, however, is Nietzschean perspectivism some kind of coherentist account of truth, where truths are true insofar as they fit together (or are harnesses within) a given socio-historical framework. Rather, the truths that pertain to a given perspective, and by extension to a given social formation, are the truths that are deserved on the basis of the encounters that give rise to the formations of the social and the self that have taken place. In a sentiment we will return to in what follows, Deleuze writes that for Nietzsche, 'The concept of truth can only be determined on the basis of a pluralist typology.'‡

Now, because truth is at issue in thinking – as we will see, it is *all* that is at issue in thinking from a certain point of view – truth too only

* Gilles Deleuze, *Difference and Repetition*, trans. Paul Patton (New York: Columbia University Press, 1995), p. 131.
† Deleuze, *Nietzsche and Philosophy*, p. 100.
‡ Deleuze, *Nietzsche and Philosophy*, p. 98.

arises in response to the shock of a sign-encounter: 'Truth depends on an encounter with something that forces us to think and to seek the truth.'* In *Proust and Signs*, perhaps Deleuze's most powerful example (and one of decisive importance for Proust himself), is that of the jealous lover: 'Who searches for truth? The jealous man, under the pressure of the beloved's lies. There is always the violence of a sign that forces us into the search, that robs us of peace.'†

Second postulate: truth is the attribute of propositions — So far, we have only identified the *origin* of truth for Deleuze. The *logical* fallacy provides us with the means to reflect on the *form* and *topos* of truth. This misunderstanding, to recall, concerns the notion that truths are propositional in nature, or (an equivalent formulation) truth is a tertiary attribution of the proposition. This is because, according to the dogmatic image, we begin with propositional assertions: she is weeping. We draw from this proposition a secondary formation, that of the question, which we arrive at by simply inverting the propositional form: is she weeping? The question of truth arises, according to the dogmatic image of thought, on this basis, and involves the determination of the relationship between the state of affairs and the inverted proposition.

This way of situating truth and the question is catastrophic on Deleuze's account: 'they can be no more than phantoms'.‡ He notes that such a conception has two sources, depending on whether we are considering the function of truth in the empirical world of social interaction or in the lineage of its concept in philosophy. In the first case, what is at issue is nothing other than the creation and maintenance of endemic stupidity as a function of social organisation. It is, he writes:

> a social prejudice with the visible interest of maintaining us in an infantile state, which calls upon us to solve problems that come from elsewhere, consoling or distracting us by telling us that we have won simply by being able to respond: the problem as obstacle and the respondent as Hercules. Such is the origin of the grotesque image of culture that we find in examinations and government referenda as well as in newspaper competitions (where everyone is called upon to choose according to his or her taste, on the condition

* Deleuze, *Proust and Signs*, p. 12.
† Deleuze, *Proust and Signs*, p. 11.
‡ Deleuze, *Difference and Repetition*, p. 158.

that this taste coincides with that of everyone else). Be yourselves –
it being understood that this self must be that of others.*

On the other hand, the subordination of truths, problems and
questions to the propositional form is already promulgated in the
philosophy of Aristotle – 'The difference between a problem and a
proposition is a difference in a turn of phrase'[†] – and in the work of
everyone who follows after him in subordinating the concept to the
form of identity as inaugural to philosophical thought. This includes,
for Deleuze, modern and contemporary logic and mathematical logic
insofar as they privilege the notion of 'solvability' over that of the
determination of problems.

Truth and sense   Now, as we have already seen in our discussion of
the event, the proposition as a form of language
and thought requires an important ontological supplementation in
order to maintain coherence: beyond denotation, manifestation and
signification, the element of sense is required. As we have also seen,
sense for Deleuze is not a representational category, but the problematic evental structure that creates openings for the reorganisation of
the alloys of bodies. A parallel claim will be advanced with respect to
the relationship between truth and the proposition – that is, truth is
a matter of sense, and cannot be accounted for either in terms of the
accuracy of a proposition's denotation, its comprehension of the
internal states manifested, nor the adequacy of its use of general
concepts (contra Aristotle, concepts cannot be 'the condition of
truth, the aggregate of conditions under which the proposition
"would be" true'.[‡]). We should only speak of true and false in terms
of problems or events, i.e., the sense of a given problem.

What the propositional view and Deleuze's account have in common
is the fact that in both cases truth ultimately concerns a relation and
not a being (we mean: the being of a truth) – and here, by the way,
is the real point of contestation with Badiou around the concept
of truth. According to the dogmatic image, the relation is between
the proposition in one or more of its three modalities (most often
designation, at least according to the widespread character of a

---

* Deleuze, *Difference and Repetition*, p. 158.
† Quoted at Deleuze, *Difference and Repetition*, p. 158.
‡ Gilles Deleuze, *The Logic of Sense*, trans. Mark Lester with Charles Stivale, ed. Constantin
  Boundas (New York: Columbia University Press, 1990), p. 14.

certain Anglo-American conception of philosophical thinking) and the state of affairs (external, internal, conceptual) to which it refers. According to Deleuze, the relation holds between the problematic sense-event and its actualisation in bodies. We should speak, therefore, of truth as adjectival, as the adjectival correlate of the infinitive status of sense-events. The truth of an event (to weep) is determined by the sense, meaning or significance of the event:

> Far from being concerned with solutions, truth and falsehood primarily affect problems. A solution always has the truth it deserves according to the problem to which it is a response, and the problem always has the solution it deserves in proportion to *its own* truth or falsity – in other words, in proportion to its sense.*

Of course, the crucial element of Deleuze's move here is to resituate truth as an ontological category rather than an epistemological one since what 'true' and 'false' characterise are not propositions but the problematic structure that gives rise to openings for the reorganisation of the alloys of bodies. An event is a true event if it makes a significant demand (shocks, constitutes a sign in need of an interpretation). That is, truth and falsity concern the degree to which an event is *decisive for me. The true, for Deleuze, is the decisive.*

Topology of truths   There is something strange about this account. How can this 'proportionality' of sense be determined, especially since (as we have seen with respect to the event) in itself sense is a state of co-existent perplication, a regime that has no intrinsic hierarchy or metric of its own (this is the feature of sense that Deleuze calls its affirmative character)? The answer lies in the way in which the world as it currently exists constitutes the conditions by which certain problems-events are exposed to it. Moreover, on Deleuze's account, this is just what Nietzsche is saying when he concludes that we get the truths we deserve. That is: we get the truths we deserve on the basis of the bodies that we currently are. Even more prosaically: the organisation of bodies in the empirical world exposes them to problems for just these kinds of bodies. This is why Deleuze speaks on occasion of two regimes of truth: 'The problem or sense is at once both the site of an originary truth and the genesis of a derived truth.'† The first, originary truth, is nothing but the problematic nature of sense, sense-events, as such, while the derived truth

---

* Deleuze, *Difference and Repetition*, p. 159.
† Deleuze, *Difference and Repetition*, p. 159.

is the truth of a specific event for this or that alloy of bodies. Put another way, the difference concerns the distance (crossed in the process of actualisation) between explicit meaning and the intrinsic sense that gives rise to it: 'truth is never the product of a prior disposition but the result of a violence in thought. The explicit and conventional significations are never profound; the only profound meaning is the one that is enveloped, implicated in an external sign.'*

Third postulate: truths are universal   The third fallacy, and its inverted, correct form, follows rather straightforwardly from what we have seen above. This fallacy contends that truths are universal in scope, and what is true for one is true for all. It requires, in order to be palatable from the point of view of common sense, the logical fallacy as its operational partner: what is universal is an empirical state of affairs that is represented in the form of the proposition. We need not suppose any intellectual intuition or collective unconscious or pan-psychism, only the neutrality, generality and homogeneity of the propositional order. The syllogism would run: 1) it is true that 'she is weeping' accurately represents the state of affairs; 2) states of affairs exist outside of the proposition, thus exist absolutely, for all equally (even though the nature of this 'exist outside' varies dramatically depending on the doctrine of language in play); and 3) therefore this truth is a universal, and the proposition 'she is weeping' is of universal validity.

For Deleuze, on the contrary, due to the differential structure of co-existing events on the one hand and the heterogeneous character of the ensemble of bodily alloys, truths must be differential in character. There is no one truth for everyone, even if everyone gets the truths that they deserve: to paraphrase the Deleuze of *The Fold*, truth is not universal, but there are truths everywhere. Truth as such is differentially actualised.

Truth and the event   This said, there is certainly a sense in which there is a category of Truth that corresponds to that of the *Eventum tantum*, another name for the originary truth proper to sense as such, and one that reflects the universal pertinence (however obscure) of every event. For Deleuze, the absolute character of any truth has as its reason the positive and real ideal co-existence of all

* Deleuze, *Proust and Signs*, p. 12.

events. Like every event, there is a non-actualised, impertinent aspect of every truth that manifests itself as the irrelevance of a given problem for bodies other than the ones for which it is decisive. But since every event is bound up with every other, the pertinence or truth of an event-problem is expressed along with its entire set of obscure connections with all other truths, that is, of the problematic character for other bodies of other events.

Case of the aphorism   Consider the example of the aphorism. While, like all uses of language, it can be treated at the level of its relationship to what is demonstrably the case (is it true that . . .?) or rephrased in other terms, the deleterious consequences of such summary manoeuvres are quickly apparent. The power of aphorisms arises in part perhaps because of their closeness in form to the bare propositional form 'S is P'. This apparent proximity is paradoxical, however, since any attempt to determine the truth and falsity of an aphorism in this way immediately robs it of its particular sense. In turn, what makes a good aphorism is not its epistemological valence, but the implicated element of sense which provides the statement with a depth that allows it a fluidity determined by the situation (which includes the reader) in which it is read. If truth is differential, the aphorism is a form in which this differential function of truths is brought to the surface in language.

Fourth postulate: truth is   The final fallacy about truth concerns the
a-temporal   a-temporal character it adopts in accordance with
the dogmatic image of thought. Essentially, it holds that time is of no consequence to the determination of the truth or falsity of a proposition *per se*. In fact, the truth-time relationship is perhaps the site of the most extended engagement with truth in Deleuze's corpus, extending beyond the Proust-Nietzsche-*Difference and Repetition* complex into the two imposing *Cinema* volumes, where he writes that 'time has always put the notion of truth into crisis'.* However, Deleuze already makes his point in a variety of ways in the trinity of texts already cited, to begin with, in *Proust and Signs*.

Truth and time in Proust   The Proustian search is a search for truth, writes Deleuze, and 'if it is called a search for lost time, it

---

* Gilles Deleuze, *Cinema 2: The Time-Image*, trans. Hugh Tomlinson (London: Athlone, 1989), p. 130.

is only to the degree that truth has an essential relation to time'.* In
this context, Deleuze will insist upon the fact that each kind of sign
Proust's narrator confronts (worldly signs, signs of love, sensuous
signs, signs of art) is significant (has decisive import, is made sense of)
only according to a certain temporal relationship. The vapid chatter
of Madame de Guermantes takes on a different sense depending on
the temporal framework adopted by the narrator, as do the various
signs emitted by Charlus or Albertine, and the narrator's love for the
latter, his effort to interpret the signs she emits, is entirely transformed after the relationship is over (two temporal modalities organised around the same signs). The bewildering sign constituted by the
madeleine takes on a different sense depending on whether it is
encountered from within the experience of memory or from the point
of view of the time proper to art. In other words, the truth – the
sense, the decisiveness – of the sign for the narrator is indexed to his
shifting temporal framework. In a text that summarises the whole
trajectory of his account of Proust, Deleuze writes that:

> To each kind of sign there doubtless corresponds a privileged line
> of time. The worldly signs imply chiefly a time wasted; the signs of
> love envelop especially a time lost. The sensuous signs often afford
> us the means of regaining time, restore it to us at the heart of time
> lost. The signs of art, finally, give us a time regained, an original
> absolute time that includes all the others. But if each sign has its
> privileged temporal dimension, each also straddles the other lines
> and participates in the other dimensions of time. Time wasted
> extends into love and even into the sensuous signs. Time lost
> appears even in worldliness and also subsists in the signs of sensibil-
> ity. Time regained reacts in its turn upon time wasted and time lost
> ... Thus the signs do not develop, are not to be explained accord-
> ing to the lines of time without corresponding or symbolizing,
> without intersecting, without entering into complex combinations
> that constitute the system of truth.†

Truth and the empty form of time   In *Nietzsche and Philosophy*, as we have also
already noted, Deleuze insists upon the untimely
situation of philosophy with respect to its time as constitutive of the
contemporary situation. In the terms of the current discussion, this
point can be rephrased in the following way: the truth of events, and
ultimately of the *Eventum tantum*, is constantly being expressed in

* Deleuze, *Proust and Signs*, p. 11.
† Deleuze, *Proust and* Signs, p. 17.

the regime of bodies as the specific problematicity or decisiveness of problems for the bodies in question. Consequently, the ultimate goal of philosophy is to insist upon the irreducible openness of every present situation – with all of its greatness and stupidity, its own panoply of masks and fools – to a future where things will be different. That is – though Deleuze never puts it like this, doubtless because of the prevalence of the dogmatic image of truth – philosophy is entirely oriented by the category of Truth insofar as it marks the openness of the future (level of the event as such), or the constitution of new configurations of bodies in relation to a true, that is to say, *decisive* problem (local level of particular bodies). Here, precisely, truths are put into crisis by time, but in the name of Truth as such, qua the evental character of truths. The present is problematised by the truths of the future always knocking on the door. There is a compact (though not an identity) between truth and time in play here, in which philosophy has a supreme interest – and what else but philosophy, Deleuze would ask, has this interest? – in recalling and continually reformulating. We must note though that all of this relies upon the renovation in the concept of truth we have been sketching. It even looks as though what Deleuze calls truth here has more in common with a rupturing of the truths of the present, a falsification of these truths, in the name of truths now unknown and yet to be. Indeed.

This shattering of present identities and forms of *doxa* is intimately connected by Deleuze, as we have already seen, to the form of time itself, the empty form of time figured in the eternal return. What this guarantees, we read in *Difference and Repetition*, is the absolute necessity of contingency, the necessary incompletion of the present-past circle. This can equally be characterised as the falsifying of the truths of the present, the rendering ordinary of contemporary singularities, required in order that other, new singularities might take on the character of the remarkable, the decisive. Another name for the form of time, then, is the False, and the necessity of contingency is nothing but the great falsifying demand, the hard law of truths.

Dissolution of the paradox of contingent futures It is at this precise point – the point of the destructive-creative intersection between truth and time in the False – that the account in the second *Cinema* work takes up. The central passage in question concerns the famous ancient paradox of future contingents, canonical since Aristotle:

> If it is *true* that a naval battle *may* take place tomorrow, how are we
> to avoid one of the true following consequences: either the impos-
> sible proceeds from the possible (since, if the battle takes place, it
> is no longer possible that it may not take place), or the past is not
> necessarily true (since the battle could not have taken place).*

This paradoxical state of affairs only arises because of a conception
of truth and time that makes them extrinsic to one another (or, as
Deleuze says, it functions as a reminder to 'keep the true away from
the existent, in the eternal or in what imitates the eternal'[†]). As he
often does when confronted with problems that involve the notion of
probability in one form or another, Deleuze finds his own solution
by passing through a partial Leibnizian response. Leibniz – and with
him contemporary modal logic – will say that there is no paradox
here, since the worlds in which the naval battle do and do not take
place are equally possible but incompossible. This means both that
the past can remain true, and that possibility is rescued from a vertiginous relationship with impossibility. This response, though, is
not ultimately correct for Deleuze. On the one hand, it relies on the
unjustified postulation of an extrinsic harmony between compos-
sibles. On the other, the (inadequate) logical register of this kind of
response has been superseded by an artistic, specifically, *cinematic*
solution. Or rather, the cinema provides us with a means of recon-
ceiving paradoxes of truth and time in a positive, creative fashion,
and thereby show a way out of the apparent impasse engendered
by the Aristotelian framework of its formulation. The key idea is
this: the cinema can organise images in ways that have no correlate in human experience. While the latter is bound by the nature
of our bodies, habitual expectations and the subtractive nature of
perception, the former is not. More importantly, whereas the human
modality of relating to the world involves the necessary but illusory
organisation of time around the category of the present, the cinema
is free to directly present time as such.

The concept of truth, consequently, undergoes a peculiar shift. The
category of the present, and experience of time that takes the present
as its locus, grounds the dogmatic view of truth, as we have seen
above, and paradoxes such as those of contingent futures (along with
many of Zeno's) mark the confounding limits of the pact between the

---

* Deleuze, *Cinema* 2, p. 130.
† Deleuze, *Cinema* 2, p. 130.

dogmatic conceptions of time and truth. However, if the cinema can deploy time in a non-human, non-linear fashion, the dogmatic notion of truth is shattered. In this sense, the reality of cinematic time is a direct refutation of the views of time and truth that populate both common sense and contemporary scientific discourse.

Dogmatic image of cinema

Nonetheless, it is certainly the case, Deleuze notes, that the cinema often reinforces the neutrality of time with respect to the truth, by organising images in accordance with the extrinsic common criterion of the sequential character of time. Such cinematic acts also give rise to the sense that the narrative is primary to both the ensemble of images and the organisation of time; conversely, the narrative organisation of image and time is wed to a representational function of the cinema, which only copies or reproduces what lies outside of it. This is the form of cinema Deleuze will dub the cinema of 'truthful narration',[*] and the entire confused mess of debates around the problems of accuracy, fidelity of documentation, and honesty that plagues so-called realist films arises on its basis – we should instead say pseudo-problems, since they cannot be resolved on their own terms are only genuinely expressed in questions.

The power of the false in cinema, photography

To this cinema of false problems, Deleuze will oppose the cinema of falsity, or falsifying cinema:

> Narration ceases to be truthful, that is, to claim to be true, and becomes fundamentally falsifying. This is not at all a case of 'each has its own truth', a variability of content. It is a power of the false which replaces and supersedes the form of the true, because it poses the simultaneity of incompossible presents, or the coexistence of non-necessarily true pasts.[†]

Now, this is not simply to note the capacity of cinema to organise images in a way that exceeds human capacity by disorganising the temporal order of images. We are not speaking of any simple rearrangement of the order of images precisely, but instead of the capacity for the assembled images of cinema to give rise to a new ways of thinking, feeling and seeing. This capacity is instituted by the incorporation of images and ensembles of images (i.e., through images and their montage) that no longer conform to the habitual

[*] Deleuze, *Cinema 2*, p. 133.
[†] Deleuze, *Cinema 2*, p. 131.

organisation of time. In the above passage, Deleuze mentions two important forms of such an institution: films in which the present moment is repeated but not identically, and those in which past events are replayed with different outcomes. In such cases, the cinema gives rise to an indeterminacy with respect to the true and the false and the consequent inability to answer the question 'what really happened?' Both approaches can sometimes be found in play in the same film, as is the case in one of Deleuze's key points of reference, Resnais' *Last Year at Marienbad*.

Again, this absolute indeterminacy is not to be taken as a negative state, as simple deception, since its consequences are not (or, at least, not only) epistemological stupefaction but, in the viewer, the experience of encountering a genuine problem, a *true* problem, whose resolution requires real change. This falsifying power is thus aligned with a higher sense of truth than that provided by the 'true narrative' approach of the classic cinema. The cinema is falsifying not merely epistemologically (in the narrow sense), but as a result of its injection of time, the necessity of becoming ('the pure force of time'*), into truth, and as such making truth into an issue of novelty rather than accuracy. And, while the link to time is more complex, the same point holds for art as such on Deleuze's account. Consider the peculiar, vertiginous effects that hyperrealist photography can have, in, for example, the work of Hannah Starkey or Gregory Kreutzen. While one can engage such work in traditional representational questions (is it faked? what argument is it making about the real world?), the source of its power lies in the way in which it undermines this problematic in its entirety.

Also at issue here is a cinematic challenge to the dogmatic conception of temporality, based upon and traced off of habitual temporal relations, which constitute, in human experience, the arrow of time and provide the basis for recollection, representation and anticipation – and for the common sense view of truth as representational and propositional. It is only insofar as time is taken to be extrinsic to truth that we are able to maintain the static and universal propositional account. But when the representational conception of truth is made subordinate to the dynamic force of time, which necessarily gives rise to encounters with problems, truth shifts over to the side of

---

* Deleuze, *Cinema 2*, p. 130.

the problem itself. Truth becomes the mark of the creative openings before us and their decisive character for us. Creation, decision: here we enter too into the worlds of Badiou.

After restoration, whence revolution? 'This took place – which I can neither calculate nor demonstrate.'[*] Badiou often refers to the period between 1975 and 1988 – between the first of the seminars which would result in 1982's *Theory of the Subject* and the 1988 publication of *Being and Event* – as the end of the 'Red Years', a period of restoration, a period, ideologically speaking, analogous to that of the Thermidorean reaction of year 2 of the French Revolution, a period when the 'brigands triumph',[†] and when what takes the place of the thoughtful, subjective production of truths is the production of the unthinkable, of what must not be thought, to the point where thought itself becomes 'suspect'. In *Metapolitics*, Badiou compares the role of the *nouveaux philosophes* of the latter part of the twentieth century with that of several figures of the Thermidor, Boissy d'Anglais most prominently.

These *nouveaux philosophes* – despised for similar reasons by Lacan, Deleuze and Badiou – are 'the name for that which, whenever a truth procedure terminates, renders that procedure unthinkable'. Such configurations, generally reactive, obscurantist at the limit, linked to interests, commercial, national, pedagogical and so on, 'constitute the unthinkable of a time', Badiou asserts, which is to say, they actively produce a knowledge of that which *must not be known* as the knowledge of the time. 'This constitution of the unthinkable', which Badiou surveys, 'can have a long-lasting power. It provides the historical matrix for a destitution of thought.'[‡]

All our thinkers – whatever the terminology used or the orientation pursued – agree with Badiou's assessment regarding the power of this destitution in the time of our time. For Deleuze, what the reactionaries produce under cover of 'big concepts' and 'small thinkers' is a thought devoid of any articulated, differential or creative concepts, attuned as it is to what he calls the 'expressing subject'. It's

---

[*] Alain Badiou, *Theoretical Writings*, trans. Ray Brassier and Alberto Toscano (New York: Continuum, 2004), p. 112.
[†] Badiou, *Logics of Worlds*, p. 26.
[‡] Alain Badiou, *Metapolitics*, trans. Jason Barker (London and New York: Verso, 2005), p. 138.

a matter of *who speaks* all over again and not of what can be said on the basis of what can be thought. Deleuze aligns this subjective emptiness, tellingly, with current curriculum reforms and provides the truth of their cumulative, reactionary 'success': marketing.* Similarly, for Lacan, such non-thought masquerading as the knowledge of thought itself, is in its very masquerade what encourages and secures the return to 'the service of goods'. The production of non-thought is, in these terms, the idiocy of equating desire with the object of that desire, the *objet a* as its real *and* its satisfaction. For this species of non-thought, which has violently produced the knowledge of all today via its success in the media, the school, the parliament, the workplace, such that to not repeat it is to be targeted for one of the various types of intervention on offer – pedagogical, legal, pastoral (the fascism of 'human resources'!) or military; collectively known as 'humanitarian' – there is no contradiction between the equation of desire with its object, thus the object with the thing 'desired', and the fact that once-requited desire never fails to not abate. For this species of non-thought, it is right and proper that desire simply shifts to another object because there is no 'thing' at all, no possible thought of what does not always already fall under the remit, the criteria of the knowledge of desire. This consumerist knowledge – one would like to say *consumptive* – was already that which ego-psychology insisted on via its 'big concept', *adaptation*. For Lacan, this was at the heart of the secure return of the thought of desire to the 'service of goods' or the 'Good Housekeeping way of life'. In short, the good is the satisfaction of an individual desire in a specific existing object. Any desire aiming at continuing – at that which cannot be seen to exist, at some truth of desire, is simply terroristic – an affront to the free reign of opinion, individuality and the consumption of knowledge itself.

---

* Gilles Deleuze, 'On the New Philosophers', in *Two Regimes of Madness*, ed. David Lapoujade, trans. Ames Hodges and Mike Taormina (New York: Semiotext(e), 2007), pp. 139–47. See also the well-known passages in Gilles Deleuze and Félix Guattari, *What is Philosophy?*, trans. Hugh Tomlinson and Graham Burchell (New York: Columbia University Press, 1994), pp. 10–12. Deleuze argues that the influence of the *nouveaux philosophes* has to do not primarily with the books they produce but with their public profile: the magazines, the articles, the TV shows, the appearances, and second with the 'versioning' of their work so there is a version for every cultural clique. There is no doubt that what still calls itself Academia has swallowed the strategy of the NP hook, line and sinker and called it engagement or service or a career, and so it's safe to say 'we are all NP now' – just as there once was only sophistry. 'What a goon squad' (Deleuze, 'On the New Philosophers', p. 142). Except that . . .

Reaction as democratic
materialism

This destitution, which Badiou names in *Logics of Worlds* 'democratic materialism', the handmaiden or 'body and language' of capital itself, has only increased in its intensity since the end of the Red Years. Nothing now escapes this knowing procedure of destitution whose genius is akin to that of Nietzsche's priest or Rancière's pedagogue who poisons as he kisses and then demands you take him on as cure too. In the world of bodies and languages there is only circulation, the repetition in one of another as the condition of recognition, of inclusion, of existence. When one returns to knowledge that which is given it to know, a new servile master is counted into history. Servile to the logic of circulation, individual master of the production of this by no means passive, by no means changeless, form of repetition – desire by desire, object by object. By this, as Deleuze notes, 'the revolution must be declared impossible' – *everywhere and for all time.* Obviously, most importantly, this 'must not be' is carried out at the level of common and indeed global knowledge.

At the same time a new anxiety, which we can call 'that which fails to know the all of this knowledge', sets to work or continues to insist. Anxiety – certainly the insistence of desire as such, which is to say, a desire *not* contained by the knowledge of desire but that insists despite that knowledge or the lack of it – is that which, Lacan says, 'does not deceive'. Anxiety is not itself true, but is a matter of truth as 'what makes doubt possible'.[†] This *insistence* manifest in diverse registers – as Deleuze also points out in music, science, painting, geography, etc. – offers itself to courage, Badiou contends in *Theory of the Subject*. Courage, intervening or supervening on the place which anxiety manifests as existing despite knowledge, will be the condition of the production of some impossible, new truth of such a world. A division thus remains registerable or we in a situation despite and ultimately because of the demand of the One (coincidence of desire and object, knowledge and subject, and the suture to finitude) – of bodies and languages and the excess they cannot fail to induce. In the history of western thought at least, this division has marked the site over and again of the disjunctive articulation of the emergence of truths and the procedures of restoration, which some

* Deleuze, 'On the New Philosophers', p. 144.
† Jacques Lacan, *Seminar X: Anxiety*, trans. Cormac Gallagher (London: Karnac, 2002), p. 51.

event will have registered anew. It can be traced all the way back to the dialogues of Plato, where a generalised sophistry – rather than any individual sophist – is the work of producing non-thought as the knowledge of the Athenian situation. For the Lacan Plato anticipates (or Socrates as analyst) sophistry is university discourse: the destitution of thought for the sake of the master who guards and who markets as 'knowledge' the knowledge of the impossibility of 'knowledge in truth'.* But as we know, the anxiety of this master-knowledge runs about Athens nevertheless interrogating every good Athenian gentleman educator as to the truth of his knowledge.[†]

The philosophical reconfiguration of truth   Badiou's conception of truths draws heavily on Lacan's de-absolutisation and subsequent dismantling of the conceits of philosophical knowledge. This procedure is carried out by way of an orientation to the unconscious of Freud: the mark of the internal and irreparable division of a subject ever incomplete, ever irreducible to itself. Badiou attributes to Lacan – who 'on the whole', he says, 'refused any compromise about the immanence of truth'[‡]– the 'forcing of [philosophy's] impasse': that 'although reducible to the depthless subset of the situation, a truth of the situation is nonetheless heterogeneous to all those subsets registered by forms of knowledge'.[§] Thus despite *and* because of Lacan's dismantling of philosophical conceit – or, at least, his disorientation of its 'concept' – truth is itself *philosophically* reconfigured by Badiou. With regard to Lacan's thesis on truth as love of castration, as a 'weakness whose veil [psychoanalysis has] lifted', Badiou reformulates matters: 'truth is bearable for thought, which is to say philosophically lovable, only insofar as one attempts to grasp it in its

---

* Badiou, *Theoretical Writings*, p. 128.

[†] In both the *Apology* and the *Meno* every Athenian citizen is counted as an educator. Socrates, we are told by these same *bon homme*, is the only one who is not (e.g., Men. 93e; Ap.25a), and, moreover, and this is the logic of the destitution of thought, if there is a citizen who unlike every citizen is not an educator then *he must not be*. Hence, the execution. Cf. A. J. Bartlett, *Badiou and Plato: An Education by Truths* (Edinburgh: Edinburgh University Press, 2011).

[‡] Badiou returns to this qualification, noting both the rather tortuous dialectic Lacan engages regarding the infinite and the finite and his oscillations around the status of Cantor's infinite. Badiou quotes Lacan from *Seminar XIX*, saying transfinite cardinals represent 'an object I would have to call mythic'. As Badiou retorts, one cannot get 'very far in drawing the consequences of the infinity of the true without insisting that non-denumerable cardinals are real'. *Theoretical Writings*, p. 126.

[§] Badiou, *Theoretical Writings*, p. 124.

subtractive dimension, as opposed to seeking its plenitude or complete saying'.[*]

The locus of its powerless power is its capacity for 'working through' or forcing: 'the point at which a truth, although incomplete, authorises anticipations of knowledge concerning not what is but *what will have been if truth attains completion*'.[†] In other words, being devoid of predication in knowledge, a truth cannot be said. It therefore has no veracity, no power in the world as such. But relative to an event and to the world for which an event is an event, it is possible, on the basis of that which the event exposes to be there for that world, to pursue its consequences from the perspective of the truth that such an exposure anticipates to have been so. 'A truth operates through the retroaction of an almost nothing' – exposed by an event – 'and the anticipation of an almost everything'.[‡] The motif of the *future anterior* and thus the infinity of the true mark Badiou's conception of truth across his oeuvre, even though it is only given a formal, non-analogical, consistency in *Being and Event*. Let's note in passing that for Deleuze in *The Logic of Sense*, castration – marking the orientation of what causes it to its own result – is thus the collapse of thought into impotence and the inscription of the metamorphosis it marks in the new 'metaphysical surface the beginning of which it brings about'. In short, then, castration effects a new 'divergent series' of evental repetition or *planar* re-inscription in which new attributes meet new expressions – 'eternal truths' – effected with sense.[§]

The dis-continuous beyond Already in *Theory of the Subject*, under the tutelage of a Lacanian advance that must be taken advantage of, and marking an avowed distance from the Deleuze of *Anti-Oedipus*,[¶] we can see Badiou attempting to find the means to

[*] Badiou, *Theoretical Writings*, p. 120.
[†] Badiou, *Theoretical Writings*, p. 127.
[‡] Badiou, *Theoretical Writings*, p. 127.
[§] Deleuze, *The Logic of Sense*, pp. 222. To this Badiou replies: 'If sense effectively possesses an eternal truth, God exists, since he was never anything other than the truth of sense. Deleuze's idea of the event should have persuaded him to follow Spinoza—who he elects as "the Christ of philosophy"—right to the end, and to name the unique Event in which becomings are diffracted as "God"', *Logics of Worlds*, pp. 386–7.
[¶] Badiou, *Theory of the Subject*, p. 115. In the 1970s, Badiou authors two scathing reviews of Deleuze and Guattari: 'The Flux of the Party: In the Shadow of Anti-Oedipus' and 'The Fascism of the Potato' (surely the greatest review title ever!). These are collected in Badiou's *The Adventure of French Philosophy*, trans. B. Bosteels (London and New York: Verso, 2012).

articulate a theory of thinking continuity *and* discontinuity (structure and subject in other words) beyond its empiricist closure.* That is, how a procedure in the real, operating in one situation, can be thought as operative in another and without either conflation under an abiding power – historical, genealogical or poetic – or as synthesis. With the benefit of a hindsight whose partiality we must admit, Badiou is here beginning to set out his most abiding line of conceptual enquiry: how can a truth procedure, specific to a particular situation (and thus not beholden to time), related to a site-specific event and convoking as its material support a finite (though not temporally constrained) subject – and so at the limit 'discontinuous' – be at the same time thought in situations entirely removed, temporally, historically and thus eventually, and so be 'continuous' with these prior 'truths'?

It becomes the very question of truth itself that it is not just 'for all', situationally speaking, but eternal or *invariant* as well, and so truths, manifest situationally, participate in their Idea – 'the intelligible has its *locus* in the sensible'† and, perhaps, the immanent has its consequence the trans-mundane. As Badiou insists, 'If an eternal truth can be appropriated by any world, including a world totally different from the one in which it was instituted, you have necessarily to think simultaneously something that is invariant and something that constitutes a break.'‡ What follows grasps Badiou's conditioning by Lacan, his vacillation with respect to Deleuze – and his absolute distinction from both.

The truth/knowledge couple   In *Theory of the Subject*, this problem of rendering truths outside knowledge, and thus as the thought of *'real* change',§ is central to Badiou's efforts to re-found the subject

* See, for example, 'Foucault: Continuity and Discontinuity', in Badiou, *The Adventure*, pp. 83–100.
† Alain Badiou, *The Concept of Model: An Introduction to the Materialist Epistemology of Mathematics*, ed. and trans. Zachary Luke Frazer and Tzuchien Tho (Melbourne: re.press, 2007), p. 92.
‡ Alain Badiou and Lauren Sedofsky, 'Matters of Appearance', *Artforum*, Vol. 25, No. 3 (2006), p. 249.
§ It is possible to begin even with *The Concept of Model* or even the shorter texts prior to it – 'Mark and Lack' or 'Infinitesimal Subversion' – as these are also structurally set out on the basis of subverting or subtracting from a dominant or predominating epistemological or empirical claim (number, logic, model) a more abstract and yet more universal determination of what is already claimed to be true knowledge. These two essays can now be found in *Concept and Form: Key Texts* from the *Cahiers pour L'Analyse*, Vol. 1, edited by Peter Hallward and Knox Peden (London: Verso, 2012), pp. 159–86 and pp. 187–208 respec-

as a category of thought. In *Being and Event*, as already noted, and taking as his denouement the limit of the nexus Descartes/Lacan, Badiou remarks 'that everything is at stake in the thought of the truth/knowledge couple'. What this amounts to, he continues,

> is thinking the relation – which is rather a non-relation – between, on the one hand, a post-evental fidelity, and on the other hand, a fixed state of knowledge, or . . . the encyclopedia of the situation. The key to the problem is the mode in which the procedure of fidelity traverses existent knowledge, starting at the supernumerary point which is the name of the event.[*]

This *diagonal* discourse – polemical on two fronts – localised in a situation despite known knowledge, holds for *Theory of the Subject* retrospectively, as for *Logics of Worlds* in anticipation: the process of truth is a 'material process' insofar as its 'subject is the body seized in its creative capacity, deploying itself in material axioms and geneses in a world. The subject is the oriented, creative name of a new body, which suddenly appears in the world around the trace of the event.'[†] Within Badiou's own development the category of truth remains *invariant*.

In one sense, *Theory of the Subject* is Badiou's own politico-philosophical 'What Is To Be Done?': a philosophical attempt to think its own time, drawing for its formal structure on productive and cumulative critiques of Hegel, Lacan, Mallarmé, Aeschylus, Sophocles, etc. That is, we pass by the philosopher, psychoanalyst, poet, tragedian, loosely organised by a somewhat still analogical use of mathematics, algebra, set and topos theory. The whole is oriented subjectively and thus politically by what was once called, beautifully we might add, 'Mao Zedong thought' – specifically, that 'one divides into two'. But it is also a work replete with conceptual and strategic inventions, which appear less as concepts in their own right and more as experiments consecrated to ridding thought of an imposture externally imposed on it and an impasse internally realised by the immanent exhaustion of a certain trajectory. Badiou is here beginning to *indiscern* in the knowledge of the time the new concepts and categories of a form of thought both timely and under condition but

tively. From this early period until today, what Badiou forges is not a true knowledge (or true opinion in Plato's terms) but 'knowledge in truth'.
[*] Badiou, *Being and Event*, p. 327.
[†] Badiou and Sedofsky, 'Matters of Appearance', p. 251.

also, as truly new, being without knowledge and yet touching on its own Idea.

Although Badiou had not yet found the materialism of the Idea, the commitment to some truth, to some point by which to hold fast, already sets this work against the flow in its anticipation of what it fails to enact.

Torsion is the key   The key 'adapted' notion is torsion.* Badiou notes that

> the term 'torsion' designates the subject point from which the other three classic determinations of truth come to be coordinated: totality, coherence, and repetition. This then reminds me that, besides its topological use (as in the torsion of a knot, following Lacan's lead), the word 'torsion' is also used in algebra in a very simple way.[†]

Without going into all the hoary details provided in the Torsion seminar – which in themselves are taut summaries of the algebraic constitution of torsion in its various configurations: elements, groups, modules, free, finite, infinite, etc. – at its most basic what torsion provides is a formalisation of the interruption of repetition and/or the forging of a divergence.

Torsion is the point at which or by which 'the cumulative is inverted into a loss'.[‡] Badiou notes that he has not attempted to mathematise anything but to 'search in existing mathematics for those places that hold in reserve the means to take a step beyond'.[§] In other words, that the impasse of a dialectical construction requires, 'unorthodoxly', that 'an unexplored mathematical lead must force the divergence' thought (or praxis) requires.[¶]

> Here we see the crossover, in a raging vacillation, between the lifeless straightness of what is missing and the vital risk of interruption. Here the subject awakens to the decision, which is purely its mode of existence. To decide always amounts to disjoin, in the determi-

---

* 'I imprudently expose myself, first to the mathematician's condemnation if I borrow metaphorically from his vocabulary and, then, to the philosopher's objection, if I give up on the idea of making the borrowed words shine in the light of pure science', *Theory of the Subject*, p. 209.
† Badiou, *Theory of the Subject*, p. 149.
‡ Badiou, Theory of the Subject, p. 171.
§ Badiou, Theory of the Subject, p. 171. These means being, *pace* Lacan, the *place* of the subject effect.
¶ Badiou, *Theory of the Subject*, p. 154.

nant unity of the serial lack, the point of destruction. This is why it is extremely rare.[*]

Torsion – given that essentially it marks what divides itself from the logic of its place(ment) – can be said to be constitutive of the subject or what the subject as such, in its 'perversity', brings to bear. That's to say, torsion is that by which force *takes* place. Force 'taking place' is what Badiou calls process and process names precisely the priority, rarely 'taking place', of force over place. These are the two critical terms/concepts of *Theory of the Subject* – force and place – subtending the articulation of several others (anxiety, superego, courage, etc.), in a work in which every concept is divided in two and sometimes divided in two again. As he says at one point 'the real that is ours depends only on this: there are two sexes; there are two classes. Busy yourselves with this, you subjects of all experience.'[†] Indeed the two that is not one, and which is so in the affirmative exclusion of any middle or (ontological) relation, is a constant in all his work. This is to say, in Badiou, the non-rapport is *thought*. Any supposed corrective needs first to deal with this.

From two not one   The question is (and remains) for Badiou 'can the subject [as the support of a truth] displace the state' from the perspective of the Two and not the One: 'What is the issue all about? It is about the topological status of truth which, as is the case in mathematics, involves the very difficult apparatus for passing from the global study to the local study.' As such, 'Truth is a function, a variety, a surface, a space. This is what is so immensely burdensome for philosophy, which would gladly want it to be nothing but a commercial code.'[‡] In the algebraic topology of *Theory of the Subject* the site of this displacement is the place of a *scission* and/or an effect of *torsion*. A *torsion* is a forced effect of the immanent disjunction between what Badiou calls the *esplace* – the space of placements – and the *horlieu* – *the outside-place*.[§] The *esplace* is the work of structure, its attempt to place within its determinate space the *horlieu*. The *horlieu* as element of this situation, of its 'proper

[*] Badiou, *Theory of the Subject*, p. 172.
[†] Badiou, *Theory of the Subject*, p. 115.
[‡] Badiou, *Theory of the Subject*, p. 120.
[§] In his *Live Theory*, Feltham translates this as 'offsite' (Oliver Felthham, *Badiou: Live Theory* [London: Continuum, 2008]). This is suggestive, insofar as it points to the later notion of site and the multiples which make it up being those that the 'state' cannot know or mark, etc., and which, then, the event mobilises as its own.

interiority', maintains, Badiou demonstrates, an integral *force*, and so the placement of these elements by the *esplace* meets not so much an opposition as its immanent lack. In this very movement of placing, the elements reveal themselves, so to speak, as 'out-placed'. The structure can never finally place these elements 'where' it determines because as elements already there, so to speak, any placement by structure produces a literally *void* 'site' of *torsion*. There is an integral disjunction between structure and element and this serves as the reservoir of force of the *horlieu* – the outplace/offsite *is a force*. *Torsion* occurs, then, when the placed element forces, so to speak, its place *as* outplace. A truth is the process of force bearing the void excess of the 'space of placements' or the *esplace* of structure.

Force, Badiou notes, denotes the 'topological side' whereas place is algebraic.[*] It is not mere opposition to the state's placement but a forceful, and thus subjective, affirmation of that (out)place as *its* place and not that of the *esplace*. This situation becomes 'historical', which is to say 'periodically heterogeneous', when the subjective force of the outplace (*horlieu*) insists on or makes manifest or 'incorporeal' the non-determination, the *scission*, of structure or *esplace*. Badiou says, 'it is a process of *torsion*, by which a force reapplies itself to that from which it conflictingly emerges'.[†] And further, 'everything that belongs to a place returns to that part of itself which is determined by it in order to displace the place, to determine the determination, to cross the limit'.[‡]

Objectively speaking, *torsion* has for its site an ambivalent 'element'. One that is determinately there, as placed *offsite*, certainly, but which, as offsite, escapes its determination. In effect it already constitutes the immanence of the rupture with the 'space of placements', and the determination of the determination, which, properly subjectivised, might displace the place of structure entirely – including its own placed place. Movement over place (arrows over objects) is the critical disjunction; in effect, this dialectic of place and order supplements the notion of class struggle. The ontological question concerns the cause of movement. In this work, Badiou, to a point, adopts an atomist conception of the moving of movement, one supplemented

---

[*] Badiou, *Theory of the Subject*, p. 10
[†] Badiou, *Theory of the Subject*, p. 11; translation modified.
[‡] Badiou, *Theory of the Subject*, p. 12; translation modified.

in its elaboration and subtlety by some very modern topos theory. Anyway, the subject is the figure who gives a minimum of consistency to this 'vanishing cause'.

The vanishing cause is here, politically speaking, the movement of the masses. The masses, as the only anti-state force, don't so much make history as make a history possible. They erupt *in* history and this eruption is divisive and destructive – formally of the *esplace*, politically of the state. The masses are in destructive excess over the state and, *pace* Marx, correlated to this excess they are the only principle of political consistency. But, Badiou remarks: 'from this we should not draw the conclusion that the theory of the subject is re-centred (on excess). There is no centre in the subjective twist. Without the anchorage of lack, the excess would be nothing but a leftist chimera, quickly reversed into its opposite, a philosophy of nature as we see in Deleuze.'* We should note that this philosophical attack against what he sees as Deleuze's vitalism remains a constant across the oeuvre and returns, after the *détente* of *Deleuze: The Clamor of Being*, with new vigour in the theory of appearing, but here it refers us back to the only other mention of Deleuze in this book, where, more in line with the political thrust of his reviews of *Anti-Oedipus* and 'Nomadology', Badiou situates Deleuze's 'leftism' as 'a radicalism of novelty', and one of two 'materialisms that treat idealinguistry by way of a drift' – as the 'combinatory of signs'. 'Materialism', the non-heretical sort, he concludes, 'is always in the position of having to resist the temptations that found it: neither atomic deciphering [Lévi-Strauss] nor liberation of the flux.'† Let's note also that while Badiou loses destruction or displaces its centrality in *Being and*

---

* Badiou, *Theory of the Subject*, p. 287.
† Badiou, *Theory of the Subject*, p. 207. See also this from 2005: 'The relation of identity between appearance and logic is supported principally by the conviction that appearance "consists". The thesis opposes the idea that the essence of the real is chaos. If the essence of the real, the effective appearance of being, were chaos, then being would not appear. It would be coextensive with its inconsistency; its appearance would itself be this inconsistency. Consequently, what I've undertaken to show is that there really is something that permits us to think being as such in its non-chaotic inconsistency, which is the pure multiplicities of mathematics. And then there is appearance, which isn't going to enter into the disorder of inconsistency but will instead be a figure of the order of intensities, what I call the "transcendental order". You're right to say that the philosophical construction is that which attributes a logic to appearance, because if you don't support that, you support the complete reduction of appearance to being in the figure of chaos. Fundamentally, my position comes down to the non-admission of chaos as the ultimate referential figure of the universe', 'Matter of Appearing', p. 250. See Deleuze, *The Logic of Sense*, pp. 253–66: It is no accident that here chaos as eternal return (or being as effect) is central in the 'most innocent of all destructions, the destruction of Platonism' (p. 266).

Event, he keeps division, and this in turn will be the basis for the return of destruction in *appearance*.*

The point is that movement escapes place but, as this is still a dialectical theory of the subject, the movement of movement can only be at the expense of place – the consolidation of one is the loss of the other. The subject, itself a composition of subjectivation and process, names a re-composition of force and place under the condition of the movement of the masses whose effect is to destroy its objective basis. The relation of subject (force) to object (place) is in essence a dialectic of destruction.

Torsion *redivivus*   In *Logics of Worlds*, this relation returns again, but again entirely renovated. Its return and its renovation are only possible, though, because of what Badiou, in fully philosophical mode, makes of torsion, place and force under the condition of set theory. In effect, Badiou comes to think that his subject of torsion is still too oriented by the state or the *splace* or, more generally, by a teleological concept of progress (albeit immanent) shackled to the One of History, whereby the subjective power of movement was subject to the objective determinations of an ever-becoming History. For Badiou, this is still too problematic – it means that in some fashion or other the subject draws something of its make up from the state and as effect can only be less than true in what it brings to bear. That is, the state's destruction is part of the subject's very constitution. In short, its genericity or generic-ness or what in *Theory of the Subject* was called its 'confidence in confidence' – its fidelity (to an event) – is compromised. Badiou needed to find a way to break with all this and yet to maintain the concept form of subjectivity as *being in truth*. Constituted on a rupture in-excess the subject of *Being and Event* is certainly subject to torsion insofar as it a-voids the state, but subject both to more formal conditions, and thus as applicable to several discursive registers or conditions, and to the event which founds it, it is a properly generic subject by whose traversal of a situation a truth of that situation is brought to bear in

---

* Badiou is clearly asserting his Platonic thesis regarding being appearing against Deleuze and in *Logics of Worlds* itself to the point of reversing the sense of the event and appropriating its (Deleuze's) concepts – bodies, organs, serialism, etc. But a note of concord: what Deleuze rescues from Plato against petit-platonism (and so anti-Platonists) is division: what Badiou insists on consistent with Deleuze is division, the basis of his Platonism of the multiple.

spite of knowledge and regardless of it, but which nevertheless returns as knowledge *in truth*.

To the invariant!   In 1976's *Of Ideology*, Badiou and François Balmès introduced the notion of the 'communist invariant' to characterise the 'basic features of a communist programme', visible in every historical resistance of 'slaves, peasants or proletarians'.* The invariant 'synthesises the universal aspiration of the exploited to have done with the principles of exploitation and oppression'.† In *Logics of Worlds*, the formally invariant, as mentioned above, goes by the name Idea. This Idea is thinkable as Idea in a world insofar as the invariant 'basic features of resistance' manifest themselves therein. This manifestation, whose work is that of the 'faithful subject', realises for thought the Idea of these basic features of resistance as they pertain to the truths of politics (in this case) vis-à-vis its immanent localisations, its collective address, its subject formations and so on. The Idea, Badiou says, 'is the mediation between the individual and the subject of a truth'.‡ This mediation Plato named 'participation'. Which is to say, through the Idea, which is in turn to say, through that which is invariant in the thought of politics, love, science and art, the individual becomes subject to the truths that mark for it its entire orientation to the world in which it finds itself. Its orientation to its world is both particular, given the world, *and* trans-mundane, given the invariance of the Idea in which it participates. This is a formal invariance insofar as it can be thought; it is not a set of sovereign conventions pertaining to content, behaviour or disposition for all time and all situations. At the same time, it is irreducible to the metaphysics of pity, or animal-humanism, characteristic of worlds such as ours today, determined secure from recourse to the Idea and the inhumanity any such ideation is supposed to engender.§

Since the victory of the sophists against Socrates, the Idea, which cannot not continue to 'accompany' this victory as its void – as the *Phaedo* cunningly insisted – has been that which must be 'educated out' in the name of our humanity. To put this another way, as Foucault shows, the nexus of knowledge and power operates on the

* Alain Badiou and François Balmes, *De l'ideologie* (Paris: Maspero, 1976), p. 66.
† Badiou and Balmes, *De l'ideologie* , p. 67.
‡ Alain Badiou, *Second Manifesto for Philosophy*, trans. L. Burchill (New York: Polity Press, 2011), p. 105.
§ Alain Badiou, *The Century*, trans. A. Toscano (New York: Polity Press, 2007), p. 177.

basis of the impossibility of there being agreement over images. The irony is that the Idea is what is real while man is image alone.*

The Idea marks the always of truths, guaranteed by nothing at all, and not of time:

> given that [the Idea] only exists in its power to bring forth the object 'in truth' and, hence, to uphold that there is something universal, it is not itself presentable because it is the presentation-to-the-true. In a word: there is no Idea of the Idea. This absence, moreover, can be named 'Truth'. Exposing the thing in truth, the Idea is true and is, therefore, always the idea of the True, but the True is not an idea.†

This constitutes the 'materialism of the Idea', whose manifest feature is a conditioned truth: singular in its site, evental in exposition, universal or 'worldly' in its trajectory, formally invariant. Thus in politics what is the truth of a political sequence is the production of the destruction of exploitation – every time. The existence of exploitation, seemingly itself invariant, politically speaking, is, however, merely what Badiou calls a modification: a simple structural variability in transcendental degrees, thus calculated, inclusive of the all, systematically and so transcendentally – a matter of the 'logic of a world', which is, as a matter of its construction, always *this* set of relations *as reaction to* this invariance of the Idea. For this reason, the logic of a world is *reversible*.

Without question this idea of truth, or more subjectively this *ideation*,‡ animates all Badiou's work.§ For Badiou, invariance¶ –

---

* See also: 'I think that, ever since Plato, philosophy has been faced with the inhuman, and that it is there that its vocation lies. Each time that philosophy confines itself to humanity as it has been historically constituted and defined; it diminishes itself, and in the end suppresses itself. It suppresses itself because its only use becomes that of conserving, spreading and consolidating the established model of humanity.' Alain Badiou and Slavoj Žižek, *Philosophy in the Present*, ed. Peter Engelmann, trans. Peter Thomas and Alberto Toscano (London: Polity, 2009), p. 75. See also Frank Ruda, *Hegel's Rabble* (London and New York: Continuum, 2011), pp. 178–9. In this section of his 'Coda' Ruda relates his discussion of Marx and truth to this same question of the human Badiou invokes in *The Century* vis-à-vis Sartre and Foucault. Ruda suggests Marx's conception of the (non)human in his early humanism is in accord with Badiou's 'formalised in-humanism' (p. 178). We would concur with this.
† Badiou, *Second Manifesto*, p. 107.
‡ See *Second Manifesto*, Chapter 8.
§ As we write he is giving his annual series of lectures on the progress of his work. The lectures, titled the Immanence of Truths, are being delivered this time at the very fitting venue of the *salle Dussane* at the ENS. These lectures are the basis for his new big book of the same name should he 'have the courage to write it'. (Indeed it is being written as we write.)
¶ 'In other words, you can take up the position to which the Greek mathematical text

the existence of which is not a fact, the effect of which is literally incalculable – effects the displacement of a temporalising or nominalising schematics, such that either, as with Ecclesiastes, nothing is ever new (no matter how different), or alternately, nothing is ever the same. At the same time, it does not accord with the wishy-washy hermeneutics of compare and contrast. In sum, all efforts to have done with the idea of the true, with truths as process in the real, merely refer back to a totality of reference no less determinist, no less totalitarian in its logic and control because it assumes the ethos of a free-range humanity, conscious of itself as the species that chooses. The remarks above affirm truths as existent in and for worlds, as exceptions to its rule *and* as that which a subject produces in, for and of a situation – point by point, or enquiry by enquiry. Given the place truth has (and doesn't have) in the history of thought, we need to note what it's not for Badiou, which entails something of its relation to philosophy.

That which is not   In the first instance, truth with a small t is distinct from Truth with a capital T. This is the relation effectively of truth procedures to their composition in a discourse, which takes account of their form and their effect, and which is itself this act of composition. As we said, philosophy does not produce truths nor does it determine what Truth is; it does not judge instances, objects or subjects as adequate to an *a priori* self-grounded concept of Truth. Truth is not founded on knowledge nor is it reducible to one or other of the sciences, mathematics included; it is not a relation to some object or other – at least in the conventional, that is to say Kantian, sense of object. It is not founded in a subject as knowledge of itself, as consciousness, as self-determined agency or as what corresponds to its essence, substance, senses, experiences, ego or its desire. Truth does not mark an ineffable presence, a whole, or a one from which what is emanates or fulgurates. There is no Truth of being though there is a being true. While it is distinct from knowledge, neither is it the unknown and unknowable horizon of all thought. There is not 'my truth' and 'your truth': it is not immanent to or trans-

constrains you without needing to modify the general subjective system of the places-of-constraint. Likewise, you can love a tragedy by Aeschylus because you incorporate yourself into the tragedies of Claudel; or evaluate the political import of the Chinese text from 81 BC, *Discourses on Salt and Iron*, without ceasing to be a revolutionary of the seventies of the twentieth century; or, as a contemporary lover, share the agonies of Dido forsaken by Aeneas', *Logics of Worlds*, p. 14.

cendent of languages, nor is it the majesty of what a body can do. It is not language nor an effect of it. Its not an *affect*, even if it is an *effect* registered by a body. Truth does not equal being; equally, truth does not equal event – even when it's written together in capitals.

In short, really, Badiou's conception of truth breaks with pretty much every empiricist, epistemological, positivist, linguistery, transcendental, metaphysical and even, finally, dialectical tradition[*]: except that he affirms *that* there are truths. As such, he also breaks with the obsession with having done with it: an obsession that mistakes its object, essentially assigning truth to preservation and authority and thus to a conservatism with regard to Being over and against the enhancement, artistic or poetic at that, of Becoming. A truth runs diagonal to all this; 'it reveals a "one-more" (or a remainder) of a procedure which is supposed exhaustive, thus ruining the latter's pretension'.[†] One cannot read denial into Badiou's conception of truth: there is only its rarity on the one side and its affirmation on the other. By contrast, he notes in *Logics of Worlds* that Deleuze – like all vitalists – is incapable of maintaining this discontinuity between 'sense, the transcendental law of appearing, and truths as exceptions'. Deleuze, he says, 'posits the One as ontological condition (chaos, the One-All, Life)[‡] and as evental result' and thus as an effect registered by a body as its actions and passions. Thereby the event is revealed as the immanent unity of the One and the body of

---

[*] Badiou summarises these under the title anti-Platonism. See, 'Pour aujourd'hui: Platon!' Seminars given at the Collège de France over three years 2007–8, 2008–9 and 2009–10, and those on the *Republic* given in 1989–90 (just after the publication of *Manifeste pour la philosophie*) are reproduced in full at http://www.entretemps.asso.fr/Badiou/07-08.htm. The notes which reproduce the seminars are by Daniel Fischer. The publication of the twenty years of these seminars is forthcoming by Fayard. See also *Manifesto for Philosophy*, trans. N. Madarasz (Albany: SUNY, 1999), *Infinite Thought*, trans. Justin Clemens and Oliver Feltham (London and New York: Continuum, 2003), pp. 45–6, and *Deleuze: The Clamor of Being*, pp. 101–2, where Badiou 'praises' Deleuze as 'the most generous' anti-Platonist, 'the most open to contemporary creations' and concludes: 'All that Deleuze lacked was to finish with anti-Platonism itself'; and 'Plato, our Dear Plato!', trans. A. Toscano, *Angelaki*, Vol. II, No. 3, December, 2006, 39–41.

[†] Badiou, *Being and Event*, p. 274.

[‡] Cf. Deleuze, *Difference and Repetition*, pp. 123–4: 'but absolutely divergent in the sense that the point or horizon of convergence lies in a chaos or is constantly displaced within that chaos. This chaos is itself the most positive, just as the divergence is the object of affirmation. It is indistinguishable from the great work which contains all the *complicated* series, which affirms and complicates all the series at once ... The trinity complication-explication-implication accounts for the totality of the system – in other words, the chaos which contains all, the divergent series which lead out and back in, and the differenciator which relates them one to another.' And 'Ontology is the dice throw, the chaosmos from which the cosmos emerges' (p. 199).

its effect, or in other words the event is what reconciles life to sense. 'He even seems to equate the two terms sense and truth', Badiou says, concluding that, as he 'once wrote to me', 'he "had no need" for the category of truth'.*

It is therefore possible to say, returning to Lacan's terminology but at one conceptual remove, that in all the above, including in the mania of their denial, truths are 'half said'. This is part of Lacan's brilliantly unconvincing anti-philosophical tirade against philosophy, whose truth lies in the notion that philosophical discourse itself is responsible for the impotence of truths, which are themselves 'potent' outside of knowledge.† That is to say, philosophy, in handling the object of its own love (or desire) displays this power as castration. Indeed, this is how philosophy displays its own power, sovereign over all discourse, as that which alone can handle the truth. In philosophy, truth advances masked. Far from wanting to or claiming to expose the full power of truths, indeed denying such a dialectic anyway, Lacan argues instead that it is this act of turning truths into knowledge, *its* knowledge, that is the key fantasy of philosophy. It is philosophy's very claims to know (the all of truth) that expose its lack of truth for Lacan, given that the knowledge of all – hence the conflation of truth and being – is already the expression of an inconsistency (given that there is the unconscious, this claim to know is excessive). In short, this knowing all in excess of knowledge is itself the symptom of its incapacity to know truth – a truth of itself that it cannot know. Hence, as Badiou phrases it, this means that for Lacan the love of truth is purely and simply the love of castration.‡ Which, lets note in passing, certainly does not equate 'truth' with the '*power* of the false'.§ Lacan's vacillation over the figure of 'Platocrates'¶ – analyst one day, know-all the next** – illustrates this unknowing, this veiling

---

* Badiou, *Logics of Worlds*, pp. 385–6. In his *Deleuze: The Clamor of Being*, Badiou, reading this lack of category *into* other of Deleuze's conceptualisations, says, e.g., 'It seems to me that Deleuze and Hegel pose, on the contrary, that truth is ultimately memory, or incorporation within Being of its own actualized fecundity' (p. 63). See also p. 65.
† See Badiou's comments on philosophy as disaster in *Conditions*, trans. S. Corcoran (London and New York: Continuum, 2008), pp. 15–21.
‡ Badiou, *Theoretical Writings*, p. 120.
§ Badiou, *Deleuze: The Clamor of Being*, p. 59.
¶ See Bartlett, *Badiou and Plato: An Education by Truths*. That Lacan entered into the 'philosopher's' game of distinguishing Plato and Socrates unequivocally is a mark against him or perhaps a mark for Plato.
** e.g., 'Plato is Lacanian', in J. Lacan, *Seminar XIX . . . Or Worse*, trans. Cormac Gallagher, available at http://www.lacaninireland.com/web/wp-content/uploads/2010/06/Book-19-Ou-pire-Or-worse.pdf, and in 1960, 'What I have called Plato's *schwärmerei*', i.e., his idea

in the guise of truth; as do the periodical efforts of philosophy to assign to some other discourse, often science, but at times politics or poetry, the task of accruing the evidence or veracity of its claims.* However, despite the scenic detours of this peripatetic, truth – acclaimed, declaimed or denied – remains in question. It remains philosophy's symptom.

To affirm the crossing of exceptions in the empty place of Truth   Badiou's schematic distinction between Truth with a capital T and truths treats philosophy as the discourse in which is exposed the *there is* of truths, that, *as exceptions*, they exist or operate in the world as such. Philosophy is the discourse that, in its own terms, affirms these truths as the truths of its time. In Badiou's words, philosophy seizes and composes truths.† It links arguments, proofs, demonstrations, etc., and sublimates or establishes, in accord with its conditions, the limits of Truth. Truth with a capital T marks the empty or void place of philosophy: it *operates*, this void (which is not the void of being), but does not *present*, does not determine what are truths.‡ Truth is the space, the empty category, within which philosophy sets to work to realise *these* truths. It is this compositional relation with truth that sets philosophy as 'a singular site of thought', invariably.§ Tellingly, as a *category*, capital-T Truth marks the open or public or discursive form not *of* Truth such that it would be Truth as such (or the Sovereign Good à la Lacan and Kant's 'two Plato's'),¶ but *for* each and every truth made manifest, for a world, or for a situation conditionally. What this 'wholly empty category' of Truth expresses, Badiou says, 'is both that "there are" truths and that these truths are compossible in their plurality, a plurality to which philosophy gives welcome and shelter'.** The singularity of philosophy as *a* site of thought is that it 'simultaneously designates a plural state of things (there are heterogeneous truths) and the thought of their unity'.†† Philosophy, then,

of the Sovereign Good of philosophy, cited in Badiou, *Conditions*, p. 240. We should note that Kant, unhappy with Plato's presumption to think the 'thing in itself' (or rather not think it but presume to it), had already called Plato 'the father of all *schwärmerei*'. See James M. Rhodes, 'Mystic Philosophy in Plato's Seventh Letter', for a discussion of Kant's attack, in Zdravko Planinc (ed.), *Politics, Philosophy, Writing: Plato's Art of Caring for Souls* (Kansas City: University of Missouri Press, 2001), pp. 179–247 (esp. pp. 242–6).

* See Chapter 6, 'Sutures', in Badiou, *Manifesto for Philosophy*.
† Badiou, *Conditions*, p. 23.
‡ Badiou, *Conditions*, p. 11.
§ Badiou, *Conditions*, p. 10.
¶ See Rhodes, 'Mystic Philosophy in Plato's Seventh Letter', p. 243.
** Badiou, *Conditions*, p. 11.
†† Badiou, *Conditions*, p. 11.

disposing as integral to it the 'void of Truth' as its site of compossibility, is an act or an operation upon truths 'that are external to it'.* Or:
'The relation of (philosophical) Truth to truths (of a scientific, political, artistic and amorous nature) is a relation of seizing.'† Seized as
such, grasped in their immanent newness, they are subtracted of
sense and meaning or from knowledge in its constructivist, empiricist
or phenomenological 'sense'. These truths are disruptive of precisely
that knowledge into which, by virtue of an event – the insistence of
the void or hole at the heart of the 'all' of knowledge – they appear.
Hence they are specific to a world or situation and are nothing to it
at once. Philosophy affirms them insofar as they *are there* (insofar as
onto-logy demonstrates what to be there is), and, from across the
situations of their appearing, composes as itself both the material
truth of their existence and the invariance of their form, as its very
own act of love: the love, precisely, of what has no 'objective' existence and thus no *worldly* or *transcendental* power;‡ of what, in
Theory of the Subject, Badiou called 'what you would never believe
twice'.§

Truth as force of change   Of course, if ' there are truths' then there is the
                           thought of the being of these truths – which is con-
secrated to ontology or mathematics which can prescribe in its own
terms the genericity of these truths, their irreducible newness, their
distinction from the constructions of known knowledge, or historically determined forms of thought – in terms of either their expression or their recognition. As exceptions, thus as inexistently 'there',
truths also require the onto-topo-logic of their exposure, which is
finally to say their *force of change*. While there are truths *of* mathematics, which is the situation of ontology as such, there is no ontological truth – being and truth are not reducible one to the other. A
truth is something new: extra-*ontological* and *onto*-logical.

Truth as errancy   What transmits, what repeats, as argued, is what
                      Badiou calls *knowledge*. Yet, as mentioned, this
knowledge, which is a form of change in its own right, is not passive
precisely insofar as it sustains everyday reproduction and everyday
representation. For Badiou, ontology is the paradigm of knowledge

* Badiou, *Conditions*, p. 12.
† Badiou, *Conditions*, p. 13.
‡ Badiou, *Conditions*, p. 14.
§ Badiou, *Theory of the Subject*, p. 331.

insofar as it is the thought of being at its most consistent, regulated and bound. What Badiou demonstrates in *Being and Event* is that this very consistency is founded on an inconsistency which only mathematics can think: rigorously, formally and as immanent to itself. For Badiou, a propos of Paul Cohen's modelling of ZF for CH, set-theory ontology formalises consistency *and* incompleteness, thus the One as result (the count-as-one) and the not-All or not-Whole. Badiou sets this generic orientation against both the constructivist and the transcendentalist orientation whose ontological *correlates* he gives as Gödel and Jensen's '*constructible* sets' and the transcendentalist 'doctrine of large cardinals'.* What ontology realises for Badiou is that there is in every situation – every situation being thinkable as a situation in its being, thus consistently – a point of inconsistency vis-à-vis the situation it is. The upshot being that every situation admits a site and a site presents the void of being as such. The void qua unpresentation, that 'unplaceable point', Badiou says a bit enigmatically, 'wanders throughout presentation in the form of a subtraction from the count'.[†] Its errancy – 'it is neither local nor global, but scattered all over, nowhere and everywhere'[‡] – is ultimately what is localised at a site *by* the event. This means that the paradigm of knowledge inscribes within itself what it cannot itself know: all knowledge operates on this non-knowledge. The event is what makes the inexistent of a site *be there:* as existent, as consistent, as its trace, and thus thinkable outside of knowledge and as indifferent to representation and its transcendental regulation. The real problem, Badiou asserts, is 'to make such truths manifest',[§] and this is because the immanence of truths requires that they come to be within and with indifferent recourse to established situations.

Truth ≠ knowledge   Badiou contends that what he calls the 'orientation of constructivist thought' is that 'which naturally prevails in established situations because it measures being to language such as it is'.[¶] The essential and familiar features are three: language, discernment and classification. The function of language is to indicate that this or that element of the situation contains a certain

---

* Badiou, *Being and Event*, p. 284.
† Badiou, *Being and Event*, p. 525.
‡ Badiou, Being and Event, p. 55.
§ Alain Badiou, *Handbook of Inaesthetics*, trans. Alberto Toscano (Stanford: Stanford University Press, 2004), p. 14.
¶ Badiou, *Being and Event*, p. 328.

property. Language effectively intercedes between presented elements and their representation. It expresses the criterion of the former's inclusion by the latter. Knowledge is the name for the capacity language has for marking out these properties.

> In the last analysis, the constitutive operations of every domain of knowledge are discernment (such a presented or thinkable multiple possesses such and such a property) and classification (I can group together, and designate by their common property, those multiples that I discern as having a nameable characteristic in common).[*]

In the case of discernment the situation itself is supposed such that its elements present properties specific to it. If an element can be discerned it is on the basis of this element belonging to the situation: it is presented as such. Thus language nominates only based on what exists. The assumption is that nothing external to the situation is (or can be) imposed in and through such discernment. This would, after all, suggest the existence (and therefore the being) of that which cannot be named. If such a property is discerned within the multiple the latter is immediately classifiable in the sense that via its 'common' name it can be included with others similarly discerned. Badiou notes that the capacity of language to achieve this commensurability between an existent or belonging multiple and an included rule of its 'inclusion' is the means by which language is able to police the excess inherent to the representative relation: 'It is this bond, this proximity that language builds between presentation and representation, which grounds the conviction that the state does not exceed the situation by too much . . .'[†]

Knowledge as control of errancy

To control errancy – the possible site of the void – by means of binding belonging to inclusion, elements and parts as tightly as possible through the specification of nomination is the goal of the 'constructivist' orientation Badiou argues against. 'Knowledge' names the coordinated movement of these three functions. The functions of discernment and classification are further grounded in capacities supposed inherent in the constructivist subject: discernment is grounded in the capacity to judge, classification in the capacity to link such judgements. To judge is not to decide but to speak correctly or to make sense insofar as what is picked out conforms to and confirms the situational order, which is

---

[*] Badiou, *Being and Event*, p. 328.
[†] Badiou, *Being and Event*, p. 288.

to say the power of language in this case, the point being that for the constructivist vis-à-vis the situation nothing else is sayable.* 'Knowledge' does not speak of what is not presented precisely because it is impossible to ascribe to 'nothing' an existent property of the situation and to count it as such: 'If all difference is attributed on the basis of language and not on the basis of being, presented in-difference is impossible.'† Thus knowledge is the 'summation of judgements' made concerning what exists for the situation such that they are all counted, or grouped by a 'common determinant'. This 'encyclopaedic' determinant organises the judged elements into parts based solely on the ascribed property. In turn, then, 'one can desig-nate each of these parts by the property in question and thereby determine it within the language'.‡ In sum, knowledge solely deter-mines existence in the form of its nomination. A consistency is sup-posed at work; or rather a law already orders the thinking of the situation such that certain (non-)attributes can have no possible means of appearing. In his critique of Leibniz, Badiou points out that what this orientation excludes as impossible to the formulas of a well-made language, a language in which what exists conforms to the reason of its existence, is the 'indiscernible'.§

The indiscernible is such that no reason for the existence of what it divides can be given and thus 'language' as nomination through rule is contradicted. As Badiou notes, Leibniz himself says, 'if the void exists, language is incomplete, for a difference is missing from it inas-much as it allows some indifference to be'.¶ Constructivist thought is founded on the impossibility of the existence of the void qua situa-tion, which is to say the indiscernible and that which presents it. As this suggests, to not know the void is not a matter of *knowledge* but of constitution – hence it falls to decision.**

* Badiou makes the point that the constructivist vision is compelling and on its own (finitist) terms irrefutable, *Being and Event*, p. 289.
† Badiou, *Being and Event*, p. 319. Plato has Protagoras put the same thing like this: 'It is impossible to judge what is not, or to judge anything other than what one is experiencing, and what one is immediately experiencing is always true' (Tht. 167ab). These several para-graphs on 'constructivism' are expanded and related to the 'state of the sophistic situation', as shown in Plato in Bartlett, *Badiou and Plato: An Education by Truths*, Chapter 1.
‡ Badiou, *Being and Event*, p. 329.
§ Badiou, *Being and Event*, p. 320.
¶ Badiou, *Being and Event*, p. 321.
** See Badiou, *Being and Event*, p. 294.

Subtractive   While the productive role of Badiou's ontology is
                immediately apparent (its vast edifice being entirely
built out of operations which are essentially performed on *nothing*),
its basic gesture is nonetheless *subtractive*. This can be understood in
a number of ways. First, Badiou's ontology is subtractive insofar as it
does not purport to convey being as presence. To the contrary, being
– *pure being* (or purely multiple multiplicity) – is that which defies
any form of presentation (or representation, for that matter).
Radically withdrawn from all unification, being is nothing other than
uncounted – and therefore unpresented – multiplicity. Thus it is also
subtractive in a second sense, in that it 'subtracts' being from its
capture by the One.* Perhaps most importantly however, Badiou's
ontology is subtractive in that its fundamental gesture is to subtract
being itself from ontology. For ontology is ultimately a discourse
which prescribes the rules by which something can be presented or
'counted' as one – its sole operation being that of the count – and the
'one' thing that necessarily *fails* to be counted is nothing other than
inconsistent multiplicity, or being itself. So, technically speaking,
being isn't actually given in ontology; rather, it is retroactively
posited on the basis of conceiving the One as a 'result' (of the operation of the count). Pure multiplicity is not something that can be
known (or again, while we certainly know that being *is*, we cannot
know *what* it is); rather, the nature of being is something that must
be *decided* upon, in an axiomatic sense.

On this basis of being not being the event of truth, the sense of truth
or the immediacy of truth and so on, but being thinkable of every
situation nonetheless, *Being and Event* opens up the analytic of truth
to four subtractive determinations, or in other words: The path of
a truth towards its incomplete universality crosses four 'negative
categories': *undecidable*, *indiscernible*, the *untotalisable* and the

---

* 'We can define metaphysics as follows: the *enframing* of being by the one. Its most appropriate synthetic maxim is that of Leibniz, which establishes the reciprocity of being and the one
as a norm: "what is not *a* being is not a *being*"', Alain Badiou, *Briefings on Existence: A
Short Treatise on Transitory Ontology*, trans. Norman Madarasz (Albany: SUNY, 2006),
p. 34; translation modified. See also the first meditation of *Being and Event*. Interestingly,
prior to his equation of ontology with mathematics (and consequent ability to align being
with pure multiplicity), in *Being and Event*, Badiou held that philosophies of the multiple
were in fact covert metaphysics of the One. Thinking in particular of Deleuze and his philosophy of multiplicities, Badiou argues in *Theory of the Subject* that such a multiple is in
truth 'never more than a semblance since positing the multiple amounts to presupposing the
One as substance and excluding the Two from it. The ontology of the multiple is a veiled
metaphysics' (p. 22).

*unnameable.** The event is linked to the *undecidable*, the subject is linked to the *indiscernible* – that which knowledge or the state does not know. Truth itself is *generic* thus infinite and untotalisable, and the *unnameable* names the point in any situation that cannot be forced by what presents it – it's a halting point. 'Nothing', Badiou remarks, 'can be granted existence – by which I mean the existence truth presupposes at its origin – without undergoing the trial of its subtraction.'†

In *On Subtraction*, Badiou is addressing this four-point subtractive affirmation to an audience of psychoanalysts. He cites Mallarmé – one of the nodal points of the non-alliance that is Lacan/Deleuze/Badiou‡ — to his 'defence' and distinguishes via this citing language and the void. As noted, it is on the basis of the void of being and not the confines of the speech/silence alternation that a truth is brought to bear in a situation. The mode of such a bringing to bear is *subtraction*, which is an act and the act par excellence is that of truth. Thus Badiou speaks to the core of psychoanalysis, the *pass-age*, so to speak, from the insistent silence of the symptom to the speech of the subject and thus its act, but he also subtly shifts the site of this truth and thus the subtractive trajectory of the act to the void of being rather than the silence of the speaking subject. No doubt this distance from Lacan, for whom ontology is just another instance of sense, again confirms also Badiou's distance from Deleuze insofar as if in the latter there is no room for the void outside of sense as such, there is also no need for truths – at least insofar as their intelligibility and sensibility (as body of thought) is composed by some subject.

---

* It is the case that the unnameable, recognized by commentators as a problematic category for some time, has been made redundant by the theory of appearing.
† Badiou, *Theoretical Writings*, p. 103.
‡ Indeed one should compare Badiou's remarks in *Theory of the Subject*, for there the poetics of Mallarmé is revealed to establish a univocity while the discourse of the psychoanalyst is established in division. Badiou evokes the 'cunning' of Lacan as 'strategist of *lalangue*', underlining that this might mean the impossibility of the *new*, such that whatever splits is mere 'iteration' and so we have simply 'the Law of splitting' as such. Or, Badiou asks, should the emphasis fall on the *one*, such that as a consequence of splitting there is no new *one*? In this case there is something new, something beyond the law of the one, and this would entail that the one of the law is not, that 'the symbolic is ruined by the real, the one ungraspable except in the process of its destruction', *Theory of the Subject*, p. 114. Badiou nominates Lacan as 'the theoretician of the true scission', of the 'one divides into two', against 'those repairmen of flat tyres, the revisionists, to whom is suited the syrupy conviction that Two fuse into one', *Theory of the Subject*, p. 113. See A. J. Bartlett and Justin Clemens, 'The Greatest of Our Dead', in ed. Sean Bowden and Simon Duffy (eds), *Badiou and Philosophy* (Edinburgh: Edinburgh University Press, 2012).

These four negative categories articulate in the following way: An event is linked to the notion of the *undecidable*. If, using the established knowledge, its rules, criteria of judgement and classification and so on, you can decide a given sentence is true or false, then there is no event, no chance supplement but only what is calculable therein. The beginning of a truth cannot be dependent on the calculations of a state knowledge. Undecidability means exactly that – one must decide, wager. Truth begins with a decision, which ontology formalises as the axiom of choice: a decision on the event; that what happened, happened. The fact that the event is undecidable, that no knowledge knows its event-ness, if you like, that contra Deleuze's impression in *The Logic of Sense*, it is not-representable, imposes the constraint that the subject of the event must appear. The subject is that which declares – in whatever form – 'this event has taken place' which 'I can neither calculate nor demonstrate, but to which I shall be faithful'*: faithful or *militant* precisely because, of the event *there is no knowledge*. Fidelity is essentially the mode of the subject insofar as it is suspended between the disappeared event and the (new) situation to come. A subject fixes an undecidable chance event because it takes the chance of deciding or wagering on it. This begins the infinite procedure of verification of this event's truth: that it is an event for *this* situation, and as such has or implies its *consequences*. The subject is the examination within the situation of the consequences of this decision, of a fidelity to this decision. This subject proceeds point-by-point establishing itself as the space of its enquiries – enquiries that come down to organising within the situation those 'elements' that can be connected to the name of the event and those that cannot – *as a body*. These enquiries establish the conditions of the new truth. It's certainly a procedure of division, yet a division whose generic form is universally inscribed, literally written on the body.

The subject, Badiou says, makes a pure choice, a choice without a concept, a choice between two *indiscernible* terms. 'Two terms are indiscernible', he argues, 'if no effect of language allows them to be distinguished.' If there is no such distinction, 'it is certain that the choice of verifying one term rather than the other will find no support in the objectivity of their difference'. Thus it will have been a pure choice, without predicate, without concept, 'free from any

* Badiou, *Infinite Thought*, p. 62.

other presupposition than that of having to choose, and with no indication marking the proposed terms, the term which will allow the verification of the consequences of the axiom will first pass'.[*] It is the 'subtraction that establishes a point of coincidence between chance and freedom'.[†]

The subject is finite yet the truth of which it is an instance is not. Being generic, it is 'beyond the reach of completion', but one can say or anticipate that if this passage of a truth were complete it would constitute a generic and thus infinite subset of the original situation.[‡] The subject, beginning in decision and confronting the indiscernible, acts to verify in the situation that for which it has decided. That there was an event, that it signifies that the state is not all, that its knowledge is partial and that its rule is excessive. These enquiries generate, as noted above, an indiscernible subset of that situation. Not being constituted by the situation's knowledge, this set is indiscernible to it and, as such, generic or new – new in the fullest sense. Further, it constitutes a universal part given that what this subset collects is that which belongs to each element of the situation – the void part, precisely, that part which escapes state knowledge, or in other words, the equal 'capacity' (retroactively speaking) of all for truth:

> Thus the universal arises according to the chance of an aleatory supplement. It leaves behind it a simple detached statement as a trace of the disappearance of the event that founds it. It initiates its procedure in the univocal act through which that valence of what was devoid of valence comes to be decided. It binds to this act a subject-thought that will invent consequences for it. It faithfully constructs . . . something for all time.[§]

[*] Badiou, *Infinite Thought*, p. 63.
[†] Badiou, *Theoretical Writings*, p. 113.
[‡] Badiou, *Theoretical Writings*, p. 113.
[§] Badiou, *Theoretical Writings*, p. 152.

CHAPTER SIX

Polemos

CIA Superior: What did we learn, Palmer?
CIA Officer: I don't know, sir.
CIA Superior: I don't fuckin' know either. I guess we learned not to do it again.
(Denouement, *Burn After Reading*, Coen Brothers [2008])

This book has been neither a variant of liturgy, nor a paean to poly-amory, nor a fake geopolitical imbroglio, nor even a contribution to gymnastic or economic improvement. Or, at least, it has attempted not to be. To that end, we have structured it as a regulated sequence of essays upon crucial conceptual problematics: the contemporary; time; the event; and truth. In doing so, we have not only exposed hitherto-disavowed complicities between our thinkers – such that even the avowed lineages of influence don't quite capture these intricacies – but have further suggested even more vicious and incommensurable differences than are usually suspected. But it is perhaps only here, belatedly, that we are able to properly repeat ourselves in a compressed and violent fashion – having, unlike our cinematic CIA comrades, not yet learned not to do it again.

Lacan   So: how would Lacan respond to the alleged 'critiques' levelled at him by Deleuze and Badiou? Regarding the rethinking of the 'contemporary', we believe his response would be clear: the contemporary can only be remade by free association. Otherwise, we will find the return of tyranny at the heart of thought, exemplified by the hypocrisy of philosophers. Free association: the impossible injunction to non-omission, non-systematisation and continuation in order to tease out the negative space of the void, of the primal repression, that founds the subject. This praxis requires a new *dispositif*, a new organisation, that in itself runs transversally to all the established institutions of modernity: not science, not arts; not a university, not a research institute; not a business, not not a business. Neither Deleuze nor Badiou

– being, as Lacan would point out, both *fonctionnaires* of the State university system – ever contributed to the invention of a single new organisation, membership of allegedly revolutionary groupuscules notwithstanding. Nor did they contribute to any real acts of dissolution. On the contrary, in their taxpayer-supported administrative duties, they extend the established system of unitising students for governmental ends; in their theories, they extend the grasp of the master with ever-more-subtle operations into the flesh of their charges.

Which is why time becomes so otiose for both Deleuze and Badiou. On the one hand, Deleuze exacerbates a fundamental psychoanalytic insight: the indifference of the unconscious to contradictions, the real-phantom persistence of memories. But he thereby mistakes the *inconsistency* of the subject for its *dissolution* and, in doing so, snaps the bond between time, thought and the subject. The priority of formalisation disappears and creation, its other, with it. At such a point, he becomes more anti-philosophical than Lacan himself – but in the service of an expanded philosophy of the master. As for Badiou, his assault on time itself in the name of the creation of a new present fails to meet the canons of anything but metaphor. The Real is the rock upon which both Deleuze and Badiou's systems shatter.

For the theories of the 'event' so beloved of our idealising philosophers not only cannot properly separate the event from novelty – an optical flaw, so to speak – but both of them succumb to a peculiar agreement on this point. Despite their own radically variant doctrines of the event – hyperintricating global singularity for Deleuze, separative vanishing for Badiou – what they share is precisely a theory of the event that is *essentially poetic*, slightly confused with other zones in Deleuze's case, very clear and distinct in Badiou's. To some extent, both derive this position from Lacan himself – witness the role of poetic creation in the psychoanalyst's work from first to last – but Lacan is more complex and subtle. For there are indeed all sorts of 'events', including the 'Cantor-event' for Lacan, but also ancient tragedy, Joyce and analysis itself, which cannot be assembled into a coherent system without falsification at every level. And this is, too, why Deleuze and Badiou cannot, respectively give any good account of sexual difference, or simply have to parasite on this matter upon the Lacanian doctrine. Everything Deleuze does works against the singularities of the feminine, desperately dissolving it into asexual connectivities, as the same moment that his swerve from 'Woman' returns in a sequence of symptomatic metaphors (such as the 'desiring machines' or 'the fold'). Whereas Badiou errs by too-enthusiastically taking the opposite route: 'woman' is primary in love, but then is only herself in love.

Unlike philosophy, psychoanalysis holds itself between science and art, mathematics and poetry in such a way as to pick up precisely the contingency of truths as without-commensurability. The logic that it *de facto* elaborates is a form of para-consistent logic: what if, rather than the laws of identity or non-contradiction, the law of excluded middle was considered primary? The entire apparatus of Aristotelian and modern logic would have to be reconsidered. For one can immediately see how excluded middle entails a pure binary without content, a pure difference as such. If we posed it as primary, we end up with the possibility of 'true contradictions' – that is, as Lacan would put it, a *subject*. Difference would then precede and condition identity, without being any less logically rigorous for all that. This would be another way, then, of phrasing the cut that is not simply a 'lack' nor a 'whole' but which makes possible as it de-totalises every possible system.

Deleuze   Pure difference! Hardly. The Lacanian position, in its attempt to instantiate a new practice on the porous rock of Freud's syncretism, swallows the Hegelian lure, hook, line and sinker. The alleged radicality of Lacan's relationship to Hegel appears in all its banality when one recognises its fundamental tenet: maintain at all costs the role of the negative. To call him anHegelian is an amusing repetition of certain of his own claims, a remarkable disavowal marked by the material absence of a void, a symptomatic collapse.

From beginning to end, Deleuze's engagement with Lacan is marked by his variable responses to the position of the negative in his thought. The cluster of texts published at the end of the '60s (in particular *Difference and Repetition* and *The Logic of Sense*) take Lacan as a definitive point of reference but only at the cost of transforming the (negative) figure of lack into the (positive) figure of the problematic virtual. This first Deleuzian portrait of Lacan is best encapsulated in the remarkable claim that 'psychoanalysis in general is the science of events'.* Any enthusiasm for this claim, though, is surely tempered by Deleuze's reflection, no more than seven years after the publication of this claim in *The Logic of Sense*, that his goal there had been 'to render psychoanalysis *inoffensive*'.†

Anti-Oedipus marks the point of transition to explicit if disguised critique. Lacan will be praised for making a central theoretical advance that Deleuze and Guattari link to the notion of the body-without-organs: 'We owe to Jacques Lacan the discovery of this fertile domain of a code of the unconscious.'‡ He is, moreover, the first anti-Oedipal reader of Freud.§ At the same time, and while not one outright critical word is explicitly addressed to Lacan himself in this book,¶ elements of his thought espoused by 'certain disciples of Lacan', in certain texts that engage in 'oedipalising interpretations of Lacan',** are mercilessly attacked, above all those that invoke the negative.†† Everything that follows with respect to psychoanalysis in the work after this – and references become, as is well-known, increasingly sparse, as though the negative and its champions, above all psychoanalysis, have entirely lost interest for Deleuze – does so in this vein.

And if psychoanalysis can consider itself the *hôte* of the quadripartite magisterium (science, art, mathematics, poetry), it is only insofar as it is the final arbiter of their now purely symptomatic significance. The consequences borne by this disavowed position of mastery are particularly disastrous for philosophy, and here, at least, Deleuze and Badiou are of one mind. Psychoanalysis always makes sure it has the last word, even and above all because this last word isn't at the end of the sequence but the very principle of its unity – and

---

*   Gilles Deleuze, *The Logic of Sense*, trans. Mark Lester with Charles Stivale, ed. Constantin Boundas (New York: Columbia University Press, 1990), p. 211.
†   Gilles Deleuze, *Deux Régimes de Fou, et autres textes*, ed. David Lapoujade (Paris: Minuit, 2003), p. 60.
‡   Gilles Deleuze and Félix Guattari, *Anti-Oedipus*, trans. Robert Hurley, Mark Seem and Helen Lane (London: Athlone, 1984), p. 38.
§   Deleuze and Guattari, *Anti-Oedipus*, p. 53; p. 175.
¶   The closest they come is to suggest that Lacan's own anti-Oedipal reinscription of psychoanalysis came at the cost of a regression to the themes of 'the Law, and the signifier – phallus and castration' (*Anti-Oedipus*, p. 217), all of which, of course, are integrally yoked to the negative for Lacan.
** Deleuze and Guattari, *Anti-Oedipus*, p. 171; p. 73. See also pp. 82–3, the most detailed text on this point.
†† They attack, for example, the figure of the big Other (in the name, notably, of *l'objet petit a*), 'which reintroduces a certain notion of lack', Deleuze and Guattari, *Anti-Oedipus*, p. 27n.

is theorised as such by Lacan himself. Deleuze repeats this point on more than one occasion: 'psychoanalysis is a complete machine, designed in advance to prevent people from speaking . . . As soon as one begins analysis, one has the impression of speech. But one talks in vain; the entire analytic machine exists to suppress the conditions of real expression.'* The *practical* lesson of psychoanalysis on this front? 'What you must be taught is Lack.'† Perhaps no symptom of this is more telling, in the current context, than the categorical assertion that philosophy is and can only be the discourse of the master, a claim that silences in advance any possibility that a philosophical discourse might even be able to respond. As Deleuze will say: the primordial act of psychoanalysis after Lacan is to crush the subject of enunciation . . . to which we might add: and then wield all of its force from the blank eye of the storm.

This makes those aspects of Badiou that are drawn from the Lacanian heritage – the Lacan that he asserts, for no reason that could be grounded in his own system, is an obligatory point of passage for contemporary philosophy – problematic from the start. But what Badiou takes from others and transforms to suit his own purpose is hardly the most troubling feature of his construction.

When Deleuze comes to directly address Badiou, it is very late, and in a context that is removed in various ways from the 'classical' positions that have for the most part guided our analysis here: *What is Philosophy?*, his last book with Guattari. This is fortunate, because Badiou's very poor understanding of Deleuze's project before, let's say, *The Fold* (published the same year as *Being and Event*), precludes the advent of any meaningful debate. Deleuze's comment on Badiou's thought there makes its own suite of errors, both about set theory and the project of *Being and Event* itself;‡ it is bizarre indeed to read Badiou's assertion that 'I do not register any incorrectness in this text.'§ But the invitation that Badiou advances

---

* Gilles Deleuze, *L'Île Déserte et autres textes*, ed. David Lapoujade (Paris: Minuit, 2002), p. 382.
† Deleuze, *Deux Régimes de Fou*, p. 80.
‡ See Gilles Deleuze and Félix Guattari, *What is Philosophy?*, trans. Hugh Tomlinson and Graham Burchell (New York: Columbia University Press, 1994), pp. 151–3. It is interesting to note that while Deleuze and Guattari incorrectly assert the parity of size between the second order of transfinite sets and the power set of the first order in their discussion of Cantor (p. 120), they manage to state it correctly when addressing Badiou (p. 151).
§ Alain Badiou, *Theoretical Writings*, trans. Ray Brassier and Alberto Toscano (London: Continuum, 2004), p. 245n3.

in the same note ('I would be grateful to anyone who could clarify this textual fragment for me, and explain what relation it bears to *Being and Event*[*]) is easily accepted – it *suffices to simply read What is Philosophy?* Badiou's claim that only 'the obstinate wish to maintain at all costs and in the face of all evidence, that every set is a number, can explain the very strange text which Deleuze devoted to my book *Being and Event* in *What is Philosophy?*',[†] clearly shows that he has not.

Here, we note only the essential: Deleuze's account of Badiou appears in the chapter devoted to the consequences that arise when philosophy is subordinated to a logicised vision of science. In turn, Badiou seems to run the risk of subordinating philosophy – since it is conditioned by science – to demands that strip it of what it enjoys by right as philosophy, a state of affairs appears only from the point of view of philosophy, since science has no interest in its role as condition. In this way, the conditioning relationship elaborated by Badiou requires a surreptitious 'logic of conditioning' that can itself only be generated from within philosophy. Badiou's position ironically threatens by way of consequence the return of 'an old conception of higher philosophy'[‡]: science conditions philosophy, on grounds and in terms that philosophy determines for science.

To this, we would simply add the following, given that Badiou's critique of Deleuze turns in no small part around the charge of mishandling the category of multiplicity. Badiou asserts that Deleuze has failed to learn the lesson of Cantor and set theory in his wake, but this is a criterion that arises only *within* the logic of conditioning we have just noted, and towards which Deleuze could justifiably remain indifferent, since he thematises the relationship of science and philosophy in different terms. And indeed, this is just what Deleuze marks at the close of his short text on Badiou: the difference lies in two ways of conceiving not just multiplicity but the status of set theory as what makes a necessary demand on the philosophical concept of multiplicity. Now, one can criticise Deleuze's concept of multiplicity for being inadequate, wrong or stupid, but to simply criticise him for not being enough of a follower of Badiou – which is the substance of

[*] Badiou, *Theoretical Writings*, p. 246n3.
[†] Badiou, *Theoretical Writings*, p. 70.
[‡] Deleuze and Guattari, *What is Philosophy?*, p. 152.

Badiou's own argument – is something altogether different. *Asylum ignorantiae?* More like a funhouse mirror.

Badiou

> You won't believe me now
> But there's been some illumination
> The wisest cops have realized
> They fucked the operation.[*]

To begin with the divergent and its lack: Castration, between body and thought, effects a new 'divergent series' of evental repetition or *planar* re-inscription in which new attributes meet new expressions – 'eternal truths' – effected with sense: 'ideal singularities that communicate in one and the same event'.[†] Lacan, most implacably, and via his drive to 'mathematical formalisation', insists on the distinction between a logic of sense and a logic of truths: castration marks the immanent lack of what (the philosophers') truth can do.[‡] In *Logics of Worlds*, Badiou writes: 'Lacan was well aware that if you consign what happens to sense or meaning, you work towards the subjective consolidation of religion, for, as he wrote, "the stability of religion stems from the fact that meaning is always religious".'[§] Yet, for Badiou, Lacan's fidelity to the subject's way out from meaning, from sensuous vitality, the unconscious, as the mark of the split subject, is ultimately reductive. This is because the unconscious is itself a logic (of) structure thus 'the infrastructure of the human animal and not', Badiou continues, 'the occurrence – as rare as it may be – of the present-process of a truth which a subjectivated body treats point by point'.[¶] Not the differentiated effect of sense, not structured like a language. The passage from the 'two effect' to thought, marked in all, is the very point of divergence. Only Badiou situates it where it cannot not be – in the gap between *ontology* and onto*logy*. Lacan and Deleuze mistake the route. 'But', Badiou continues, 'the break is really quite complex. In terms of heritage, the two with whom I am in dialogue are Deleuze and Lacan, who were on the extreme internal

---

[*] The Clash, 'Midnight Log', *Sandinista*, CBS, 1983.

[†] Deleuze, *The Logic of Sense*, pp. 253–5.

[‡] Badiou, *Theoretical Writings*, p. 126. Cf. *Logics of Worlds*, trans. Alberto Toscano (London: Continuum, 2009), p. 39: 'As Lacan says, "*mathematical* par excellence," means "transmissible outside of meaning."' And: 'We must recognize that we are indebted to Lacan – in the wake of Freud, but also of Descartes – for having paved the way for a formal theory of the subject whose basis is materialist; it was indeed by opposing himself to phenomenology, to Kant and to a certain structuralism, that Lacan could stay the course', *Logics of Worlds*, p. 48.

[§] Badiou, *Logics of Worlds*, pp. 386–7.

[¶] Badiou, *Logics of Worlds*, p. 480.

edge, the border between democratic materialism and the materialist dialectic I propose.'*

In an interview with Lauren Sedofsky in *Artforum*, Badiou notes that 'there are immediate adversaries and, perhaps, in effect, deep ones. The immediate adversaries fall into two principal groups: all those aligned with the tradition of the *"nouveaux philosophes"* in France and the analytic philosophers, where the coupling of philosophy and democracy is flagrant.'† Setting aside the analytic philosophers, the difference between a *nouveau philosophe* – for whom truths in their universal sense are destitute fictions or authoritarian Idealisations and for whom the slew of democratic opinions, self-interest and consensual majorities mark the paramount arbiters of the good – and an anti-philosopher, such as Lacan, for whom conceits are deposed in the name of what a truth aims at, is marked in this very conditioning. As an anti-philosophy, psychoanalysis traverses the history of philosophy (among other things – it is a poacher's discourse) as its own and as a thought to whose unconscious it attests. Badiou's slow turn towards Deleuze qua philosopher, marked in the review of his book on Leibniz and in Badiou's *Deleuze*, has to be seen in terms of what are for Badiou the three orienting categories of philosophy – being, truth and subject – which in turn bring to bear an orientation to them, and with regard to these this 'turn' is also the denomination and delimitation of a distance from Deleuze, subject to a distinct difference in orientation – the formalisation (or 'actualising') of the infinite and the (Hegel inspired and Lacan dodging) 'every atom is real' being only two marks of their obverse orientation.‡ Even more finely tuned, and with regard to truth especially – and particularly insofar as for Badiou it is subtractive of being, thus *eventally* divided from it (the event itself *not being* qua being) and (thus) subjective, Ideal and material at once – is the question of immanence. That there is no All, that the multiple of multiples is the 'empty set' or void, means that immanence is actual. Thus, immanence can be said, *not* contra

<hr>

* Alain Badiou and Lauren Sedofsky, 'Matters of Appearance', *Artforum*, Vol. 25, No. 3 (2006), p. 248. Also: 'it was by conceding too much to [democratic materialism] that Deleuze – having started from the project of upholding the chances of a metaphysics against contemporary sophistry – came to tolerate the fact that most of his concepts were sucked up, so to speak, by the *doxa* of the body, desire, affect, networks, the multitude, nomadism and enjoyment into which a whole contemporary "politics" sinks, as if into a poor man's Spinozism', *Logics of Worlds*, p. 35 and cf. p. 387.
† Badiou and Sedofsky, 'Matters of Appearance', p. 248.
‡ Badiou, *Logics of Worlds*, p. 251.

but *beneath* its romanticist or constructivist thinking in Deleuze as a transcendental empiricism, the ground-logos of sensations as the force of *life* (hence a bio-logic).* Immanence insists as a question for Badiou because he has never resiled from thinking philosophy under the double articulation of structure and subject or form and truths, being and existence, in which there is no place for either a natural, omnipresent immanence nor a potential, ineffable thus *relational* infinite.† In contrast, the virtual qua multiplicity straddles this double as the All of what is 'between elements' and not what founds them.

In Badiou these two fronts are diagonalised. 'One divides into two': formally, mathematics is ontology / mathematised logic (as category theory and so not as a logic of mathematics) thinks appearing; truly, it is under the condition of the two that the force of the generic, singular in becoming, universal by a *formally* (and not thereby virtual) immanent prescription, produces in-situ, as generic for it, what is true of it. A rival – if not necessarily 'crucial' – philosophy (Deleuze's) is subject to two conditioning moves: establish its veracity at the limit; intervene or recommence to think at *that* void point (whether excess or lack). It is not enough just to read. One must be read as oneself. Badiou reads Deleuze rhizomatically, or rather, as if his work is as he desired it to be: *rhizomatic*. The excerpts from Deleuze's oeuvre that Badiou appends to his *Deleuze* are Deleuze's 'subterranean tendrils', not branches on a tree to be set in a one-to-one correspondence: 'a line does not go from one point to another'.‡

Lacan, then – insofar as he suspends the question of truth in the constitution of a subject qua 'lack of rapport' – is conditional, *but not final*. Deleuze – insofar as he suspends the question of truth as an affect/effect of sense (bodies), and for whom the event returns always as the immanence of life as such (the being of the sensible as that

---

* In his 'Preface to the American Edition of *Difference and Repetition*', in *Two Regimes of Madness*, Deleuze says that under the constraint of an understanding of philosophy as conditional – vis-à-vis Science and Art – he tried to conceptualise repetition in terms of a relation between a mathematical function and a biological function. Gilles Deleuze, *Two Regimes of Madness*, ed. David Lapoujade, trans. Ames Hodges and Mike Taormina (New York: Semiotext(e), 2007), p. 306. Note also that in this preface to his 'first work of philosophy' (p. 305), Deleuze consecrates Chapter 3 as the key to his later work, including with Guattari: the work on the vegetable as model of thought (p. 308).
† The references to Deleuze here are from 'Immanence: A Life', in *Two Regimes of Madness*, pp. 388–93.
‡ 'Preface to the American Edition of *Difference and Repetition*', in *Two Regimes of Madness*, p. 312. When one hears the word 'rhizomatic' one cannot resist appending the denouement: 'greased lightning'?

which can only be *sensed*), as the product of its 'state of things' – is rival.* It is not impossible to say here that what unifies Lacan and Deleuze, beyond the diversity of their shared ambivalence towards what Badiou names 'Plato' and everything which holds them apart, is the placement of the void (and thus the treatment of the infinite and thus 'mathematics'), marked as castration or as the instance of what separates a body from thought, an attribute from its expression, the subject from its discourse. Thus, 'beyond being'.

Let's phrase it this way: to not know the void is not a matter of *knowledge* but of constitution – hence it falls to decision.† Both Deleuze and Lacan might acquiesce in the first instance of the claim and maybe the second at a pinch – so long as the decision is not framed by any experiential or consciousness nonsense (*not* non-sense). Lacan might see the 'ground' (or to use Hegel's pun on *daimon*, 'fall to ground')‡ for this as the unconscious – what precisely, à la Freud, denudes philosophy of its absolute power or knowledge (to which Lacan is hysterically faithful) – and Deleuze, at least in *The Logic of Sense*, might see it in the immanent non-sense of sense as the lacunae of his temporal schematic. For Badiou, this decision – on the advent of the nothing that is – marks the matter-reality of a truth, its implication or consequences and thus its subject, devoid of all knowledge and so the rationality or consistency of being without sense.

The operation of the void, the real of an immanent division and hence the place of the subject's 'displacement'§ is precluded in all (*ultimately*) Aristotelian arrangements.¶ (This claim in no way 'forgets' the strenuous efforts of both Deleuze and Lacan to put Aristotle at a distance: indeed what's suggested in this 'comment' is that it's the *manner* [ultimately, onto-*logical*] of this putting that returns Aristotle to us.)** Deleuze's own vitalism precludes the conceptualisation of the

---

* Gilles Deleuze, *Difference and Repetition*, trans. Paul Patton (New York: Columbia University Press, 1994), p. 68, and 'Immanence: A Life', in *Two Regimes of Madness*, p. 392.
† See Alain Badiou, *Being and Event*, trans. Oliver Feltham (London: Continuum, 2005), p. 294.
‡ We owe this to Z. L. Fraser. See his 'Go Back to An Fang' (p. 44), 4 June 2012, available at http://formandformalism.blogspot.com.au
§ Cf. Badiou, *Logics of Worlds*, p. 390: 'Under the names of "singularity", "event", "point" and "body", from now on it will be a question of what is neither being nor appearing, neither ontology nor logic, but rather the aleatory result of what happens when appearing is unsettled by the being that it localizes.'
¶ Badiou, *Being and Event*, p. 77.
** Cf. Frank Ruda's subtle review of the volume *Badiou and Philosophy*, edited by

void as real or 'rational', so to speak, on the basis of its too close association with the negation of the necessary relation between limit and (what is) thought (for Deleuze), thus, Badiou argues, the void threatens the thesis as to the univocity of being.* In Deleuze, the void cannot be thought *with* the infinite – they mark two distinct forms of judgement. The latter, the paradigm of any 'constructivism'. Thus (later, returning to the actuality of Leibniz) the Fold rather than the void-site comes to mark the disjunctive relation or non-relation between being (whose proper name is void for Badiou) and thought (the mark of the subject for Badiou) in Deleuze – between 'outside' and 'internal-to'. Hence to fold at the limit is to think as the force of the outside, but, despite everything, from within the vitality of the One or, it's the same, from the impossibility of the non-naturality or non-virtuality of the void.† In other words, only the void is unique, punctual, unpresentable, and thus thinkable without *place*.‡

Certainly, for Deleuze, invoking Lévi-Strauss's 'degree zero', an *appearance* can be excess in one and lack in an other,§ and perhaps this crossing of the threshold between being and appearing is already marked in his claim that it is 'imprecise to oppose event and struc-ture' given that for Deleuze the latter 'includes a register of "ideal" *events* [emphasis in original], that is, an entire history internal to it'. 'The situation is very similar to that of differential calculus, where the distributions of singular points correspond to the values of differ-ential relations.'¶ The key here, however, key that is to the difference we are marking, is that for Deleuze this wandering void or displaced degree zero or 'differentiator' has the '*property* [emphasis added] of always . . . being absent from its own place'.** The rational inconsist-ency which 'grounds' the decision in Badiou's sense is precisely the placing of the void – which is not an effect of calculation, thus not a property – and thus the precise imposition of the irreducibility of

   Sean Bowden and Simon Duffy (Edinburgh: Edinburgh University Press, 2012), in *NotreDame Philosophical Reviews*, 27-3-2013, available at http://ndpr.nd.edu/news/38530-badiou-and-philosophy

* Alain Badiou, *Deleuze: The Clamor of Being*, trans. Louise Burchill (Minneapolis: University of Minnesota Press, 2000), pp. 88–9.

† There is some irony here, then, in Deleuze's ostensible rewriting of Heidegger's opening chapter of *Being and Time* as his own introduction to *Difference and Repetition* as a critique of Aristotle. We can't follow that here.

‡ Badiou, *Being and Event*, p. 76.

§ Deleuze, *The Logic of Sense*, pp. 59–61.

¶ Deleuze, *The Logic of Sense*, p. 60.

** Deleuze, *The Logic of Sense*, p. 61.

event to structure – the formal mark, which insists as the evental trace, of their non-relation. Deleuze rejects Aristotle's rejection of the void insofar as for the latter the void is impossible because it would require, so to speak, no place and non-place, which for Aristotle is ontologically inconsistent, but returns to an Aristotelianism via the constructivist attribution of property (later, territory). He cannot, despite *himself** (which is to say, the *expressed* ontological field), think the non-place as punctuation and thus the consistency of unpresentation without recourse to a serial logic or analogic. Deleuze is a great thinker of appearing: forces, intensities, modes of existence, aggregates, vegetables.

In Lacan, the void marks division in the subject as that of the non-rapport whose recourse qua suture or *point de capiton* is always to language or the *logic* of the signifier. The latter constraint, or fidelity, limits Lacan's intuition towards the matheme to a secondary function, that of confirming in formal language the impossibility of the subject being other than that of the *knowledge* of the unconscious. In other words, the failure to place the void on the side of being (a philosopher's conceit, anyway, for Lacan), following the very mathematics Lacan invokes to his cause, means that the subject, as what speaks, remains terminally enframed by language even if he marks some 'hole' in it. Ironically, the anti-philosopher's recourse to mathematics mirrors the philosophers he rebukes insofar as qua discourse it remains incapable of its own thought and must in the end be spoken of, spoken by or spoken for. For Lacan, we could say, ontology's very intelligibility – that it thinks the nothing that is, as subtracted from the logic of the signifier – is its symptom. And as we know, the symptom or mark of lack is always the moment of recapture or return, the *moment* of psychoanalysis in fact, which is not to say, for the analyst at least, aporia or recommencement. Thus Lacan is less 'the *educator* to every philosophy to come' than the pedagogical reminder of the *pensum*, to borrow Beckett's usage, the philosopher must not repeat qua philosophy – and this, ironically, insofar as mathematical formalisation is his *goal*. For Lacan, as the mathemes, knots and inadequate topologies show, anti-philosophy really is *conditional* and a philosophy exists as such insofar as its act is decisive

---

* In 'Preface to the American Edition of *Difference and Repetition*', in *Two Regimes of Madness*, he claims, among other things, to break with 'the classical image of thought', specifically of truth as adequate to propositions 'serving as answers' (p. 308). Maybe this is the case for truth and perhaps not for that which functions as its place?

vis-à-vis this formalisation, this act of recommencement, this recomposition. Hence, leaving repression in its wake, the philosophical act par excellence since Plato: Mathematics is ontology insofar as truths exist.

We can posit: Badiou's relation to the philosopher Deleuze is conditioned by what Deleuze does not know he can do. His relation to the anti-philosopher Lacan is conditioned by what Lacan does not know he cannot do. Two absolutely different aporias that nevertheless share a knowledge of mathematics they don't have. Both – Deleuze via the proposition, Lacan via the indubitability of linguistic structure – submit one way or another to the indistinction of logic and mathematics.

As much as mathematics is ontology is the science of being qua being and thus is irreducible to sense, onto-*logy* is the science of appearing and thus is irreducible to language.* As much as the subject is, and is thus an effect of neither sense nor structure, but is the finite form or body a new truth takes in a world, its irreducibility to either is guaranteed only by an event which is neither inscribed in a series nor confined to an analytical act. The truth of the subject is the impossibility of knowledge, whose most rigorous instance is mathematics and whose own consistency derives from the very inconsistency by which exceptional truths are possible for animals like us.

> Socrates: One, two, three; but where, my dear Timaeus, is the fourth of those who were yesterday my guests and are to be my entertainers today?
> (Opening line, Plato, *Timaeus*)

---

* Badiou and Sedofsky, 'Matters of Appearance', p. 250.

Bibliography

Agamben, G. *The Kingdom and the Glory: For a Theological Genealogy of Economy and Government*, trans. L. Chiesa and M. Mandarini, Stanford: Stanford University Press, 2011.

Agamben, G. *What is an Apparatus?*, trans. D. Kishik and S. Pedatella, Stanford: Stanford University Press, 2009.

Badiou, A. *The Adventure of French Philosophy*, trans. B. Bosteels, London and New York: Verso, 2012.

Badiou, A. *Being and Event*, trans. O. Feltham, London and New York: Continuum, 2005.

Badiou, A. *The Century*, trans. A. Toscano, New York: Polity Press, 2007.

Badiou, A. *Concept of Model*, trans. Z. L. Fraser and T. Tho, Melbourne: re.press, 2011.

Badiou, A. *Conditions*, trans. S. Corcoran, London and New York: Continuum, 2008.

Badiou, A. 'The Courage of the Present', *The Symptom*, available at http://www.lacan.com/symptom11/?p=163

Badiou, A. *Deleuze: The Clamor of Being*, trans. L. Burchill, Minneapolis: University of Minnesota Press, 1999.

Badiou, A. *Ethics: An Essay on the Understanding of Evil*, trans. P. Hallward, London: Verso, 2001.

Badiou, A. *Logics of Worlds*, trans. A. Toscano, London and New York: Continuum, 2009.

Badiou, A. *Manifesto for Philosophy*, trans. N. Madarasz, Albany: SUNY, 1999.

Badiou, A. *Metapolitics*, trans. J. Barker, London and New York: Verso, 2005.

Badiou, A. 'Of Life as a Name of Being, or, Deleuze's Vitalist Ontology', trans. A. Toscano, *Pli, Warwick Journal of Philosophy*, No. 10 (2000), pp. 191–9.

Badiou, A. 'On Contemporary Obscurantism', *The Symptom*, available at http://www.lacan.com/symptom11/?p=163

Badiou, A. 'Plato, our Dear Plato!', trans. A. Toscano, *Angelaki*, Vol. II, No. 3 (2006), pp. 39–41.

Badiou, A. *Polemics*, ed. and trans. S. Corcoran, London: Verso, 2006.

Badiou, A. et al., *The Rational Kernel of the Hegelian Dialectic*, trans. T. Tho, Melbourne: re.press, 2011.

Badiou, A. *Second Manifesto for Philosophy*, trans. L. Burchill, New York: Polity Press, 2011.

Badiou, A. *Theoretical Writings*, trans. R. Brassier and A. Toscano, New York: Continuum, 2004.

Badiou, A. 'We Need a Popular Discipline', *Critical Inquiry*, No. 34 (2008), pp. 645–59.

Badiou, A., J.-C. Milner and P. Petit, *Controverses*, Paris: Seuil, 2012.

Badiou, A. and L. Sedofsky, 'Matters of Appearance', *Artforum*, Vol. 25, No. 3 (2006), pp. 246–56.

Bartlett, A. J. *Badiou and Plato: An Education by Truths*, Edinburgh: Edinburgh University Press, 2011.

Bartlett, A. J. 'Innovations in Incapacity: Education, Technique, Subject', *Digital Culture and Education*, Vol. 5, No. 1 (2013).

Bogost, I. *Alien Phenomenology, or, What It's Like to Be a Thing*, Minneapolis and London: University of Minnesota Press, 2012.

Bowdler, S. *The Priority of Events*, Edinburgh: Edinburgh University Press, 2011.

Brassier, R. 'The Enigma of Realism: On Quentin Meillassoux's *After Finitude*', *Collapse* II (2007).

Brassier, R. *Nihil Unbound*, Houndsmills: Palgrave Macmillan, 2007.

Bryant, L. *A Democracy of Objects*, Ann Arbor: Open Humanities Press, 2011.

Bryant, L. et al. eds. *The Speculative Turn: Continental Materialism and Realism*, Melbourne: re.press, 2011.

Cassin, B. *Jacques le Sophist*, Paris: EPEL, 2012.

Certeau, M. de. *Heterologies*, trans. B. Massumi, Minneapolis: University of Minnesota Press, 1987.

Chiesa, L. 'Hyperstructuralism's Necessity of Contingency', *S*, No. 3 (2010), pp. 159–77.

Chiesa, L. *Subjectivity and Otherness: A Philosophical Reading of Lacan*, Cambridge, MA: MIT, 2007.

Clemens, J. *Psychoanalysis is an Antiphilosophy*, Edinburgh: Edinburgh University Press, 2013.

Clemens, J. *The Romanticism of Contemporary Theory*, Aldershot: Ashgate, 2003.

Clemens, J. and O. Feltham, 'The Thought of Stupefaction; or, Event and Decision as Non-ontological and Pre-political Factors in the Work of Gilles Deleuze and Alain Badiou', in R. Faber et al. eds. *Event and Decision*, Newcastle: Cambridge Scholars Press, 2010, pp. 16–47.

Deleuze, G. *Cinema 2: The Time Image*, trans. H. Tomlinson and R. Galeta, Minneapolis: University of Minnesota Press, 1989.

Deleuze, G. *Deux Régimes de Fou et autres textes*, Paris: Minuit, 2003.

Deleuze, G. *Difference and Repetition*, trans. Paul Patton, New York: Columbia University Press, 1995.

Deleuze, G. *Essays Critical and Clinical*, ed. and trans. D. W. Smith and M. Greco, New York: Verso, 1998.

Deleuze, G. *The Fold: Leibniz and the Baroque*, trans. T. Conley, London: Athlone, 1993.

Deleuze, G. *L'île déserte et autres textes*, Paris: Minuit, 2002.

Deleuze, G. *Kant's Critical Philosophy*, Minneapolis: University of Minnesota Press, 1984.

Deleuze, G. *The Logic of Sense*, trans. M. Lester with C. Stivale, ed. C. V. Boundas, London: Athlone, 1990.

Deleuze, G. *Masochism*, trans. J. McNeil, New York: Zone Books, 1991.

Deleuze, G. *Negotiations*, trans. M. Joughin, New York: Columbia University Press, 1995.

Deleuze, G. *Nietzsche and Philosophy*, trans. H. Tomlinson. New York: Columbia University Press, 1983.

Deleuze, G. *Proust and Signs*, trans. R. Howard, Minneapolis: University of Minnesota Press, 2000.

Deleuze, G. *Pure Immanence: Essays on a Life*, trans. Anne Boyman, New York: Zone Books, 2001.

Deleuze, G. 'Réponse à une série de questions', in Arnaud Villani, ed. *La Guêpe et l'Orchidée. Essais sur Gilles Deleuze*, Paris: Belin, 1999.

Deleuze, G. *Two Regimes of Madness*, ed. D. Lapoujade, trans. A. Hodges and M. Taormina, New York: Semiotext(e), 2007.

Deleuze, G. and F. Guattari, *Anti-Oedipus: Capitalism and Schizophrenia*, trans. R. Hurley, M. Seem, H. R. Lane, London and New York: Continuum, 2000.

Deleuze, G. and F. Guattari, *A Thousand Plateaus*, trans. B. Massumi, Minneapolis: University of Minnesota Press, 1987.

Deleuze, G. and F. Guattari, *What is Philosophy?*, trans. H. Tomlinson and G. Burchell, New York: Columbia University Press, 1994.

Deleuze, G. and C. Parnet, *Dialogues*, trans. H. Tomlinson and B. Habberjam, London: Althone Press, 1987.

Derrida, J. *Resistances of Psychoanalysis*, trans. P. Kamuf et al., Stanford: Stanford University Press, 1998.

Detienne, M. *The Masters of Truth in Archaic Greece*, trans. J. Lloyd, New York: Zone Books, 1996.

Dosse, F. *Deleuze and Guattari: Intersecting Lives*, New York: Columbia, 2010.

Duve, T. de. *Kant After Duchamp*, Cambridge, MA: MIT, 1998.

Feltham, O. *Alain Badiou: Live Theory*, London and New York: Continuum, 2008.

Foucault, M. *The Government of Self and Others: Lectures at the College de France, 1982–1983*, ed. and trans. A. Davison and G. Burchell, London: Picador, 2011.

Foucault, M. *The Order of Things*, trans. A. Sheridan, New York: Pantheon Books, 1970.

Foucault, M. *Power/Knowledge: Selected Interviews 1972–1977*, ed. C. Gordon, New York: Pantheon Books, 1980.

Freud, S. and J. Breuer, *Studies on Hysteria, The Standard Edition of the Complete Psychological Works of Sigmund Freud*, Volume II (1893–1895), ed. J. Strachey et al., London: The Hogarth Press and the Institute of Psycho-Analysis, 1955.

Freud, S. *The Standard Edition of the Complete Psychological Works of Sigmund Freud*, Volume XXI (1927–1931), ed. J. Strachey et al., London: The Hogarth Press and the Institute of Psycho-analysis, 1961.

Grigg, R. *Lacan, Language and Philosophy*, Albany: SUNY, 2008.

Groys, B. 'Comrades of Time', *e-flux journal*, No. 12 (2009).

Harman, G. *Prince of Networks: Bruno Latour and Metaphysics*, Melbourne: re.press, 2009.

Harman, G. *Quentin Meillassoux: Philosophy in the Making*, Edinburgh: Edinburgh University Press, 2011.

Harman, G. 'The Well-Wrought Broken Hammer: Object-Oriented Literary Criticism', *New Literary History*, No. 43 (2012), pp. 183–203.

Hegel, G. W. F. *The Phenomenology of Spirit*, trans. A. V. Miller, foreword. by J. N. Findlay, Oxford: Oxford University Press, 1977.

Hegel, G. W. F. *Science of Logic*, trans. A. V. Miller, Atlantic Highlands: Humanities Press International, 1989.

Heidegger, M. *Being and Time*, trans. J. Stambaugh, Albany: SUNY Press, 1996.

Johnston, A. *Time Driven: Metapsychology and the Splitting of the Drive*, Evanston: Northwestern University Press, 2005.

Kant, I. *The Critique of Pure Reason*, ed. and trans. P. Guyer and A. W. Wood, Cambridge: Cambridge University Press, 2000.

Koyré, A. *Etudes d'histoire de la pensée philosophique*, Paris: Gallimard, 1971.

Koyré, A. *From the Closed World to the Infinite Universe*, Baltimore and London: The Johns Hopkins Press, 1957.

Koyré, A. *Galileo Studies*, trans. J. Mepham. Sussex: The Harvester Press, 1978.

Laplanche, J. and J.-B. Pontalis, 'Fantasy and the Origins of Sexuality', *IJP*, No. 49 (1968), pp. 1–18.

Lacan, J. *Ecrits*, trans. B. Fink with R. Grigg and H. Fink, New York: Norton, 2006.

Lacan, J. *Encore: The Seminar of Jacques Lacan, Book XX: On Feminine Sexuality: The Limits of Love and Knowledge 1972–1973*, ed. J-A. Miller. trans. with notes B. Fink, New York: Norton, 1998.

Lacan, J. *The Ethics of Psychoanalysis 1959–1960*, trans. D. Porter, New York: Norton, 1992.

Lacan, J. *The Four Fundamental Concepts of Psychoanalysis: Seminar XI*, trans. A. Sheridan, London: Penguin, 1994.

Lacan, J. *The Other Side of Psychoanalysis: Seminar XVII*, trans. R. Grigg, New York: Norton, 2006.

Lacan, J. *The Psychoses: The Seminar of Jacques Lacan, Book III 1955–1956*, trans. R. Grigg, New York: Norton, 1993.

Lacan, J. *Seminar XIX*, ed. J.-A. Miller, Paris: Seuil, 2011.

Lacan, J. *Le Séminaire XXIII: Le sinthome*, Paris: Seuil, 2005.

Lacan, J. *Le triomphe de la religion*, Paris: Seuil, 2005.

Lundy, C. 'Deleuze and Guattari's Historiophilosophy: Philosophical Thought and its Historical Milieu', *Critical Horizons*, Vol. 12, No. 2 (2011), pp. 115–35.

Lundy, C. *History and Becoming: Deleuze's Philosophy of Creativity*, Edinburgh: Edinburgh University Press, 2012.

Malabou, C. *The New Wounded: From Neurosis to Brain-Damage*, trans. S. Miller, New York: Fordham University Press, 2012.

Malabou, C. 'Post-Trauma: Towards a New Definition?', in T. Cohen, ed. *Telemorphosis: Theory in the Era of Climate Change, Vol. 1*, Ann Arbor: Open Humanities Press, 2012, pp. 226–38.

Meillassoux, Q. *After Finitude: An Essay on the Necessity of Contingency*, trans. R. Brassier, London: Continuum, 2009.

Meillassoux, Q. 'The Contingency of the Laws of Nature', *Society and Space*, Vol. 30, No. 2 (2012), pp. 322–34.

Meillassoux, Q. 'History and Event in Alain Badiou', trans. Thomas Nail, *Parrhesia*, No. 12 (2011), pp. 1–11.

Miller, J.-A. 'Mathemes', in E. Ragland and D. Milovanovic, eds. *Lacan: Topologically Speaking*, New York: Other Press, 2004.

Milner, J.-C. *L'Oeuvre claire: Lacan, la science, la philosophie*, Paris: Seuil, 1995.

Morton, T. *Realist Magic: Objects, Ontology, Causality*, Ann Arbor: Open Humanities Press, 2012.

Nietzsche, F. *Thus Spoke Zarathustra*, trans. R. J. Hollingdale, Harmondsworth: Penguin, 1961.

Noys, B. *The Persistence of Negativity: A Critique of Contemporary Continental Theory*, Edinburgh: Edinburgh University Press, 2010.

Roffe, J. 'Time and Ground: A Critique of Meillassoux's Speculative Realism', *Angelaki*, Vol. 17, No. 1 (2012), pp. 57–67.

Roudinesco, E. *Jacques Lacan*, trans. B. Bray, New York: Columbia, 1999.

Roudinesco, E. 'The Mirror Stage: An Obliterated Archive', in J-M. Rabarté, ed. *The Cambridge Companion to Lacan*, Cambridge: Cambridge University Press, 2003. pp. 25–34.

Ruda, F. *Hegel's Rabble*, London and New York: Continuum, 2011.

Smith, T. *What is Contemporary Art?*, Chicago: University of Chicago Press, 2009.

Tomsic, S. 'Three Notes on Science and Psychoanalysis', *Filosofski Vestnik*, Vol. XXXIII, No. 2 (2012), pp. 127–44.

Volbers, J. 'Natural Conditions of (Kantian) Majority', in V. Brito and E. Battista, eds. *Becoming Major/Becoming Minor*, Maastricht: Jan van Eyck Academie, 2011.

Widder, N. *Reflections on Time and Politics*, University Park: Pennsylvania State University Press, 2008.

Wittgenstein, L. *Culture and Value*, trans. G. H. Von Wright, London: Blackwell, 1998.

Žižek, S. 'Descartes and the Post-Traumatic Subject', *Filosofski Vestnik*, Vol. XXIX, No. 2 (2008), pp. 9–29.

Žižek, S. *Did Somebody Say Totalitarianism?*, London: Verso, 2001.

Žižek, S. *For They Know Not What They Do*, London: Verso, 1991.

Žižek, S. *In Defense of Lost Causes*, London: Verso, 2007.

Žižek, S. *Living in the End Times*, London: Verso, 2010.

Žižek, S. *The Metastases of Enjoyment*, London: Verso, 1994.

Žižek, S. *The Plague of Fantasies*, London: Verso, 1997.

Žižek, S. *The Sublime Object of Ideology*, London: Verso, 1989.

Žižek, S. *Tarrying with the Negative*, Durham, NC: Duke University Press, 1993.

Žižek, S. 'Why Lacan is not a Heideggerian', *Lacanian Ink*, 3 (2008), pp. 134–49.

Žižek, S. ed. *Lacan: The Silent Partners*, London: Verso, 2006.

Index